What people are saying about

Ugly Beauty

Phil Freeman has always been a free-thinking jazz critic, wary of majority opinion and allergic to conventional wisdom. In *Ugly Beauty* he applies that sensibility to a series of dispatches from a fast-moving scene, portraying some of the most vibrant artists of our time. A welcome addition to the growing literature around 21st century improvised music, with a crucial awareness of its relationship to a broader culture.
Nate Chinen, author of *Playing Changes: Jazz For the New Century*

Phil Freeman composes a much-needed text pointing towards the futures of an important art form while making connections to its origins and histories over a century. He doesn't only touch on the telling of a jazz story in the 21st century, but also prescribes a soundtrack within which to situate a time in history. His register of writing flows with rhythm, and this is a definite must get!
Nduduzo Makhathini, improviser, healer and scholar from South Africa

Ugly Beauty: Jazz in the Twenty-First Century

Ugly Beauty: Jazz in the Twenty-First Century

Phil Freeman

zer0 books

Winchester, UK
Washington, USA

JOHN HUNT PUBLISHING

First published by Zero Books, 2021
Zero Books is an imprint of John Hunt Publishing Ltd., No. 3 East St., Alresford,
Hampshire SO24 9EE, UK
office@jhpbooks.com
www.johnhuntpublishing.com
www.zero-books.net

For distributor details and how to order please visit the 'Ordering' section on our website.

ISBN: 978 1 78904 632 8
978 1 78904 633 5 (ebook)
Library of Congress Control Number: 2021931083

A CIP catalogue record for this book is available from the British Library.

Design: Stuart Davies

UK: Printed and bound by CPI Group (UK) Ltd, Croydon, CR0 4YY
Printed in North America by CPI GPS partners

Contents

For Izalia

I stand outside music and from this standpoint I observe it. That this standpoint is very imperfect I freely admit; that I am able to see very little in comparison with those fortunate people who stand inside I do not deny; but I still continue to hope that from my standpoint I too may be able to impart some odd piece of enlightenment on the subject, although the initiated could do it much better – yes, to some extent even understand what I say better than I do myself...The difficulty the following must contend with is really that since what the music under discussion expresses is essentially music's proper object, this music expresses it far more perfectly than does language, which makes a very poor showing in comparison...So what remains to be explained can only have meaning for the person who has listened and who continues constantly to listen. For him it may perhaps contain a suggestion or two that may move him to listen once more.
Søren Kierkegaard, *Either/Or*

Introduction

When I started writing this book, I expected to spend 2020 as I'd spent every previous year: going out a few times a month to jazz clubs, hanging out with musicians backstage or at the bar before or after their sets, talking to them by phone here and there. That didn't happen, obviously. The last jazz show I saw was February 1, 2020, and as I type these words in October 2020, I don't know when I'll be in a jazz club again. Some venues are starting to creep open, inviting no more than 20 people into spaces that previously only held 100 or so anyway, or allowing bands to take the stage with no audience present, and record sets which are then streamed. Some musicians are playing outdoors, in parks and other public spaces. But none of that is the same.

Before 2020, jazz had been feeling truly vital for several years. I'd been actively writing about the music since roughly the turn of the century, and amazing things happened every year, but it really seemed like beginning in 2015, to borrow bassist Melvin Gibbs' evocative phrase, the universe decided to care. That, after all, was the year that Kamasi Washington's triple CD *The Epic* caught the ear of listeners and critics who'd never before shown the slightest interest in jazz. While that had happened before — Miles Davis, Herbie Hancock, Keith Jarrett, Charles Lloyd and the Mahavishnu Orchestra, among others, had successfully sold records and concert tickets to non-jazz listeners — the cultural environment was vastly different.

The record industry has been in free fall since about 2001, and attitudes have changed quite a bit as a result. There's no such thing as "selling out" anymore. Thus, when Washington broke through, far more people within the jazz community saw it as a victory than as a capitulation to anything. Of course, there were a few artists who griped that he couldn't "really play," or that his band, with its synth player and its two drummers who clearly spoke the languages of rock and funk, didn't swing, but virtually everyone else recognized not just a validation, but an opportunity.

What did it actually mean that Kamasi Washington had so thoroughly broken out of jazz's tiny corner of the music world? Was this a sign of a broader movement, or was he a one-off?

In 2020, it's obvious that he's not a one-off, but he's also not a synecdoche for jazz as a whole. His commercial success is still unmatched, but an entire generation of artists has emerged in his wake and is performing to audiences weaned on indie rock and hip-hop, and making music that reveals that they're steeped in those sounds themselves.

At the height of the hippie era, saxophonist Charles Lloyd's quartet, which featured Keith Jarrett on piano, played the Fillmore in San Francisco, and their album *Forest Flower* — the second of eight they'd release between 1966 and 1968, all but one recorded live — went platinum. In the late 1990s, David S. Ware's quartet, with Matthew Shipp on piano and William Parker on bass, and a series of drummers, signed to Columbia and opened for Sonic Youth. (Their second and final release for the label, *Surrendered*, featured a version of Lloyd's "Sweet Georgia Bright.") Ware didn't go platinum, but he did get reviewed in *Rolling Stone*. Neither Lloyd nor Ware played music that conceded anything to rock audiences, and yet they connected with the people who heard them, especially onstage.

There's also always been a sizable, if critically overlooked, audience for music that blurs the lines between jazz, soul, funk, and R&B. In the 1970s, the Blue Note and CTI labels released albums by players like Donald Byrd, Hank Crawford, Freddie Hubbard and Stanley Turrentine that were sophisticated yet gritty, combining deeply soulful playing with lush string arrangements and a willingness to embrace pop songwriting and craftsmanship. "Soul jazz" and later "smooth jazz" was received coolly at best by (mostly white and male) critics, but it has always drawn in listeners who don't want to be screamed at — they want to have fun.

There's a whole world between these two poles, and a new generation of musicians have begun to populate it. In the twenty-first century, jazz has a higher public and critical profile than ever before. Jazz releases are routinely covered on Pitchfork, Stereogum, Noisey, Popmatters, the Quietus and other websites catering primarily to open-eared pop and rock fans, and magazines from *The Wire* to *Rolling Stone* interview and profile young jazz players with a regularity that would shock fans whose memories stretch back as far as the 90s. The annual Winter Jazzfest, a week-long collection of performances held in lower Manhattan every January and centered around a massive weekend marathon, sends eager listeners sprinting from club to club, art gallery to theater, to hear and see as much music as possible by performers from around the world. In recent years, the organizers, recognizing the power in the sheer numbers of people they attract, have begun adding themes, panel discussions and seminars, attempting to engage the audience beyond the level of mere entertainment and draw their attention to the political issues attached to forward-thinking art in a rapaciously post-industrial capitalist society.

The primary reason for this is not a concerted media campaign, though of course publicists are working as hard as ever to push their clients on the ever-diminishing number of freelance music writers. No, it starts from where you'd expect: great music being made by musicians who know how to navigate the modern world, and who share the social and political concerns that directly impact their generation.

In the pages that follow, I will explore the landscape of twenty-first century jazz — the music and the people who make it, as well as the issues that surround it. I will focus on four key zones:

In London, a school of players, most of them from immigrant

families, are combining the lessons learned in traditional music schools and the Tomorrow's Warriors program with the sounds they hear — and make — on the streets and in clubs. Their music is driving, optimistic and celebratory of their cultures and histories, but they're clear-eyed about the world they live in. (They saw Brexit coming, no mistake.)

In Los Angeles, a spiritual, Afrocentric scene has existed since the 1960s, combining a sense of unity and collective mission with music that looks forward while honoring the past. This is the milieu that produced Kamasi Washington and the members of his band, each of whom has struck out on his or her own, while also returning home to preserve the community that built them.

In Chicago, the lessons of the Association for the Advancement of Creative Musicians (AACM) — write your own music, create on your own terms, work together for the benefit of all — have been internalized by younger players. They find unorthodox venues for long-term residencies; they appear on each other's records, and recommend their peers to open-minded labels; and they acknowledge their status as points on a line, rather than radical individualists.

In New York, multiple scenes exist in parallel, only rarely meeting. One club, or one Brooklyn neighborhood, houses arty composers whose music is dense and fully notated, while another showcases classicist players who, heard with one's eyes closed, could be live-streaming from 1959, and still another features performers fully conversant in R&B, hip-hop and contemporary electronic music and production methods.

That said, geography means less than one might think in a digitally dispersed world where albums can be made via iPhone and Skype and Dropbox, and this book is not a travelogue. Rather, I have chosen several dozen of the most interesting musicians of the moment and dealt with them in sections. Each of these is loose, at best; many artists travel between creative zones depending on the mood of the moment. But in general, there's a group of players who wear suits, play standards, and look and sound like "jazz musicians" to non-jazz fans. Another group creates complex, frequently through-composed music that owes as much to modern composition as to swing or the blues — at certain performances, everyone on the bandstand has sheet music in front of them, including the drummer. Of these five groups, they're also the most overwhelmingly white.

Yet another group seems to be reviving and maintaining the tradition of spiritual jazz that began with artists like Pharoah Sanders, Alice Coltrane, Yusef Lateef and others in the late 1960s and early 1970s, while adding modern touches drawn from across the Afro-Caribbean diaspora. I have put a group of trumpeters into their own section, because while each is unique, they have much in common, particularly their fascination with the creative possibilities of hip-hop and modern, high-tech production. Finally, there are a loose assemblage of artists who are pushing harder at jazz's boundaries and borders than anyone else around. Their music is arty and often aggressive, blending jazz, rock, metal and noise with multimedia presentations, hacked technologies and anything else that will get their messages across.

Each of these approaches to jazz raises deep and serious questions. What is the relevance of traditional jazz in 2020? What does it benefit anyone, musicians or listeners, to pretend the last 60 years haven't happened? On the other hand, does the music written and performed by the second group stray too far from jazz's vernacular, African-American roots? Is it something else entirely? And what about the modern spiritualists? What does their borrowed/inherited pan-Africanism and Afrocentrism mean, in a world where Nigeria is more identified with email scammers than Black liberation? Do the trumpeters who have never known a world without hip-hop hear and understand music differently than their forebears, or are they returning it to its roots — a drum and a horn? And are the last group building a new world because there's no place for them in the current ecosystem of club gigs and festivals? Or are their multimedia performances just a way to sneak into art gallery-land via the side door?

In September 2000, the late Stanley Crouch wrote in *JazzTimes* magazine:

> The term "mainstream jazz" probably means less now than it ever has. Jazz is, now, itself and whatever else you can get away with. You can now play New Orleans-style music and just about anything else, including twentieth-century European concert music clichés as well as snippets — or an abundance — of ethnic music, and find yourself included in a jazz festival or written about in a jazz magazine. These days you can be given an award by jazz critics...even if you play with no feeling of swing, no feeling for the blues and make use of hardly anything from the great canon of jazz technique. Mainstream jazz can now mean anything.

For the record, I think he meant all that as a criticism. But his argument is exactly the one I'm advancing in this book, and to me it proves jazz's continued vitality. It's hard to say what jazz's place is in the twenty-first century. Indeed, it's difficult, nigh impossible, to even say what a "jazz musician" is now. Perhaps that's because like all musical styles, it's a mosaic, not a monolith. Although collaboration abounds, jazz is ultimately a vehicle for individual voices, and every performer in this book has something different to say, and their own way of saying it. So yes, jazz in the twenty-first century is a massive subject, one that resists in-depth analysis by never staying still long enough to be pinned down.

Still, we can try. In the pages that follow, which I encourage you to think of less as an encyclopedia and more as a collection of postcards, I will offer my interpretations of the music based on personal experience (listening to albums, attending live performances and conducting interviews) and research. But the sociopolitical atmosphere, and the capitalist ecosystem that leaves musicians increasingly on their own and scrambling from gig to gig, record date to record date, teaching job to freelance publicity side hustle to bartending shift, are factors that must be taken into account, and discussed, as well.

The class structure that walled jazz off as music for elites, immune to the vagaries of the market thanks to academic support, has largely collapsed. Popular songs are streamed, not purchased. Even before COVID-19, touring was already hampered by the closure of borders and hostility not just to long-term immigrants, but to visiting artists; visas are expensive and hard to come by. Social media is an advertising platform disguised as a community space, and the potential marketing benefits must always be weighed against the flood tide of racism, sexism and general abuse that will greet almost any statement from an artist, especially one that touches on politics. It's a rough world out there, but that only makes these artists' work more important. They are citizens of their time, speaking to and for their communities (racial, sexual, political), and audiences that might never have considered jazz to be "for them" are finding the music a welcoming space. If you're reading this, you're one of them. So...welcome.

PART I

JD Allen; Jeremy Pelt; Wayne Escoffery; Victor Gould; Ethan Iverson; Orrin Evans; Jason Moran

Introduction

When listening to the music made by Jeremy Pelt, JD Allen, Wayne Escoffery, Orrin Evans, Victor Gould, Ethan Iverson and Jason Moran, along with many other performers in their age cohort and even younger, it is possible to draw a straight line back to recordings and performances from 60 years earlier, if not much longer — decades before they were born, in any case. They record their own versions of standards which were initially drawn from a variety of sources, but most often from musicals of the 1920s, 30s and 40s. They also write new tunes which either borrow from the melodies and chord structures of those old songs, or hold to the same compositional principles that animated them.

To some, this may seem paradoxical. If the mission of jazz is to "make it new," in the phrase popularized by Ezra Pound, then why this focus on the music of the past? But this constant reckoning with the past is for men like these the central mission of jazz. A player hears something. It inspires him. He formulates his own response to it, or makes his own version of it. He uses the same tools as those who came before him, in the same combinations. It is tradition. It is the way things are done.

There is value in traditionalism. For one thing, it makes it easier to present the music. You can play any album by any of these artists for a listener, even one who professes ignorance of jazz, and there will be no confusion; whether they like it or not, they will almost certainly nod and agree, "Yes, that sounds like jazz to me."

From an artistic perspective, too, traditionalism has a certain nobility. An artist must be willing to create a border and stay within it, saying in effect, "I do *this* — I don't do *that*." The rejection is as important as the affirmation. I once asked Cecil Taylor if he had ever played an electric keyboard. I was not goading him; I was genuinely curious. He looked at me as if I had suggested he consider growing a third arm and replied, "Why would I do that? That's not a piano."

These performers also declare themselves to be jazz musicians through their visual presentation. They wear tailored suits on stage, or jackets, button-down shirts and trousers at least. Their album covers feature somber portraiture, with names and titles picked out in classicist fonts. In so doing, they once again make it easy for the casual or uninformed listener, saying in effect, *This is what a jazz musician looks like.*

This is an approach which works well if your goal is to appeal to existing jazz fans, many of whom are middle-aged or older and many of whom believe jazz to be innately superior to other, more commercially successful forms of music. But what message does it send to a teenager or young adult who hears something that interests them, but doesn't have the slightest idea what the next step might be? It can create an unconscious suspicion that *maybe this isn't for me,* a sort of imposter syndrome. That's an uncomfortable feeling, and not one somebody's going to subject themselves to willingly more than a few times. By presenting themselves in such a traditionalist — even retro — manner, these artists can be seen as buying into aesthetic tropes and marketing paradigms that carry classist baggage that are at best irrelevant to the twenty-first century, and at worst harmful. It could even be argued that it's a form of self-sabotage. Which, given the brilliance of their music, is a shame.

On the other hand, there is an appeal for certain young — or just new — listeners in embracing the traditions of a somewhat closed community. Learning the "rules" can feel like being accepted into a fraternity. It's no different from getting a pair of boots and a spiky haircut when you first embrace punk rock, or sewing patches on your jacket to signify your love of metal. To some, there's no point in being into jazz if no one can tell. So why not make it apparent at a glance?

JD Allen: Just Keep Going

Queens, New York seems purposely designed to confuse travelers. It's January 2, 2020, a brisk but sunny day, and I'm to meet saxophonist JD Allen at Samurai Hotel Recording Studio. To get there, I ride the N train from Manhattan, then walk up Broadway (a different Broadway) to 21st Street, where I make a right and pass, in order, 31st Road, 31st Drive and 31st Avenue. The building that houses the studio bears no sign and could easily be a residence. I press the buzzer beside the door, and am admitted.

Allen makes an album a year, and he likes to get an early start so the music will reach the public in late spring or early summer. (This album will be delayed until the end of August.) I arrive before he does, and watch the engineers set up microphones around bassist Ian Kenselaar and drummer Nic Cacioppo. The studio owner and lead engineer shows me a beautiful vintage RCA microphone that Allen will be using. It belonged to John Coltrane, whose son Ravi donated it to the studio.

There's some brief confusion, because when Allen and company recorded last year, Cacioppo had three toms on his kit, and this year he has only two. Soon enough, though, the levels have all been tested, the sound dialed in, and when Allen arrives at 12:30 and begins passing out sheet music, everyone's ready to get to work.

A typical jazz recording session takes a day, or two at most, and it goes like this: if they're a working band, the musicians have probably been playing the tunes for a while on gigs, and if they've been called together specifically for the session, they've spent the previous day rehearsing, enough to get a general idea and lock in a collective approach. They'll do a take or two, maybe three, of a tune, and when they're satisfied with it, they'll move on to the next one.

That's not how JD Allen works. He prefers to record in what he calls "sets," giving the band all the tunes at once and playing them one after another in sequence, as though they were onstage in a club. They record all day and sometimes into the night, tracking between two and five complete "sets" of music, and then he takes it all home and digs in, picking out the best performances of individual pieces.

"I tell the guys, 'If you make a mistake, don't stop, just keep going.' And usually the mistakes are pretty hip," he told me in 2019. "By the time the day's over, we're crawling out of the studio, but then there's no need to go in the next two days, or the next week, because we've done it all in one day."

This working method gives his albums immediacy and cohesiveness. The music is all of a piece, even when it's not. This is, in turn, a mirror of his live performances, during which he blends tunes together into nearly seamless suites, one hooky, bluesy melody feeding into the next. As he told me the first time we ever spoke, in 2011:

> We average about 15 to 20 tunes a set. We stretch it out — if it feels like we can go farther, we take it farther, but on average I have 15 tunes per set. If we can go longer, like if we have to play for 75 minutes, then I'll throw in a couple of standard ballads. I like ballads. But for our usual 45-minute set, 15 tunes.

Allen's voice on the horn is huge; he's part of a long tradition of big-toned tenor saxophonists that includes Coltrane, Joe Henderson, Sonny Rollins, David Murray, David S. Ware and others. His lines are steeped in the blues, and he has a deep sense of swing nurtured during an early apprenticeship with singer Betty Carter.

I was a fan of his for years before seeing him live, because his shows were always inconvenient in one way or another:

location, date, time of night...somehow, I didn't get to a gig until early 2019, by which time he'd dissolved his longtime trio with bassist Gregg August and drummer Rudy Royston. The eight albums they made together, beginning in 2008 — *I Am I Am, Shine!, Victory!, The Matador and the Bull, Graffiti, Americana: Musings on Jazz and Blues, Radio Flyer* and *LoveStone,* the last two with guitarist Liberty Ellman added to the lineup — were as strong a body of work as any twenty-first century jazz group produced, and some of my favorite albums of the era. Live performances on YouTube proved that they were locked-in tight onstage, too, keeping the tunes concise for maximum impact and never slowing down or giving the audience time to breathe.

The first time I saw Allen perform, at the Jazz Gallery in Manhattan, he had Kenselaar — a tall, skinny blond kid of 25 — on bass, and an equally young man named Malick Koly on drums. Both were significantly younger and less experienced than Allen, who's in his mid-forties and had been on the scene since the late 1990s, and there was an element of coaching as he guided them through the set, pointing to one or the other when he wanted them to solo and making sure they listened closely to each other.

A few months later, on a Wednesday night in June 2019, I trekked out to Bar Bayeux, a narrow venue tucked between a hair salon and a deli on Brooklyn's Nostrand Avenue. Another saxophonist of my acquaintance, Jerome Sabbagh, was booking a weekly series of performances, one of which was to feature Allen and his new trio (now with Cacioppo behind the kit), to celebrate the release of their first album together, *Barracoon.*

The bar provided just enough room for a few people to congregate in the front, by a big window, and another small area of open floor in the back. Cacioppo was setting up in the corner as Allen made the rounds, shaking hands with the small group of friendly faces who'd made the gig. When Kenselaar turned up, wheeling an upright and lugging a bass guitar and a small amp, the three leapt into action.

The set was slightly more structured than the onstage practice session I'd witnessed at the Jazz Gallery, but there were similarities. The pieces flowed together with few pauses, forcing Kenselaar and Cacioppo to watch carefully and listen closely. Allen started each tune from the embers of the one before, like a chain-smoker. His melodies were short and mantra-like, drawn from the blues and burnished by his tone, which combines elements from the John Coltrane of *Crescent* and the Sonny Rollins of *East Broadway Run Down*, but peppered with a sly phrasal invention all his own.

Midway through the second or third tune, Cacioppo took a solo that exploded with a furious energy, but was nevertheless deployed with precision. His sticks danced across the snare and tom, leaving sonic craters in their wake, as he stared ahead with the impassivity of an assembly-line worker snapping parts together. Later, when he suddenly let his mouth fall open and his tongue loll nearly to his collar in mid-tune, it was so startling it was almost hilarious.

At Samurai Hotel, Cacioppo's drums sound massive; his toms boom like Elvin Jones's on Coltrane albums from the 1960s. Kenselaar's bass is huge, too, a thick strumming sound. Allen stands in the big central room, turned sideways so he can see each of them in their small isolated chambers, and he gives them room to run. One track, "Die Dreaming," includes a bass solo, and another, "Elegua (The Trickster)," is kicked off by a drum solo. (In 2011, Allen had told me he often leaves room for drum solos when composing his tunes.)

This group is looser than the previous trio with August and Royston had been. Those two always had a coiled tension to their interactions; the drummer's snare snapped and rang sharply. Cacioppo, on the other hand, is as interested in creating effects as in keeping time or driving the trio. He has a fascination with pitch bending, a technique that gives a drum more of a bowed sound than the traditional percussive strike. It's a subtle thing, but when combined with his busy approach to the kit – he's as big a fan of the holistic free playing of Milford Graves as of the fierce swing of longtime Count Basie drummer Papa Jo Jones – it makes the trio's taut, bluesy workouts endlessly compelling.

When the first set of tunes has been tracked, Allen heads outside for a smoke. I follow him, and we hang out and talk, swapping stories of encounters with Cecil Taylor while he smokes and a photographer takes pictures of him, potentially for the CD booklet. I duck out before the trio returns to work, listening to a previous Allen album – 2015's *Graffiti* – on my way back to the subway.

The next time I see Allen is at the Jazz Gallery again, on February 1, 2020. He's joined a band led by fellow saxophonist Marcus Strickland called Ghidorah, named for the three-headed dragon from the Godzilla movies; the third head is Stacy Dillard. Onstage, Strickland is in the center, and Allen and Dillard are at stage right and left, respectively, with Eric Wheeler on bass and Rodney Green on drums. A video screen behind them shows clips of their namesake monster, as well as dance performances by the Nicholas Brothers and tribute footage of Kobe Bryant, who had died 5 days earlier.

The band plays four sets over the course of two nights, with each saxophonist bringing in original music; this is not a "let's stretch out on some standards" gig. Nevertheless, they are explicitly grappling with the legacy and lineage of the jazz tenor saxophone, and particularly the Black male voice on that horn. Before the first set on the second night, Strickland discusses the history of the tenor and shouts out a litany of legends, including Coleman Hawkins, Lester Young, Don Byas, John Coltrane and Sonny Rollins, and paying special tribute to Jimmy Heath, who had died on January 19.

The first piece the group performs is by Allen, and his compositional voice – those hooky melodies, steeped in the blues, but with a steely core — is instantly recognizable, and an ideal way to start the night. The sound of three tenor saxophones biting into a powerful melody is spine-tingling, and Wheeler and Green launch into a loose but hard-swinging rhythm.

A self-effacing player, Allen lets both Dillard and Strickland solo before him, each man establishing his lane in the process. Dillard is the fiercest, as he'll remain throughout the night. His solo is raucous and even shrill at times, recalling David Murray's punishing squalls of sound. Strickland, by contrast, burrows into the lower end of the tenor's range, with a thick tone like a bubbling cauldron. When Allen takes his turn in the spotlight, he too uses his first solo to make a statement of identity, defining himself for anyone present who doesn't know his name or his work. The oldest of the three co-leaders at 47 (Dillard is 45, Strickland 40), his playing is just slightly more restrained than the other two men's, hewing closer to the melody — he wrote it, after all — but deploying a few fleet-fingered phrases, almost as a form of humblebragging.

The second piece comes from Dillard's pen, and keeps the excitement level high. It almost has an old school R&B feel, with a jumpy, vibrant energy befitting its origins in a trip he'd taken to South Africa. Strickland gets the first solo this time, followed by Allen, with Dillard batting cleanup. Wheeler takes an extended bass solo, as he'd done on the first piece.

The quintet could easily opt for an hour of these bluesy rave-ups; that strategy had worked for Johnny Griffin and Eddie "Lockjaw" Davis, after all. But on the third number, Allen's "G Thing" (which appears on *Toys/Die Dreaming*, the album I'd watched them record at Sorcerer Sound), they shift gears, offering a simmering, mournful ballad in the mode of John Coltrane's "Alabama." Strickland is up first, and switches to bass clarinet, playing an Eric Dolphy-esque solo with a questing feel. Allen is next, followed by Dillard, who opts for soprano, continuing the Coltrane-ish mood but playing in a more abstract manner. At one point, he takes a wrong turn that requires a second of silence to recover from, but the vocal and enthusiastic crowd is with him — and everyone else — all the way.

The last piece of the night is a Strickland composition, "Pivotal Decision." It's a fast bebop burner, and a perfect closer, with all three men back on tenor and tossing the tune back and forth like NBA all-stars. The leader is up first, followed by Allen, then Dillard, and to cap things off, Green takes his only drum solo of the night, a too-brief, kit-rattling eruption that has as much in common with hard rock as jazz. The three heads of the dragon wind things down in thrilling, high-speed harmony, each man's unique voice making up one-third of a powerful chorus.

As the show progresses, more names than those Strickland listed pop into my head: Charlie Rouse, Archie Shepp, Albert Ayler, Dewey Redman, David S. Ware...not because what the members of Ghidorah are doing is in any way derivative of their forebears, but because the tenor saxophone is the beating heart of jazz, and these men are keeping the blood pumping and then some.

Essential Listening

JD Allen Trio, *Victory!* (Sunnyside, 2011)
JD Allen Trio, *Graffiti* (Savant, 2015)
JD Allen Trio, *Americana: Musings on Jazz and Blues* (Savant, 2016)
JD Allen, *LoveStone* (Savant, 2018)
JD Allen, *Barracoon* (Savant, 2019)
JD Allen, *Toys/Die Dreaming* (Savant, 2020)

Jeremy Pelt: You Eventually Sound Like Yourself

Turbaned organist Dr Lonnie Smith usually performs at New York's Jazz Standard a couple of times a year. He's made some good albums in the twenty-first century, especially 2013's *In The Beginning* and 2016's *Evolution*, so when he showed up there in July 2019, leading a largish band (it was billed as an octet, but for most of the shows it was actually a septet), I decided to check it out.

The first three nights of his six-night stand featured him with a trio that included guitarist Jonathan Kreisberg and drummer Xavier Breaker. On the night I went, four horn players were added: Jeremy Pelt on trumpet, Joel Frahm on tenor sax, Alexa Tarantino on alto sax and Jason Marshall on baritone sax. For the final night of shows, which I didn't attend, Chris Potter came in on tenor, making it a full eight-piece.

The set began with a spacy trio jam featuring some nasty guitar work from Kreisberg. He was capable of a broad range of sounds, from biting blues-funk to weird synth-guitar stuff like imitation Kurt Rosenwinkel. The horn players filed to the front on the second number, a version of Smith's "Falling in Love" that featured fierce fanfares and hot solos. The band also played a version of Paul Simon's "50 Ways to Leave Your Lover," a surprising choice but one that they funked up very nicely. Breaker gave it a New Orleans second-line feel, and the horns responded accordingly. Frahm's solo was just a little too busy and too long, though, full of houserockin' clichés that the audience didn't really respond to the way he probably intended.

The fifth and final piece of the night was a long, hard funk jam with plenty of wah-wah guitar and fierce drumming. Smith's organ became positively piercing at times, like he was leaning on the keys with both elbows, and he was grinning broadly at the horn players as they soloed. Frahm was up first, and went long again, heading into a zone of almost free jazz shrieking at times, while Maxwell went low and farty, with Smith and the drummer dropping in and out behind him like a live dub mix. Tarantino seemed tentative at first, but gradually ascended from funk riffs to the speedy bebop runs that are her real strength, and Pelt closed it all out with a red-hot blast.

The band seemed lightly rehearsed to me; they spent a fair amount of time staring at their sheet music, and probably wouldn't have let Frahm dominate the way he did with a little more time to get things together. But overall, it was a fun show, and I'm glad I got to see Dr Lonnie. Afterward, I approached the stage to shake hands with Pelt, a frankly stunning trumpeter who works constantly and, like JD Allen, makes an album a year under his own name.

A stocky, always nattily dressed player, Pelt has been recording since the turn of the century; his first album under his own name, *Profile*, was released in 2002. Six years later, he formed the group that would make his name – a quintet featuring Allen on tenor sax, Danny Grissett on piano, Dwayne Burno on bass and Gerald Cleaver on drums. Between 2008 and 2012, they recorded four albums, but eventually Allen and Cleaver in particular were busy enough that the band drifted apart. In 2013, Burno died of kidney disease.

The quintet's recordings bore superficial similarities to the work of the Miles Davis quintet of 1965, but around the time of their third album, *The Talented Mr Pelt*, the trumpeter told me that "a lot of what's happening in the music, in my music, comes from a lot of different points of view that maybe weren't expressed in any of the recordings of the Miles Davis group. We use that, we've listened to it, we've all soaked it in, but...we're not practitioners of garnering that sound."

Indeed, the comparison is really only valid in regard to the instrumentation and some of the compositions. JD Allen has none of Wayne Shorter's tentative, questing style in his playing, and Pelt has more in common with Freddie Hubbard or Woody Shaw than the reserved Davis. Like those predecessors, he's a technical master of the horn, but one with a romantic side — he really loves to play ballads. His 2020 album, *The Art of Intimacy, Vol. 1,* was a collection of slow standards featuring bandmates older than himself: pianist George Cables, bassist Peter Washington and no drummer.

Pelt studied at Berklee College of Music in Boston, Massachusetts, taking mandatory courses in instrumental technique and whatnot but focusing on film scoring. At the time, a generation of very strong players were making their debuts, and he was listening. "Nicholas Payton was about three years older than me, so he was starting to become a big thing, and I admired his playing quite a bit," he told me in 2018, "but I think Roy Hargrove had the biggest impact when I was in high school and going into college. He was a big hero of mine. And Terence Blanchard, but more so Roy."

Hargrove, who died in November 2018, covered a tremendous amount of stylistic ground in the 1990s, moving from hardcore acoustic jazz to funk and R&B with his band the RH Factor, and playing on D'Angelo's *Voodoo,* Common's *Like Water for Chocolate* and Erykah Badu's *Mama's Gun, Worldwide Underground* and *New Amerykah Vol. 1.* He was also well known as a bridge between generations. Bassist Christian McBride, who collaborated with Hargrove in the 1990s, told me that the trumpeter always sought out older masters of the horn, whether they were beboppers like Clark Terry or avant-gardists like Lester Bowie of the Art Ensemble of Chicago. He was eager to learn, but also eager to pass on his own knowledge; in his final years, he would offer advice and support to younger players at jam sessions or in master classes.

While he hasn't jumped into R&B and soul with both feet the way Hargrove did, Pelt has made albums — most notably

2013's *Water and Earth* and 2014's *Face Forward, Jeremy* — that incorporated electronics in thoughtful ways. He's also got the other man's interest in learning from elders while also mentoring the next generation.

Having spoken to Pelt several times, I can hear his personality through his horn. He has an almost conversational style when he plays; he rarely goes all the way out, but neither is he a whispering seducer. He says what he has to say calmly, and there's a lot of intelligence and wisdom in his statements. And he knows — and acknowledges — where he came from. During that same 2018 conversation, he told me, "I don't think anybody, no matter how much they try, or what hype they subscribe to, is completely original. I don't believe in that. So I'm listening to myself, and yeah, there are obvious influences there, but then the more you start to play, and the years go by, you eventually do sound like yourself."

Several years after his quintet split up, Pelt told me that he knew they were a huge part of his legacy:

> I felt like the quintet was the band at this point, so if I don't ever play the trumpet [again] and somewhere in a new jazz history book for modern times, they talk about Jeremy Pelt, they'll say his important band, the same way they say Trane's important band or Miles Davis's important quintet — that would be the band, with JD and everybody. And even though I tell you that I didn't see it lasting for much longer than it did, it still left a huge void in my soul when it did disband.

In 2016, Pelt formed a working band for the first time since the dissolution of the quintet. (In between, he'd experimented with this and that, even fulfilling a longtime dream by recording with legendary bassist Ron Carter on 2016's *#jiveculture*.) He made 2017's *Make Noise!* with pianist Victor Gould, bassist Vicente

Archer, drummer Jonathan Barber and percussionist Jacquelene Acevedo, and took that group on the road, releasing *Noir en Rouge: Live in Paris* the following year.

"At a certain point, I decided I wanted to have a band again," he told me:

> The funny thing is...trumpet is always thought of, especially if you have solo recordings and you've kind of made a name for yourself in a certain type of way, you're always expected to be the leader of a gig. So it was almost that I *had* to form a band, because I'm always hustling to get gigs. Every tour I do, I book myself. So to make it interesting for the person that's buying the band, I decided to go ahead and start writing more original music and conceptualize putting together a new band.

In 2018, he shuffled the lineup somewhat, replacing Barber with Allan Mednard, Acevedo with Ismael Wignall, and adding vibraphonist Chien Chien Lu, guitarist Alex Wintz and synthesizer player Frank LoCrasto for one of his most ambitious albums, *Jeremy Pelt, the Artist*.

The record's first five tracks are a suite, commissioned by FONT (the Festival of New Trumpet Music) and inspired by the work of sculptor Auguste Rodin. The first section, "L'Appel aux Armes," begins with slowly pulsing piano and vibraphone, more like the music of composer Steve Reich than jazz. After a minute or so, the trumpet, guitar, bass and drums enter, and the music surges. Eventually, LoCrasto appears, on Fender Rhodes, and he and Gould take turns in the spotlight, as Lu's vibraphone dances around them over a hard-slapping groove from Archer and Mednard. After the initial melodic statement, Pelt himself doesn't reappear until the fourth minute of a 7-minute track.

The suite's third segment, "I Sol Tace (Gates of Hell)," is shockingly abstract for Pelt. It begins with electronically warped trumpet straight out of Miles Davis circa 1969, layered over vibes and percussion, before Archer's positively booming bass enters. Ultimately, the swirling acoustic music provides a bed for Pelt's smeared trumpet lines, and he hits some uncharacteristically piercing high notes.

In the album's second half, he returns to more familiar territory. "Feito" is a bouncing post-bop number of a type he's recorded many times. His rich, full trumpet sound keeps the energy level high, with just a piano trio behind him. At the piece's midpoint, Lu appears, taking a fast, Milt Jackson-esque solo as Mednard hammers the kit.

The album ends with "As of Now," a lush slow blues played by the core quartet, reminiscent of Woody Shaw's late 70s work. Pelt starts things off, then Archer takes a short but potent solo before the leader returns to the spotlight. Gould is the final soloist, his florid romanticism the perfect closing statement.

If Jeremy Pelt has made a bad album, I've never heard it. He's one of the most technically impressive and lyrical trumpeters around, and in recent years, particularly on *Jeremy Pelt, the Artist*, he's allowed his skills as a composer and bandleader to come forward like never before.

Essential Listening

Jeremy Pelt Quintet, *The Talented Mr Pelt* (HighNote, 2011)
Jeremy Pelt Quintet, *Soul* (HighNote, 2012)
Jeremy Pelt, *Water and Earth* (HighNote, 2013)
Jeremy Pelt, *Make Noise!* (HighNote, 2017)
Jeremy Pelt, *Jeremy Pelt, the Artist* (HighNote, 2019)
Jeremy Pelt, *The Art of Intimacy, Vol. 1* (HighNote, 2020)

Wayne Escoffery: We All Learn Lessons in Life

Wayne Escoffery has worked as a fashion model. The first time I saw him glowering at the camera in a magazine advertisement, it surprised me, but only for an instant. He's very tall and extremely handsome, with a penetrating gaze. It's hard not to stare at him, and when he's playing, he seizes the spotlight almost effortlessly, even though he's been one of the most respected sidemen on the New York scene for 2 decades. He's a veteran of the Mingus Big Band, which performed almost every Monday night in the city, until March 2020; he's played with trumpeter Tom Harrell for over a decade; and he's worked with drummer Ben Riley, playing the music of Riley's former employer, Thelonious Monk.

As a leader, he's made somewhere around ten albums, plus a few more in collaboration with his now ex-wife, singer Carolyn Leonhart. Their son Vaughn appears on his 2020 album *The Humble Warrior*, singing the "Benedictus" section of a radical interpretation of composer Benjamin Britten's *Missa Brevis in D*.

Although Escoffery records and performs regularly (while also teaching at Yale, a school where his mother worked when he was a child), his name doesn't seem to pop up in conversation as often as those of his peers. Perhaps that's because his music is slippery and hard to categorize. At first, it can seem like conventional post-bop, "just" acoustic small group jazz played at as high a level of technical skill as anyone since Joe Henderson, but there's often a lot more going on, as one realizes after multiple listens.

I first became aware of Escoffery in 2009, when his fifth album, *Uptown*, was released on the Posi-Tone label. It was a soulful, groove-heavy outing that positioned him firmly within the tradition of hard bop blowing — I later learned he'd been heavily influenced by alto saxophonist Jackie McLean, serving in the older man's band for several years in the 1990s — but also made a case for him as a better-than-decent composer. Pieces like "No Desert" and the questing "Maya's Waltz" recalled Wayne Shorter's mid-60s compositions, and Escoffery's hoarse tone and meditative phrasing can bring Shorter to mind, too. But the album was arranged for an organ quartet with guitarist Avi Rothbard, drummer Jason Brown and Gary Versace at the keys, and pieces like "Nu Soul" and a version of Duke Ellington's "I Got It Bad (And That Ain't Good)" seemed aimed at jazz radio, while the two-part "Road from Eilat" and "Gulf of Aqaba" had a psychedelic, spiritual edge reminiscent of Larry Young's Blue Note albums.

Three years later, I interviewed Escoffery and learned that the album wasn't even intended to come out under his name.

He told me:

> What happened was a great friend of mine, Avi Rothbard, is the guitarist on that recording. Avi and I actually moved to New York together, and we used to play at a club called St Nick's Pub in Harlem. So Posi-Tone had approached me about a recording, but I couldn't record for them as a leader because I was obligated to Joel Fields at Savant Records, so what I offered them was, I said, look, there's this great guitar player, a friend of mine named Avi, and we play together a lot, we have an organ group together. And I've always wanted to record some organ music, because that's kind of where I came from, so it would be a lot of fun for Avi and I to do a project together. But ultimately what ended up happening was due to some savvy business dealings, they put the record out as my recording. That's why half the music is Avi's music, because it was supposed to be a collaborative recording that actually featured Avi more than me, but I think they felt it was more marketable to make it

> my album. We all learn lessons in life, and I learned a big one for sure.

At the time of our conversation, he had just released an extremely personal album, *The Only Son of One*. Orrin Evans was on piano, teamed up with synth player Adam Holzman, a veteran of Miles Davis's late-80s bands. Hans Glawischnig played bass on some tracks, Ricky Rodrigues on others and Jason Brown was back on drums. Escoffery wrote all the music, assembling an instrumental chronicle that began with his London childhood and the abusive man his mother fled, taking him to Connecticut when he was 8. The album paid tribute to his mother, explored the multiple dimensions of racism and colorism the relatively light-skinned saxophonist encountered in America, and dealt with an encounter Escoffery had with his father's ghost during high school.

He told me:

> All the pieces really do come from the stories that I'm telling with them. But with instrumental music, it doesn't really matter what I think the songs mean. They're gonna speak to the listener how they do, and the listener's going to interpret them how they do. So I'm just telling you, the listener, what the music means to me and where it comes from. And it doesn't mean that's the only thing that's supposed to be thought about. I mean, I expect and I hope that the music is going to inspire other thoughts and other feelings in people. Music's not one-dimensional.

In 2014, after years of changing musicians on every album, Escoffery put together a working band. To date, he's made three albums with pianist David Kikoski, bassist Ugonna Okegwo and drummer Ralph Peterson Jr. They started with a live disc, recorded at Smalls in Greenwich Village. That was followed by *Vortex*, a studio disc released in 2018. Like *The Only Son of One*, it was a deeply personal album — "Tears for Carolyn" was a ballad mourning the dissolution of his marriage, "The Devil's Den" was a musical portrait of Donald Trump and those around him, and "In His Eyes" was a meditation on how his son might see the changes in America and the world beginning in 2016. The latter two tracks featured Kush Abadey subbing in on drums, and Jeremy Pelt, also a father, played on "In His Eyes." Jacquelene Acevedo, percussionist on Pelt's *Make Noise!* and *Noir en Rouge*, appeared on three tracks.

The Humble Warrior, released in spring 2020, brought in more guests — trumpeter Randy Brecker and guitarist David Gilmore — to accompany the core lineup of Kikoski, Okegwo and Peterson. The 22-minute, four-part Britten piece took up a full third of the album, and had the stately feel of the classic John Coltrane quartet's work, especially when Escoffery switched to soprano on the opening "Kyrie" section. On the subsequent "Sanctus," Brecker, Gilmore and Escoffery were effectively performing three-part harmony on their various instruments, making the music soar. Behind them, the trio swung in a regal manner, with Peterson keeping his usual apocalyptic approach to the kit just slightly in check. He made sure the listener knew the bombs were there, should he choose to drop them, though.

The title track also featured Brecker; he and Escoffery played off each other beautifully, dancing confidently through the complicated but serene melody before stepping out with graceful but fierce solos. "AKA Reggie," composed by pianist George Cables, was a slow, bluesy ballad on which Escoffery's half-murmured phrases slid smoothly across the perfectly locked-in rhythm laid down by the trio.

In 2013, Escoffery, Jeremy Pelt and drummer Johnathan Blake debuted a new project, the Black Art Jazz Collective, at Jazz at Lincoln Center. The initial lineup also included James Burton III on trombone, Xavier Davis on piano and Dwayne

Burno on bass.

He told me in 2020:

> I wanted to put together a band that would celebrate the origins of the music, would talk about the history of Black culture, would talk about important Black figures in the music and [the fight] for social justice and social change throughout history, and I wanted to do it in a positive way with musicians of my generation who I knew were amazing musicians...and also upstanding citizens. People you would see on the stage and would offer a certain kind of respect and dignity, kind of like my teacher, Jackie McLean.

The group was pushed back a step when Burno died, but they recruited Vicente Archer and continued, making their debut on disc with a 2016 album recorded at the Side Door Jazz Club in Old Lyme, Connecticut. Everyone but Archer wrote for the album, and they included one of Burno's compositions, "Devil Eyes."

The BAJC, like many jazz groups whose name can be turned into an acronym, made their agenda explicit. They were honoring Black culture, specifically the ultra-high-level acoustic jazz played by masters like Woody Shaw, Joe Henderson, McCoy Tyner and others in the 1970s and 80s. The compositions carried dedications to WEB DuBois, Barack Obama, Sojourner Truth and Henderson, and the performances, while kept at a low simmer, nonetheless showed anyone paying attention exactly how high modernist hard bop should be played. Watching a 2017 performance from Jazz at Lincoln Center's Dizzy's Club Coca-Cola (with Darrell Green subbing in on drums) was a reminder that the phrase "America's classical music" is awful, but the reverence it's meant to inspire is hard-earned. The tight harmonies of the three horns and the intricate swing of the rhythm section, as perfect as a choreographed dance routine even as it was being reshaped moment by moment, were a reminder of exactly how glorious jazz is and can be. It's a tradition, but a living one.

The second BAJC album, *Armor of Pride,* was released in 2018, and retained all the power and gravitas of the debut, but the energy level might have been even more ferocious, thanks to Blake's hard-driving work behind the kit. A track like "The Spin Doctor" was typical of the album. A triumphant eruption, it launched with a high-speed three-horn melody that downshifted into a zone of abstraction before Escoffery dove into a fast, gritty solo. Pelt was up next, his full tone and impeccable command of the horn allowing him to spit out long, complex lines that sounded like verses by Black Thought of hip-hop group the Roots, while Burton's trombone pulsed and swelled without ever devolving into smears. Like his bandmates, he is a precise and energetic player. Blake's drumming was key to the whole exercise; he drove the band hard at all times, chopping up the beat and keeping the other players on their toes.

The group's third album, *Ascension,* brought major personnel changes. The entire rhythm section was replaced by pianist Victor Gould, bassist Rashaan Carter and drummer Mark Whitfield Jr. The mood stayed the same, though; the goal was to honor the tradition while putting their own stamp on it. One piece, "Twin Towers," was written by Jackie McLean as a tribute to Escoffery and Jimmy Greene, both of whom were in his band at the same time in the 1990s. He never recorded it, though, so Escoffery pulled it out of a drawer. It starts with a beautiful intro from Gould, but the horns come in fast and furious, pushing through a spiraling, complicated melody, and the bass and drums drive hard and emphatically.

Wayne Escoffery is highly regarded on the jazz scene, but there's always a sense that he's in the shadows, watching with those dark, penetrating eyes, waiting for his moment. He's been hard to market, because his personal version of the traditionalism-originality tightrope walk makes so few concessions to the world outside jazz.

"I think one thing that's always tough for people to market is a thorough musician, though I hate to say it that way," he told me in 2020.

> I came up studying bebop music, traditional music, and I love that music. It's an important part of what I do. Blues and bebop...is an integral part of being a creative modern musician. That being said, when I do a gig, I'm not gonna go up there and just be a Dexter Gordon or a Sonny Stitt clone, even though I could do that. Because Jackie McLean didn't do that. He studied Charlie Parker and Dexter Gordon, but he wasn't a Charlie Parker clone. He wanted to be an artist, and he wanted to create and keep adding different devices and sounds and concepts to make art, and that's what he did.

Between his work as a leader and the Black Art Jazz Collective, the time is now to recognize what should have been obvious long ago. Wayne Escoffery is a serious artist, and attention must be paid.

Essential Listening

Wayne Escoffery, *The Only Son of One* (Sunnyside, 2012)
Black Art Jazz Collective, *Presented By the Side Door Jazz Club* (Sunnyside, 2016)
Wayne Escoffery, *Vortex* (Sunnyside, 2018)
Black Art Jazz Collective, *Armor of Pride* (HighNote, 2018)
Wayne Escoffery, *The Humble Warrior* (Smoke Sessions, 2020)
Black Art Jazz Collective, *Ascension* (HighNote, 2020)

Victor Gould: A Challenge To Be Embraced

Singer Jazzmeia Horn is aptly named. Her voice, even when she's not scatting (singing non-verbal syllables in imitation of an instrumental solo), has the quality of an alto saxophone, or perhaps a bass clarinet — a gently moaning sound, slightly hoarse at the edges and with an implicit vulnerability that occasionally becomes explicit. Onstage at Dizzy's in May 2017, she's backed by the trio of pianist Victor Gould, bassist Noah Jackson and drummer Henry Conerway III. At various points during the set, trumpeter Josh Evans, trombonist Frank Lacy and tenor saxophonist Stacy Dillard will bolster the ensemble. All of these men save Jackson and Conerway played on her debut album, *A Social Call*; there, as on her 2019 follow-up *Love and Liberation*, Ben Williams was on bass and Jamison Ross on drums.

Horn is wearing a blue and green dress like a West African kimono, and a matching headwrap. Her bandmates are in matching vests, navy blue with a pattern of red and yellow rectangular shapes. When she's not singing, and sometimes when she is, she nestles up against the outward curve of the piano, swaying gently and raising the microphone insouciantly to her lips like a champagne flute — on the verses, anyway; when she starts scatting, she grips it in both hands like a saxophone, and turns her head at a slight angle, like Lester Young.

During a performance of "East of the Sun (and West of the Moon)," she glides to far stage left, so that each member of the trio can solo with the audience's full attention on them. Still, she can't resist dancing, and offering vocal encouragement as Gould and Jackson take short but potent solos. When it's Conerway's turn, she trades fours with him, raising the energy level somewhat but still keeping it at a cool simmer.

That's followed by her arrangement of urban gospel singer

Kirk Franklin's "Up Above My Head," on which she's joined by all three horns. The rhythm hits hard, but Gould's exploration of the melody is done with a light touch, more nightclub than church.

Throughout the hour-long set, Gould is a gracious accompanist, always serving the band without ever seeming like he's waiting his turn to solo. At times, he seems curiously distant from what's going on, gazing out the massive window behind the stage, which overlooks New York's Columbus Circle and Central Park.

Almost exactly 2 years later, in May 2019, Gould was onstage at the Jazz Standard as part of an entirely different band. Jeremy Pelt was celebrating the release of his album *Jeremy Pelt, the Artist* with a septet performance that included Gould, guitarist Alex Wintz, vibraphonist Chien Chien Lu, bassist Corcoran Holt, drummer Allan Mednard and percussionist Ismael Wignall. Over the course of an hour, they played the entire five-part "Rodin Suite" from the album, and more.

There, Gould was a more assertive player, striking the keys with assurance and settling into a deep groove dug by Holt and Mednard, with Wignall adding accents not only from congas but a variety of shakers as well. Lu and Wintz soloed before he did, but when the pianist finally dove in, he ran the keyboard with an almost McCoy Tyner-esque blend of lyricism and power. Through it all, nearly 7 minutes of music, Pelt remained stock-still and silent at center stage, blowing one quick fanfare then letting his band run. Finally, he took a solo of his own, but it was much more rooted in the piece's theme than what Gould and the others had played; it was almost as if he was attempting to rein them back in with his own statement.

Gould is very much an up-and-coming performer, having only appeared on about two dozen albums since the mid-2000s. Still, he's worked with saxophonist Donald Harrison, drummer Ralph Peterson Jr., the late trumpeter Wallace Roney and others.

But his three recordings as a leader showcase his talents better than anything he's done as a sideman. That's often true, but in Gould's case the difference is stark.

His 2016 debut album, *Clockwork*, was released on the Fresh Sound New Talent label from Spain. There are several forms a pianist's first album can take; one of the most common is a simple trio date, preferably one with a rhythm section composed of better-known veterans. Gould dispensed with two traditional practices in one. While he was joined throughout by Ben Williams — the bassist in Jazzmeia Horn's group — and drummer E.J. Strickland, on eight of the album's eleven tracks, there were horns present as well. Jeremy Pelt, who also co-produced the record, was on trumpet, Godwin Louis played alto saxophone and Myron Walden was on tenor. And even more surprisingly, a string trio — violinist Yoojin Park (on whose 2013 album *West End* Gould had played), violist Heejin Chang and cellist Veronica Parrales — showed up on three tracks. With the addition of Anne Drummond on flute and Pedrito Martinez on percussion, the ensemble grew to an impressive 11 members, all working together on a blend of jazz and modern chamber music.

The album's centerpiece was the two-part "Apostle John," running nearly 12 minutes in all. The sound of the strings swirling and zinging around Gould's rippling, McCoy Tyner-esque piano, and surging behind Walden's surprisingly fierce tenor solo, was enough to make one's pulse quicken and heart soar. But "The Return," on which Louis's alto was the only horn, was equally exciting, a quick-footed post-bop excursion with a twitchy energy.

The Tyner influence was extremely strong on *Clockwork*. The music seemed to recall particularly albums the late pianist made shortly after leaving John Coltrane's band, like 1967's *The Real McCoy* and 1968's *Tender Moments*. Walden's tenor playing also sounded influenced by Joe Henderson's work on the former disc. But Gould's own voice came through with equal clarity, in the compositions and especially the orchestrations. Even when he adapted Wayne Shorter's "Nefertiti" toward the end of the disc, it was still possible to hear a unique musical mind pondering the thoughts of another.

The horns were absent; Gould explored Shorter's mantra-like melody with just Williams and Strickland behind him, and he spun it out into complex but never meandering extrapolations (unlike the original Miles Davis quintet version, on which the horns repeated their line over and over again as the bass and particularly the drums went ever farther out). When Williams took a forcefully plucked solo, that famously keening melody returned, soft, in the background, as Strickland danced on the cymbals.

"I was completely floored, man," Pelt said of *Clockwork*. "I didn't know that he had this much depth. I was very impressed with the whole thing."

Gould's second album, 2018's *Earthlings*, showcased his skills as an interpreter rather than as a composer. He wrote or co-wrote only four of the ten tracks; the others included versions of Mulgrew Miller's "Farewell to Dogma," Horace Silver's "Love Vibrations," Bobby Hutcherson's "Roses Poses," and the title track, a piece by saxophonist Joe Ford, revealing the depth of his listening in the process, as these were not obvious or overly familiar tunes. Criss Cross sessions are typically stripped-down affairs, and the core group on *Earthlings* consisted only of bassist Dezron Douglas, drummer Eric McPherson and percussionist Kahlil Kwame Bell. Alto saxophonist Godwin Louis and soprano saxophonist Tim Warfield appeared on five tracks between them, overlapping on only one, the bouncing "Blues On Top," a Gould original that sounded like a cross between the 1980s music of Wynton Marsalis and that of clarinetist Don Byron from a decade later.

In 2019, Gould released his third album, *Thoughts Become*

Things, on the upstart Blue Room Music label. From its cover art down, it was a counterpart to *Clockwork*, again featuring an expanded ensemble with Pelt on trumpet, Drummond on flute and alto flute, Louis on alto saxophone, Dayna Stephens on tenor saxophone, Lucas Pino on bass clarinet and Aaron Johnson on bass trombone, Vicente Archer on bass, Rodney Green on drums, Wignall on percussion and a string quartet featuring Yoojin Park and Jim Tsao on violins, Jocelin Pan on viola and Susan Mandel on cello. It was a more somber and individualistic statement than its predecessor, though.

The opening track, "Brand New," was a solo piano piece, and on the tracks that featured horns, only one player per piece was permitted a solo. Toward the end of the album, Gould and Pelt played a duo version of the Jimmy Van Heusen/Johnny Burke standard "Polka Dots and Moonbeams." But "October" was a true highlight. It was a fantastically lush, intricately arranged composition that recalled the late 70s/early 80s work of trumpeter Woody Shaw in the way it blended romanticism with high-level instrumental technique, but Shaw never had a string quartet behind him that I know of. The chamber music atmosphere was strengthened not only by the presence of the string quartet, but also by the thrilling alto flute solo from Drummond — exactly the kind of surprising choice that makes his work so unique and breathtaking.

In 2020, Gould is one of the new members of the Black Art Jazz Collective, and according to BAJC co-founder Wayne Escoffery, the choice was obvious.

> Victor had subbed in Black Art Jazz Collective many times, when Xavier Davis couldn't do it. So he was definitely one of the first choices when we thought about changing the rhythm section, because he'd played the music a few times and kind of had an idea of the concept and energy of the band. He's an amazing composer and I was really eager to have some of

> his music represented on Black Art Jazz Collective's album. His compositions are challenging. Not all of them, but some of them are, particularly "Ascension," the title track. There's some intricate rhythms there, and the piece doesn't really lay how you expect it to lay, and that's what I wanted; I wanted musicians to come in and throw stuff at us that would challenge us.

Gould doesn't just challenge his bandmates, he challenges listeners, but never in a harsh or assaultive way. And he throws down a gauntlet for other musicians, who must recognize that there's a major new composer on the scene.

Essential Listening

Victor Gould, *Clockwork* (Fresh Sound New Talent, 2016)
Jazzmeia Horn, *A Social Call* (Prestige, 2017)
Victor Gould, *Earthlings* (Criss Cross, 2018)
Jazzmeia Horn, *Love and Liberation* (Concord Jazz, 2019)
Victor Gould, *Thoughts Become Things* (Blue Room Music, 2019)

Ethan Iverson & Orrin Evans: In Two Notes I Could Tell

Since about 2005, drummer Billy Hart has led a quartet with saxophonist Mark Turner, pianist Ethan Iverson and bassist Ben Street. They have recorded two albums for ECM and one for HighNote. I saw a variation of the group at the Village Vanguard in 2016. Turner was absent, replaced by Houston Person. A bluesy soul jazz player with a feel for ballads, Person played like he should have been wearing a ruffled tuxedo. He talked to the audience between songs, particularly the ladies seated at tables in the front, and every song — most of which were well-known jazz standards — had a beginning, a middle, an end and a melody you could hum. All four musicians on the stage were having a good time, playing songs they either knew well or could make a meal out of, or both, particularly Iverson. It was one of the most traditional, old-school shows I'd ever seen, and one of the best I saw that year, by anyone.

Ethan Iverson's position in the jazz world is an odd one. He rose to fame, and commercial success, as one-third of the Bad Plus, a collective trio with bassist Reid Anderson and drummer Dave King. Together, they made twelve studio albums and two live releases between 2000 and 2016, including collaborations with singer Wendy Lewis and saxophonist Joshua Redman. They earned critical acclaim and an audience outside the jazz scene, largely through their interpretations of rock and pop songs by Nirvana, Rush, ABBA, the Pixies, David Bowie, Black Sabbath, Yes, Pink Floyd, Heart and many others. They also recorded several albums that contained only original material, though, and a surprising and strong interpretation of Igor Stravinsky's *The Rite of Spring*. And in 2014 and 2015, they expanded to a sextet featuring alto saxophonist Tim Berne, soprano saxophonist Sam Newsome and cornet player Ron Miles for a tour on which they performed music from Ornette Coleman's 1971 album *Science Fiction* and other contemporaneous tunes from his book.

They never looked like they belonged in the same band. Iverson is a short, stout, professorial fellow with a shaved head, pink as a brand-new pencil eraser. Anderson is of medium height and clean-cut in the manner of a retail store manager, while King, heavily tattooed and with a wild gleam in his eye, looks like he loads and unloads trucks for a living. (He has a side band called the Dave King Trucking Company that has made three albums.)

I didn't listen to the Bad Plus much when they were at their most popular. I reviewed their fourth album, 2005's *Suspicious Activity?*, but other than that, I was merely aware that they existed and had an audience. Iverson interested me, because he seemed to want very badly to be a "real" jazz musician. He's a focused and earnest student of the music, to the point of a kind of genial snobbery; he's stated often that the rock tunes were not familiar territory for him. He also built a parallel career during his tenure with the band, recording with masters like drummers Albert "Tootie" Heath and Billy Hart, and alto saxophonist Lee Konitz. He also launched a blog, Do The Math, on which he wrote long essays and conducted in-depth, discographically and historically focused interviews with players of previous generations.

Around the time I saw Iverson play with Houston Person, he published a conversation between them on the blog. Among other things, Person said, "I tell young people they should search for their own sound, and see what they hear. Everyone looks for different things. Me, I just want beauty. I want a pretty sound. It should also fill the room. A big, pretty sound that fills the room, that's what I want to do."

In April 2017, Iverson left the Bad Plus, by mutual decision. In an article by Nate Chinen, Anderson and King delineated the differences that had arisen among the three men. "Ethan started to have an agenda, especially critically," he said:

> That was a little bit uncomfortable for us, because all of a sudden we're in a band with a guy who's essentially a jazz critic. We're used to him throwing his opinions around the van, but having his opinions out there in the world so strongly all the time, it started to reflect on people thinking it was *all* of our opinions.

He added that "it felt a little bit like we became a bankroll for his desires to play with the old masters."

Since departing the trio, Iverson has continued writing, for magazines as well as online. He also teaches at New England Conservatory in Massachusetts, and has recorded for ECM, first in a duo with saxophonist Mark Turner and then in a quartet with trumpeter Tom Harrell, bassist Ben Street and drummer Eric McPherson.

The duo with Turner was a reunion of longtime friends. They had first played together at the turn of the century, and had been members of the Hart quartet for a decade and a half, off and on. But playing duets allowed them to dive deeper than ever into the things they had in common, including an innate sensitivity well-suited to ballads and spacious improvisations, and a general disinclination to explode. Turner is both a Buddhist and a vegan, and you can hear it in every note he plays.

On "Turner's Chamber of Unlikely Delights," they wound their way through a highly complex, ever-shifting series of melodic ideas. Turner spun out long lines on the tenor that were closer to the soprano's range, while Iverson delivered heavy, almost liturgical blues behind him and really seemed to think about every note. It was challenging music in the sense that if I were a saxophonist or a pianist, the idea of attempting to play it would terrify me, but as a listener, it was beautiful.

By contrast, I was prepared to dislike the quartet album, *Common Practice*. A set of standards and blues tunes, recorded live at the Village Vanguard, it seemed like an invitation to wallow in cliché, and a concept that held very little appeal for me in 2019. Some of the pieces performed were ones I would have been happy to never hear again in my life, like "All the Things You Are," "I'm Getting Sentimental Over You," and "I Can't Get Started." The fact that the band's work on two Iverson originals, "Jed From Teaneck" and "Philadelphia Creamer," was an order of magnitude more energized than on the standards only solidified my belief that they should have recorded nothing but new music. But by the time I finished listening to it, *Common Practice* had won me over, because the musicians were clearly, audibly taking pleasure from playing these old songs. There was nothing rote about their approach to the material, even if one had heard most of the songs a hundred times before. The version of "Sentimental Journey" was a particular highlight. Harrell's slightly squeaky, slightly smeared trumpet soared over Iverson's slow-dancing piano and the rhythm section's tick-and-boom.

Iverson's replacement in the Bad Plus, announced at the same time as his departure, was Philadelphia pianist Orrin Evans. When I read the news, I was immediately fascinated by the choice. To put it rudely, there had always been something white and nerdy about the Bad Plus, starting with their taste in covers and extending to their jackhammering version of swing. Dave King is a powerhouse drummer with tremendous technical skill, but he's not the most subtle dude to ever get behind a kit. And while their original compositions were enjoyable, their reliance on interpretations of pop and rock material, however creative, had led to them being perceived by a lot of folks, fairly or not, as a "safe" entry point into jazz.

Evans is almost the opposite of that. His music is deeply rooted in the African-American vernacular tradition of jazz. Temperamentally, he's an old-school swinger who came up playing with Ralph Peterson, a drummer who consciously strove to claim Art Blakey's mantle. So Anderson and King must have known the band might go in a very different direction with him in the piano chair.

He had a personal connection to the bassist, who was a groomsman at his wedding and played on his album *Listen to the Band* in 2000. They were both also members at one time of a collective known simply as the Band, with JD Allen on tenor sax, Sam Newsome on soprano and Nasheet Waits on drums. That group released a double CD, *Live at Widener University*, on Imani, a label Evans ran with his wife, Dawn.

I've only seen Evans live once, in a band led by tenor saxophonist Bill McHenry, with bassist Eric Revis and drummer Andrew Cyrille. They performed at the Village Vanguard, celebrating the release of the excellent album *La Peur du Vide*, recorded at the club in 2012. (McHenry had previously led a quartet with Reid Anderson on bass. Jazz is a small world, have you noticed?) I've interviewed him twice, though. In our first conversation, he told me about the roots of his style, which come directly from his hometown.

"There's a certain type of approach that I've only heard coming out of Philadelphia pianists," he said, adding:

> I know it's me 'cause it's me, but other people, I think they listen and hear what they think is my touch, that is similar to what some other pianists might play. And also how you interpret time. I think I have a really different approach to time, touch and feel. And I base a lot of that on my life experience — the music I grew up listening to, the people I checked out like Shirley Scott, Trudy Pitts, McCoy Tyner, Sid Simmons, all these people who are from Philadelphia. Sid Simmons was a great pianist from Philly who didn't blow up to international fame but still recorded a lot, and in two notes I could tell it was him, and that's because of that Philly sound that I heard resonating from the piano.

In the same conversation, he expressed misgivings about trio playing in general. On many of his albums, he's added horns to the band, and he leads a large ensemble, the Captain Black Big Band, whenever possible. "There's a sense of freedom that I do enjoy about playing trio, but there's also a sense of vulnerability that is extremely intimidating. And that's something I've always shied away from...you're out there, and you have to pull the cats along. But the same thing that intimidates me also intrigues me."

The Bad Plus is not the Orrin Evans Trio, though, just as it wasn't the Ethan Iverson Trio. It's a collective, with Reid Anderson and Dave King in the driver's seat most of the time. "There's a definite respect for how they've done it, and I have to be aware of it," he told me in 2018. One major adjustment was dealing with the band's no-sheet-music policy:

> I've never really memorized music; that wasn't a thing I had to do, but they memorize music. So hey, you're joining the Bad Plus, you've got to learn how to memorize music. I'm respecting that it's their house, and they have always made me feel at home, and each day I get more comfortable at leaving my shoes at the door, going and getting a glass from the cupboard. They've already said, "Make yourself feel at home."

In his own way, Evans was already familiar with that group dynamic, having formed Tarbaby with Eric Revis and Nasheet Waits in 2009. Their four albums, of which 2010's *The End of Fear* and 2013's *The Ballad of Sam Langford*, named for an early-twentieth century boxer, are the best, are aggressively political, deeply Black and utterly lacking in self-deprecating humor, pop-friendliness or ironic distance. Indeed, while he's more conventionally melodic and swinging than Matthew Shipp or Cecil Taylor, Evans' catalog is suffused with a seriousness of purpose equal to that of either man.

Thus far, his tenure with the Bad Plus has been marked by a sharp turn away from interpretations of outside material. Both of the two albums to include him as pianist, 2018's *Never Stop II* and 2019's *Activate Infinity*, have featured all-original music. Evans wrote two pieces for each.

Never Stop II (its title marking it as an explicit sequel to their first all-original set, from 2010) began with "Hurricane Birds," a jazz trio-does-Radiohead number that might seem clichéd, until you remember that the Bad Plus were more or less the inventors of that sound. Evans took the heavy chords and ostinato-ish pattern, written by Anderson, and transformed them into a bouncing, chopped-up cross between Vince Guaraldi and Thelonious Monk, something that shouldn't have worked but did.

For his first contribution as a writer, "Boffadem," he started out on a toy piano, pinging out tiny notes over a bouncing bass line from Anderson. It sounded like a synth patch from a Björk album. He switched back and forth repeatedly between the toy and a full-sized instrument, allowing the latter to serve as a kind of emphatic sonic punctuation. Behind him, King's rock-solid and heavy beat provided ideal support.

"Commitment," Evans' second piece, was the penultimate track on the LP, and seemed to be his way of welcoming the other two into his world, rather than vice versa. He opened it up for a King solo early on, and the drummer dominated the later passages, too, driving hard as the pianist spun through rapid, seemingly disjointed phrases. Then it all stopped dead, and the final minute-plus was an ultra-gentle ballad.

Throughout *Never Stop II*, Evans proved to be a lighter and more conventionally swinging pianist than his predecessor, while making it clear that he recognizes that it wasn't his band; he adapted to the new environment very well.

"The Red Door," one of his two contributions to *Activate*

Infinity, was an uptempo piece that began with a single, low chord followed by a dancing, almost Thelonious Monk-ish melody. When Anderson and King locked in, though, they were playing a light, flickering rhythm that swung but also seemed to bounce. The middle section took a sharp left turn into almost free playing, with Evans' piano suddenly diverging from the core melody entirely, like he'd passed through the titular door into an unlit room and was wandering around bumping into things, as King's drumming took on a scurrying, almost Rashied Ali-esque aspect. Eventually, of course, things came back into line, with Evans returning to the melody while King was still soloing. It took a few seconds for him to re-establish the groove, but when he did, it was even more energetic than before.

Evans continues to maintain a parallel career as a leader, and as a sideman. He has released two albums with the Captain Black Big Band since joining the Bad Plus, and intends to continue working on his own. It's a source of some frustration to him, though, that even after nearly 25 years and more than 20 albums, he's not the draw he'd like to be outside New York.

He told me:

> Although yes, I've got a 20-year career, that career didn't present a lot of situations for me to play as a leader outside New York or outside of Philly. Ninety percent of my work has been as a sideman, that has been notable as far as touring and the times that I've spent on the road. In the past 20 years, I've gone to Europe as a bandleader maybe five times. But because I've put out different records and I've really worked hard to be known as a leader, and I've played in New York as a leader...it makes me laugh, because...I can quote a direct conversation with Bob Bennett [owner of the Jazz Bistro in St. Louis, MO] from two years ago when he said, no one will come out to see you, Orrin Evans. Like, literally.

In 2018, Anderson and King revived their Ornette Coleman project in slightly different form. I went to the Jazz Standard one Wednesday night in May, to see the second of two shows by a new band called Broken Shadows. Like the Bad Plus's *Science Fiction* tour, it featured Tim Berne on alto sax, but he was joined by tenor saxophonist Chris Speed (who also plays in the Dave King Trucking Company), and there was no pianist. This time, they were paying tribute not only to Ornette, but to two other artists from Fort Worth, Texas: Julius Hemphill and Dewey Redman. They also performed Charlie Haden's "Song for Ché," but they modeled their version on the one heard on Ornette's 1969 album *Crisis*, not the large ensemble arrangement recorded by the late bassist's Liberation Music Orchestra.

Ornette Coleman compositions may be the most instantly recognizable in jazz. Even if you don't know the name of a given tune, you can tell in 2 seconds that it came from his pen. Broken Shadows played four of his pieces in an eight-song set, along with the aforementioned Haden tune, one by Redman and two by Hemphill. They mostly opted for relative obscurities, so we didn't get versions of Hemphill's "Dogon A.D." or Coleman's "Lonely Woman," but that choice actually allowed the audience to focus on what the musicians were doing to make these performances live, rather than mentally comparing them to the records.

Perhaps it was the way the microphones were positioned, but the bass and drums often seemed louder than the horns. Speed's solos were more fluttery and meandering than Berne's, even when King was driving him ferociously hard. But the way the alto and tenor sang the complex melodies together was truly beautiful, in a just-this-side-of-unfettered manner that conjured the spirit of Coleman, Hemphill and Redman more than anything else. King offered entertaining banter every couple of tunes, and the whole thing was raucous and thrillingly alive.

Tradition and originality must be carefully balanced in jazz.

Live and on record, all four current and former members of the Bad Plus deploy their compositional and interpretive skills in a kind of never-ending tightrope walk between those two poles. They know where they came from; where they're going remains to be seen.

Essential Listening

The Bad Plus, *These are the Vistas* (Columbia, 2003)
Orrin Evans, *Flip the Script* (Posi-Tone, 2012)
Tarbaby, *The Ballad of Sam Langford* (HiPNOTIC, 2013)
Orrin Evans' Captain Black Big Band, *Mother's Touch* (Posi-Tone, 2014)
The Bad Plus, *The Rite of Spring* (Sony Masterworks, 2014)
Mark Turner/Ethan Iverson, *Temporary Kings* (ECM, 2018)
The Bad Plus, *Never Stop II* (Legbreaker, 2018)
Ethan Iverson Quartet with Tom Harrell, *Common Practice* (2019)
Chris Speed/Dave King/Reid Anderson/Tim Berne, *Broken Shadows Live* (Screwgun, 2020)

Jason Moran: How Do You Value Your Work?

The first time I saw pianist Jason Moran play live, he was a member of alto saxophonist Greg Osby's band, along with vibraphonist Stefon Harris, bassist Lonnie Plaxico and drummer Eric Harland. Osby and Moran (and sometimes Harris) worked together frequently for several years, on the pianist's 1999 debut *Soundtrack to Human Motion*, the vibraphonist's *A Cloud of Red Dust* and a string of Osby albums including *Zero, Banned in New York, Friendly Fire, New Directions, Symbols of Light (A Solution)* and *Inner Circle*.

Moran broke out on his own quickly, though. I saw him a second time a couple of years later, leading the Bandwagon, his trio with bassist Tarus Mateen and drummer Nasheet Waits, with legendary avant-garde saxophonist Sam Rivers as their guest. The four men had recorded an astonishing album together, 2001's *Black Stars*, and appeared at New York's Iridium to celebrate its release. The thorniness of Rivers' saxophone style meshed with the Bandwagon's equally challenging, but different approach, creating something that was simultaneously modern and classic, declaring that the so-called avant-garde had long since become a codified language...and that was a *good thing*.

During his 15-year tenure with Blue Note Records, which encompassed nine albums as a leader and appearances on discs by Osby, Harris, singer Cassandra Wilson and clarinetist Don Byron, Moran took his music in many directions, showcasing and synthesizing a broad range of inspirations. His follow-up to *Black Stars* was *Modernistic*, a solo disc that included interpretations of pieces by James P. Johnson, avant-garde composer Muhal Richard Abrams of the Chicago-based AACM, and hip-hop pioneer Afrika Bambaataa.

His final Blue Note album was 2014's *All Rise: A Joyful Elegy for Fats Waller*, an outgrowth of a live "Fats Waller dance party" he had been performing since 2010. On it, he took the stride pianist's compositions and brought them into the modern era with a band that included three horns (trumpet, trombone and alto sax), Mateen switching between electric and upright bass, and Moran himself jumping to Wurlitzer or Fender Rhodes electric piano as the moment demanded. A stripped-down piano-drums version of "Lulu's Back in Town," a song also recorded by Thelonious Monk, seemed to draw the straightest line from past to future.

After leaving Blue Note, Moran began to focus on unique events rather than the recordings-and-gigs cycle that is the average jazz musician's lot. He wrote specially commissioned pieces for festivals like Other Minds, documenta and the Whitney Biennial, often in collaboration with his wife, soprano Alicia Hall Moran; accompanied theatrical productions and ballet companies; and in 2013 and 2014, soundtracked skateboarding shows at San Francisco's SFJAZZ Center. He also toured extensively as a member of saxophonist Charles Lloyd's New Quartet with bassist Reuben Rogers and drummer Eric Harland, and was one of two pianists (David Virelles was the other) on Henry Threadgill's 2016 album *Old Locks and Irregular Verbs*.

In 2018, Moran launched his most ambitious project, a self-titled museum exhibition and massive multimedia work. Premiering at the Walker Art Center in Minneapolis, then moving to the Institute for Contemporary Art in Boston and the Wexner Center in Columbus, Ohio, it finished its run at the Whitney Museum in New York.

The exhibition included three installations modeled on historic New York jazz venues: the Savoy Ballroom in Harlem, the Three Deuces in midtown Manhattan and Slugs' Saloon in Greenwich Village. Each of these had an audio component as well. Work songs from the Louisiana State Penitentiary in Angola droned from the Savoy; a player piano at the Three Deuces played improvisations by Moran; and the Slugs' Saloon set featured a jukebox that emitted audience sounds recorded at the Village Vanguard, where the Bandwagon has played every Thanksgiving weekend for years. Works on paper, including scores and abstract drawings, were also displayed, as were films and recordings of various Moran collaborations and theatrical projects.

During the course of the exhibition, which ran from September 2019 to January 2020, musicians were invited to perform live, including saxophonist Archie Shepp in duo with Moran, vocalist Fay Victor with saxophonist Darius Jones and cellist Christopher Hoffman, and drummer Jamire Williams with dancer Marlon Taylor-Wiles.

When Moran returned to releasing music as a leader, in 2016, he launched a Bandcamp page instead of signing with a label. The first release, *The Armory Concert*, was his second solo recording, and where 2002's *Modernistic* had featured interpretations of others' music, *Armory* was a collection of ten new original compositions. That was followed by a live Bandwagon disc, *Thanksgiving at the Vanguard*.

I spoke to Moran by phone one afternoon in 2017, and he told me that "part of [the Bandwagon's] strength is that we don't tour all the time. It's in spurts. And I have so many different special projects that will sometimes spur from how the Bandwagon works...that helps us to keep our perspective."

Moran called their collective language "slippery," and told me he felt like their sound was "something that's still, I don't want to say raw, but it's definitely still got some soil attached to the vegetables, you know what I mean?" He also ascribed a great deal of freedom to each member, saying, "Although we might assume our roles much of the time, we also know that we can leave that role at any moment, and change the direction of the song." Indeed, for a player with so much stride, blues and church music in his style, Moran is remarkably free.

That freedom manifested itself quite strongly on his third Bandcamp release, *BANGS*. It was a trio recording featuring cornet player Ron Miles and guitarist Mary Halvorson, whose style is an often startling blend of sharp edges and strange, off-kilter ripples and squiggles. I would never have picked her as someone who traveled in the same circles as Moran, but New York is a very small town sometimes.

"My wife and I heard Mary playing with Vernon Reid, Marc Ribot, and Elliott Sharp at [the Museum of Modern Art] maybe 10 or 11 years ago, and we thought she outplayed everybody," he told me with a laugh.

> There was such originality, really, in her entire approach to the instrument. So...Alicia first started working with her on some stuff that was never released, except one song that was on her record *Heavy Blue*. And this trio with Ron Miles is something we've been doing off and on [since 2012]. But *really* off and on — like, once every year and a half, we'll play. And the last time we played, I said, "We should really make this a record."

BANGS was a remarkably visceral set of ten compositions — Moran wrote five, Halvorson three and Miles two — that left plenty of room for fierce improvisation. On the guitarist's "Red Sky Green," Moran's piano rang out with sharpness and clarity, his fast, extrapolating melodic runs echoing the language of Cecil Taylor as Halvorson and Miles played staccato phrases on either side of him. By contrast, Miles' "Cupid" was a ballad so tender and sketched-out, it could have been a Coldplay song. Some of Moran's pieces, like "Crops" and "They Come to Us Theme," featured programmed percussion; on the latter, Halvorson's guitar sounded like Delta blues played on a detuned zither, while the pianist pounded out huge, booming chords and Miles raced along beside them, his notes soft but emphatic.

One of the most startling things about Moran's new independent releases was the price point. The digital-only Bandcamp releases were $20 each (with physical CDs available for $25 from a separate website), where most artists asked between $5 and $12 for an album, with some allowing listeners to name their own price. And where albums could usually be streamed in their entirety on the Bandcamp site before a listener decided whether or not to buy, Moran enabled streaming for just one or two tracks at most.

He told me:

> I think about music as, "What do you value it at?" and that's basically it. I've often been asked this very question, and my immediate response is, look at the back of a slave that's been whipped, and ask yourself, 'How do you value your work?' That's the end for me. I could charge $50 for this, and if a person wants it, they want it. If they don't, they don't. It's totally fine.

The next time I saw Jason Moran perform live was in January 2019. He was accompanying drummer Kassa Overall at the Jazz Gallery. Overall had booked a 6-month residency at the venue; once a month, he would come in with a different pianist and perform improvised duos. These were recorded, and some of the music ultimately became part of his 2020 album *I Think I'm Good*. The set with Moran kicked off the series; it turned out to be a trio performance, because bassist Evan Flory-Barnes was added to the lineup.

They played a surprisingly long set — almost 90 minutes — that included music by composer Maurice Ravel and jazz pianist Geri Allen, and also featured some sound manipulation from the board, in the manner of a live dub mix. Overall seemed happier locking into a hip-hop groove with Flory-Barnes than swinging, and his drum solos had a thick, muscular aggression, including barrages of tom and snare. Moran met him on his chosen ground, clanging out powerful runs and keeping the energy level high, even when journeying into more romantic zones. It reminded me that while he's as tied into the jazz tradition — including some of its least fashionable parts, like ragtime and the specific blues traditions of his native Texas — as anyone, he is also very much a man of the twenty-first century, living in the moment and interacting with the world around him as it is.

Essential Listening

Jason Moran, *Soundtrack to Human Motion* (Blue Note, 1999)
Jason Moran feat. Sam Rivers, *Black Stars* (Blue Note, 2001)
Jason Moran, *Modernistic* (Blue Note, 2002)
Jason Moran, *All Rise: A Joyful Elegy for Fats Waller* (Blue Note, 2014)
Jason Moran, *BANGS* (Yes, 2017)
Jason Moran, *Looks of a Lot* (Yes, 2018)

PART II

Vijay Iyer; Taylor Ho Bynum; Tomeka Reid; Nicole Mitchell; Mary Halvorson; Linda May Han Oh; Tyshawn Sorey

Introduction

Many years ago, the writer Frank Kogan came up with the idea of the Superword, which he describes as:

> a battleground, a weapon, a red cape, a prize, a flag in a bloody game of Capture the Flag. To put this in the abstract, a Superword is a word or phrase that not only is used in fights but that is itself fought over. The fight is over who gets to wear the word proudly, who gets the word affixed to him against his will, etc.

Kogan used the words "punk" and "metal" as his primary examples, but to my mind jazz is one of the all-time Superwords. It is freighted with so much cultural and even psychological baggage that its impact on us is practically subconscious — as discussed in the first section of this book, there are records you can play for someone who claims to know nothing about jazz, and upon hearing them they will say, "Yes, that's jazz." But how much of the work of Taylor Ho Bynum, Mary Halvorson, Vijay Iyer, Linda May Han Oh, Tomeka Reid or Tyshawn Sorey can you say that about? The majority? In some cases, but not all. Iyer has written string quartets and entire albums of electronic music. Oh blends jazz rhythms with string arrangements pulled from modern chamber music. Sorey has written massive, multi-hour works that fit no category at all.

For decades, musicians identified with jazz by critics and scholars have rejected the label, with varying degrees of vehemence. They see it as limiting, patronizing and possibly racist. And there's truth to all of that. Even if you're being generous, you must recognize that "jazz" is nothing but a marketing term like "hip-hop," "country," "rock 'n' roll" or worst of all "world music," and denotes no actual musical qualities, or at least no absolutes. For every sonic trope that you can assert as definitive to a particular genre, you can tally up a thousand examples of records that don't have that thing, but are unmistakably of that genre.

Still, you must also accept that jazz is one of the most successful marketing terms of all time. Want proof? Start with the fact that it's been adjective-ized. If someone says the word "jazzy" to you, you immediately have a vague sense of what they mean. It refers to a set of musical signifiers (loose, swinging rhythm; bluesy melodies; piano and probably horns) but also to a set of non-musical signifiers, some material – sunglasses, cigarettes, late nights in cities – and some psychological or attitudinal: a particular sort of relaxed, "cool" performance of the self.

But let's stick with those musical signifiers for the moment. If an artist is known for making music that can be identified as jazz with relative ease, even if it's free or avant-garde jazz, and then they release a piece of work that has none of the musical qualities associated with jazz, are they still a jazz musician? The answer should be yes. But what if we approach it from the opposite angle? What if someone known as a classical composer creates a piece scored for trumpet, tenor saxophone, piano, upright bass and drums, and says that, as part of the score, the musicians will be improvising based on pre-determined melodic structures? There is room for improvisation in classical music, even more so in modern composition; they just call it "indeterminacy." But is that piece a classical composition, or a jazz tune? And does it matter?

Perhaps it doesn't, in the grand scheme of things. But how about this: if someone chooses to self-identify as a jazz artist, but makes music which does not possess the commonly understood qualities of jazz – improvised solos, blues forms, swinging rhythms – are they really jazz artists? Can they be written out of the genre at a certain point, if they have traveled too far from jazz's vernacular roots? If their music, to put it crudely, isn't Black enough? And how far is too far, anyway? All of the artists discussed in this chapter have pushed right up against jazz's apparent boundaries. They have written through-composed music for unorthodox combinations of instruments, eschewing traditional structures and recording it knowing that it will likely never be performed live.

Many of the artists in the pages that follow, who dwell on this particular branch of the jazz tree, are connected with Anthony Braxton and/or Roscoe Mitchell; they've played in one or the other man's bands, if not both. But Braxton and Mitchell were hardly the first to embrace composition and "non-jazz" ideas in this way. It's been part of the music since the beginning. Duke Ellington wrote "Reminiscing in Tempo," a through-composed piece, in 1935. Eric Dolphy was performing the music of Edgard Varèse at the same time that he was making jazz records under his own leadership and with John Coltrane and Charles Mingus. Ornette Coleman wrote a symphony, *Skies of America*, and multiple chamber music works. Charlie Parker was obsessed with Stravinsky, and likely would have explored much more broadly had he lived longer. These musicians are points on a line, and if "jazz" doesn't encompass what they do, it is only a sign that the word is inadequate to the task.

Vijay Iyer: On the Either-Or Side

On a warm Friday evening in October 2017, I took the subway uptown to 129th Street, to the Lantern, a small upstairs room in Columbia University's Lenfest Center for the Arts. The Art Ensemble of Chicago were performing in New York for the first time since 2004. I'd seen them that time, too, at Iridium, the Midtown club where I'd seen Jason Moran and Sam Rivers, and, a few years later, Cecil Taylor.

The Art Ensemble's original bassist, Malachi Favors, had died just 3 months before that Iridium show, so it was something of a memorial to him. Jaribu Shahid, who had worked with Art Ensemble founder Roscoe Mitchell going back to 1981, had filled the bass chair. Trumpeter Lester Bowie, another founding member of the group, had died in 1999; Corey Wilkes, substantially younger than the other members of the band, subbed for him. The two shows they played were recorded for a 2006 double CD, *Non-Cognitive Aspects of the City* (named for a Joseph Jarman composition), which was the last Art Ensemble album to be released until they returned with *We Are On the Edge: A 50th Anniversary Celebration* in 2019.

For a long time, the group had gone quiet. Jarman had retired from music entirely, but Mitchell and drummer Famoudou Don Moye stayed active as solo artists or leading other ensembles, the former in particular. The Columbia show had come as a major surprise, especially once it was announced that Jarman would be appearing. Tickets sold out fast.

There were a lot of musicians and other avant-jazz figures of note in the audience. I was seated next to Vijay Iyer and his daughter. There was a spot directly behind me reserved for Henry Threadgill; he didn't make it, but when I turned around at the end of the show, fellow alto saxophonist Darius Jones was there. And while waiting around outside beforehand, I met drummer Tyshawn Sorey, whose work I had been listening to for years but with whom I had never spoken before that night.

The performance itself was quite something. At their peak in the 1970s and 1980s, Art Ensemble shows were theatrical extravaganzas. Members wore costumes (Bowie a lab coat; Jarman, Favors and Moye robes and face paint) and chanted, and the stage was covered with a vast array of horns, percussion equipment and "little instruments" which were used to create a constant, fluid chatter, a jungle of sound that suited their motto, "Great Black Music: Ancient to the Future." This twenty-first-century incarnation of the Ensemble, though, was often closer in spirit to Mitchell's solo work, which blurs and even erases the lines between avant-garde jazz and modern composition.

The lineup featured Mitchell on alto and soprano saxophones, Hugh Ragin on trumpet, Tomeka Reid on cello, Jaribu Shahid and Junius Paul on basses, and Moye on drums. Ragin kicked things off with a gentle and quite beautiful trumpet solo, which Mitchell countered, playing the high-pitched soprano sax like something was stuck and he couldn't quite get the notes to come all the way out. (This is in line with his main musical obsessions, which are improvisation, pure sound and opposition. It's also extraordinarily difficult, and hearing him do it was almost dizzying.) Slowly, the rest of the group came in, playing together in a way that almost swung but still retained an avant-garde energy. And then, midway through the set, an old man in a baseball cap stood up and took a seat with the group. I hadn't even recognized Joseph Jarman!

He read from a notebook for quite a while, as Moye moved to congas and the band dropped the intensity level just enough to provide a backdrop for his verses, which returned again and again to themes, more like chanted incantations than poems. (Jarman, who was an actual Buddhist monk and aikido teacher, used to deliver an invocation to begin each year's Vision Festival. My first encounters with any members of the Art Ensemble came in 1998, when he opened the festival's first night, and Roscoe Mitchell performed in a trio with vocalist Thomas Buckner and pianist Borah Bergman.)

After Jarman finished, the set rose to a crescendo that was like an old-school free jazz blowout, everyone all in, but it never had the wild abandon of a set by saxophonists Charles Gayle or the late Frank Wright. Mitchell's demeanor is professorial; he was wearing a really nice shirt and tie, and always maintained a posture that implied that everything was going exactly how he'd planned it. In a way, it was like he was saying that "free" was just one more way of making music, no different than any other, and that's sort of been the philosophy behind the Art Ensemble's music for the entire 50 years of their existence. They'll pull from anywhere, low or high, and put it all on the same plane. They're amazing synthesists, creating something uniquely their own out of wildly disparate elements.

Vijay Iyer had been a member of one of Mitchell's bands, the Note Factory, in the 2000s, playing on 2002's *Song for My Sister* and 2010's *Far Side*. I'd also heard him on several CDs by Burnt Sugar the Arkestra Chamber (a large improvising ensemble conducted by music critic Greg Tate) and trumpeter Wadada Leo Smith's Golden Quartet. I first met Iyer in 2006, when I was editing the "world music" magazine *Global Rhythm*. He'd made a duo album, *Raw Materials*, with saxophonist Rudresh Mahanthappa, and they'd come by the office to talk to me about it.

That afternoon, we discussed the idea of Indian-Americans as the "model minority," and how that tied into the idea of jazz becoming a gentrified, academic music, moving ever farther from its vernacular Black roots. He said:

> One thing that you see is...that Asian-Americans become the boundary by which American identity is defined. So we are always the people who are on the either-or side of the American fence. I see it happening almost in the way we're

> included in the jazz world, which is often that we're included by saying, 'This is part of this international movement in jazz,' when both of us have grown up here.

Just over a decade later, in May 2017, I visited Iyer in his Harlem apartment. We sat in his airy, sunlit kitchen on a Tuesday afternoon, a load of laundry running behind him as we talked. He'd just finished recording *Far From Over*, an album featuring cornet player Graham Haynes, alto saxophonist Steve Lehman, tenor saxophonist Mark Shim, bassist Stephan Crump and Sorey on drums, for ECM Records, and was preparing for a trio engagement at the Village Vanguard, with the latter two.

Prior to signing with ECM, Iyer had released a string of critically acclaimed albums on the German label ACT Music, beginning with 2009's *Historicity*. That disc, with Crump on bass and Marcus Gilmore on drums, was a wide-ranging collection that included four original tunes and six covers, including versions of avant-garde touchstones like Julius Hemphill's "Dogon A.D." and Andrew Hill's "Smoke Stack," as well as adaptations of "Somewhere" from the musical *West Side Story*, Stevie Wonder's "Big Brother" and, most surprisingly, MIA's "Galang." It received nearly universal acclaim from jazz and, perhaps more importantly, rock critics; for a few years, it seemed like Iyer was the only jazz artist being reviewed on Pitchfork.

"I suppose from the outside it seems like working with a label is some kind of big artistic choice," he told me, "but what it actually is, is just a set of transactions." For him, signing with ACT was a way of gaining an audience outside the US. "You'll pay for this, you'll promote it when I'm there, I'll have more press in Europe, so then it'll be easier for me to get more gigs in Europe. Cool, let's give it a try."

Between 2009 and 2012, Iyer's profile grew year after year, and in 2012, he swept critics' polls; his trio album *Accelerando* was named *DownBeat*'s Album of the Year. In 2013, he received a

MacArthur Fellowship, a so-called "genius grant." And in 2014, he left ACT for ECM. His first release for them was *Mutations,* an album of compositions for piano, electronics and string quartet. That was followed by another trio disc, 2015's *Break Stuff,* and 2016's *A cosmic rhythm with each stroke,* a set of duos with Wadada Leo Smith.

Iyer seems to consider his work an extension of ECM's avant-garde 1970s output. "You can't really summarize them," he says of the label. "But there's this sort of cliché way of talking about ECM in the last 20 years that actually erases all this other stuff that happened...my relationship to ECM was like, Dave Holland's *Conference of the Birds,* Wadada's *Divine Love,* the Art Ensemble of Chicago's *The Third Decade,* Jack DeJohnette's stuff, Don Cherry, Lester Bowie..."

Watching a pianist play can give you real insight into their personality. Iyer sits up straight on the bench, eyes halfway or entirely closed, chin tucked down toward his chest. He sometimes strikes the keys with his fingers splayed wide and flat, the way Thelonious Monk did, but his notes are clean and precise, ringing sharply like McCoy Tyner's. A self-taught pianist (his first instrument was violin, which he played for 15 years), he always seems to be enjoying himself. He'll suddenly lean backwards at times, as though in excited surprise at what he's just played. While his lines have a lyrical flow, rhythm is extremely important to him, and his attack often has the machine-gun percussiveness and obsessive repetition of drum programming.

I saw him play twice in the span of 3 months. The first was in November 2019, at ECM's fiftieth anniversary concert, hosted by Jazz at Lincoln Center. The show featured close to a dozen acts, each getting 10-15 minutes of stage time. It began with Brazilian pianist Egberto Gismonti, performing solo in an extremely lyrical and romantic manner. That was followed by the trio of saxophonist Joe Lovano, pianist Marilyn Crispell and drummer Carmen Castaldi, playing two pieces from their 2019 album *Trio Tapestry*.

For me, the most thrilling portion of the concert was two back-to-back sets. The first was a duo performance by Iyer, who started out on electric piano, and Smith. The two improvised together for about 10 minutes in a way that was simultaneously soft and gentle, but throbbing with energy. Then Iyer left the stage, but Smith remained. He was joined by guitarist Bill Frisell and drummer Andrew Cyrille, and they performed a piece from *Lebroba*, an album they'd made in 2018. It was louder and more aggressive than what Smith and Iyer had done, but his stunningly beautiful trumpet playing, much of it with the horn pointed straight down at the stage, was the common factor. Each note was like an ice-cold dagger fired straight through every audience member's heart.

In late January 2020, I saw Iyer again, playing in a trio with Linda May Han Oh on bass and Sorey on drums, at the Jazz Standard. They were premiering new music, seven pieces in all, with Iyer addressing the audience at the beginning and end of the set. In between, it was all business.

The first piece was a strutting vamp, as much a showcase for Oh and Sorey as for Iyer — the pianist played very softly at first, then struck harder; the effect was like he was being faded in by an engineer. Sorey took a big solo, Oh a shorter one. This led into a gentle ballad, with the drummer switching to brushes at first, but halfway through, the music erupted, leaping into double time and getting seriously loud. Oh was dancing with her bass as she played, and Sorey's attack was astonishingly precise, but as forceful as death metal.

The next few numbers were a journey through various piano styles, all delivered with Iyer's mix of focus and ebullience. They played a bouncy and swinging but complex piece that sounded like what might have happened if Chick Corea, rather than Vince Guaraldi, had gotten the gig composing music for the *Peanuts* animated cartoons; Sorey's drumming was like Roy Haynes playing breakbeats. That transitioned seamlessly into a calmer, midtempo piece with a very Keith Jarrett feel and lots of space for Oh to wander and explore. After that, the trio entered an almost Thelonious Monk-ish zone, with Sorey playing like an angry Questlove, knocking out a steady soul beat punctuated by fierce snare rolls. Iyer, meanwhile, was hitting in such a disjointed style he sounded like chopped-up samples of piano at times.

The set ended with another ballad, very soft and slow, with Sorey using mallets on the toms and hi-hat, and Oh offering little beyond the occasional boom, and then a big McCoy Tyner-esque closer. Iyer was all over the keyboard and Sorey was almost martial, as Oh bounced and danced between them, sounding like Dave Holland. Eventually, pianist and drummer began trading fours, hard and heavy, before the piece — and the evening — ended in an almost Latin zone.

"I don't know how to set out to develop an individual voice on the piano, but I also don't know how not to," Iyer told me in 2017.

> I mean, I've studied very carefully and closely and for decades the music and playing of Thelonious Monk and Duke Ellington and Andrew Hill and Cecil Taylor and McCoy Tyner and Herbie Hancock and Herbie Nichols and Randy Weston and Ahmad Jamal, Alice Coltrane, Geri Allen, Hank Jones — I've gone in detail, transcribed and analyzed and tried to learn details about what they're doing, but not with the aim of imitating them. I mean, I *wish* I could do what McCoy Tyner did — it was mostly just, I hope one day I'll be able to make good music.

When Iyer's albums balance original pieces with versions of songs by Stephen Sondheim, Stevie Wonder and MIA, and he composes for string quartet as capably as for piano trio (or sextet), and creates electronic music on laptop and synthesizer, is he a jazz musician? Is he making "new music" in the modern-classical sense? Does interpreting the Michael Jackson hit "Human Nature" make him a pop performer? Or is he in a territory all his own, the borders of which encompass all these things and leave room for further exploration yet to be revealed?

Essential Listening

Vijay Iyer Trio, *Historicity* (ACT Music, 2009)
Vijay Iyer Trio, *Accelerando* (ACT Music, 2012)
Vijay Iyer, *Mutations* (ECM, 2014)
Wadada Leo Smith/Vijay Iyer, *A cosmic rhythm with each stroke* (ECM, 2016)
Vijay Iyer Sextet, *Far From Over* (ECM, 2017)

Taylor Ho Bynum: Blurring Lines, Upending Expectations

One of the things I find most fascinating about avant-garde jazz and improvised music is the methods people use to impose structure, while still allowing room for players to run free. In August 2019, I went to the Jazz Gallery to witness a performance by cornet player Taylor Ho Bynum's 9-Tette. They were premiering music from the album *The Ambiguity Manifesto,* which would be released the following month.

The group featured alto saxophonist Jim Hobbs, tenor and soprano saxophonist Ingrid Laubrock, bass trombonist Bill Lowe, guitarist Mary Halvorson, cellist Tomeka Reid, electric bassist Stomu Takeishi, upright bassist Ken Filiano and drummer Tomas Fujiwara. Many of these players had been working with Bynum in one context or another for years; his relationship with Fujiwara went back to the early 1990s.

Bynum explained that while they would be presenting a continuous performance of the music from the forthcoming album, that didn't mean a straight run through the tunes. Rather, there were four basic themes that would be explored in various ways by the ensemble during the course of the next hour or so. And with that, they were off.

What resulted was as fascinating to watch as it was to hear. The themes were performed as unison melodies by the ensemble, with the saxophones dominating in traditionally "jazzy" fashion. Takeishi and Fujiwara were a surprisingly powerful, even rocking rhythm section; the bassist kept returning to a riff that was almost a rewrite of Henry Mancini's chugging theme to the 1950s TV show *Peter Gunn*. But in between those anchoring passages of collective music-making, the group broke down into subdivisions of two or three players. The most common combinations were Bynum/Hobbs, Laubrock/Cole and

Halvorson/Reid/Filiano, but other pairings emerged throughout the evening.

There were musical passages on separate sheet music pages, and they seemed to be numbered, because I kept seeing one player look across the stage at another, point to that person and hold up two or three fingers to indicate which passage or idea they wanted to play (with). The other person would nod, and at the next opportunity, when the music seemed to be opening up, they'd launch into the bit they'd decided to work on.

Laubrock and Cole, because they were standing side by side at the front of the stage, played together a lot, as did Bynum and Hobbs, who was immediately to his left. Halvorson and Reid, who were seated together at stage right, next to the piano, had to look all the way across to connect with Filiano, who was at stage left, beside Fujiwara's drum kit.

There were relatively few traditionally "jazzy" solos, but lots of duets or at least simultaneous playing in a conversational manner. In the beginning, there was a lot of pointillist squawking and tootling, as players tossed short phrases or individual notes out in a staccato manner like bait on a fishing line, waiting to see who would leap out to engage. But after a few minutes, they'd all established their own zones, and knew who they wanted to team up with, and there was no audible hesitation as one team took the handoff from the one before, or the entire nine-piece band came together for fanfares. Some of the best passages were almost orchestral.

I first heard Bynum — though I didn't know his name — as a member of the Sound and Vision Orchestra, a large ensemble that performed with Cecil Taylor at the Knitting Factory on Leonard Street in Manhattan in June 2002. The pianist, three female singers and a double rhythm section (two bassists, two drummers) filled the stage; the rest of the instrumentalists — five trumpeters in all, two trombonists, two tuba players and ten saxophonists (three alto, five tenor, one baritone, one bass) sat where the audience would normally have been, only with the seats flipped around.

The piece Taylor composed for the occasion, "With Blazing Eyes and Open'd Mouth," began with him standing behind the piano, declaiming poetry which was echoed in call-and-response fashion by the singers. After a few minutes of this and some percussive clatter from the back of the stage, he sat down at the keyboard and the music began in earnest. Within moments, the ensemble was at full roar.

The performance was described as being for "improvising orchestra." Great masses of sheet music adorned each player's stand, seemingly containing individual motifs, which any section could play, in any order it saw fit. There was no overarching score in the traditional orchestral manner. This was both interesting and ultimately disappointing. While it allowed for some fascinating interplay as, say, the tenor saxophonists worked through a melodic idea and the trumpeters flipped through their scores seeking something with which to counter, it also left the ensemble vulnerable to indulgence and flailing. And at nearly 90 minutes, there was more than a little indulgence.

After a half hour or so, the sound of two dozen instrumentalists playing at full force became simply too much. The few moments of high-level musical achievement were lost in drenching blasts of sound. Even Taylor seemed swamped. His piano was sometimes barely audible amid the blare of the horns. And I was watching from the balcony; I can't imagine what it must have been like on the floor.

The improvisatory nature of the piece led inexorably to bloat. Natural ending points emerged about eight times, but the band cruised blithely on, finding its way to one more solo, one more crescendo or a little more chanting from Taylor and his female chorus.

It took several more years for me to start really picking up on Bynum. He worked with trumpeter Bill Dixon on another large ensemble work, *17 Musicians in Search of a Sound: Darfur*, recorded at the Vision Festival in 2007, and on *Tapestries for Small Orchestra*, a studio album released in 2009. The latter ensemble also traveled to Victoriaville, Canada to perform at the 2010 Festival de Musique Actuelle, and released a recording of the concert, *Envoi*. He was also working regularly with saxophonist and composer Anthony Braxton, as he'd been doing since the 1990s; he can be heard on close to 50 of Braxton's recordings going back as far as 1996, including several duo performances.

Bynum's style can be hard to pinpoint, because so much of what he plays goes beyond conventional instrumental technique. He employs effects that have been popular since the 1920s, like the growls heard on early Duke Ellington records, but he also emits hisses and kissy sounds that require close miking and amplification to even be audible. At the same time, he displays speed and precise articulation when that's what's called for. And he draws lines between his own forward-looking music and the past. On 2007's *The Middle Picture*, the debut album by his sextet, they transform Miles Davis's "In a Silent Way" into a clattering, psychedelic jam closer to Amon Duul II than jazz-rock. And on *The Double Trio*, a disc recorded in 2006 with trumpeter Stephen Haynes (also of the Sound and Vision Orchestra, and Bill Dixon's groups), Allan Jaffee and Mary Halvorson on electric guitars, and Warren Smith and Tomas Fujiwara on drums, the ensemble performs a version of Ornette Coleman's "Broken Shadows" that has a delicate, even cautious feel, as though they're learning the melancholy melody note by note as they play it.

Bynum is not just a student of Anthony Braxton's music, he's been instrumental in preserving and promoting it through the Tri-Centric Foundation, a nonprofit dedicated to premiering Braxton's music live and documenting it on record. He was the foundation's executive director from 2010 to 2018. He's also one of the co-founders of the Firehouse 12 label, affiliated with a performance space of the same name in Connecticut. He has released much of his own music on that imprint, as well as work by Braxton, Dixon, Halvorson, pianist Myra Melford, Tyshawn Sorey and others. He publishes the journal *Sound American*, to which I once contributed an essay on the ritualized nature of metal performance. And he teaches at Dartmouth College.

More than just a musician, Bynum is a cultural engine. He explores his own concepts by sharing them with others, and allowing their input to shape the final product. He is a leader, seemingly never as happy making music on his own (for a performer on the border between jazz and non-idiomatic improvised music, he's released shockingly little solo material) as assembling a like-minded group for a collective endeavor. As such, he's tied into a tight-knit network of performers that includes Fujiwara, Halvorson, Reid, Laubrock and others. They appear on each other's albums, perform together in a broad variety of contexts, and separately and together are presenting a particular version of jazz that owes as much to free improvisation and to modern composition as it does to the blues and swing and other traditional forms.

In the liner notes to his 2011 album *Apparent Distance*, Bynum writes:

> My goal is not just to blur the lines between composition and improvisation (a longtime pursuit), but to try to upend the listeners' expectations in other ways: circular melodies without beginnings or ends, disguised unisons and non-repetitive vamps, transitions that are simultaneously jarring and organic. Most importantly, I want to spotlight the striking individuality and virtuosity of all the players, albeit in a context where the needs of the ensemble reign supreme — a concerto for sextet, if you will.

This is not a new or revolutionary practice. Indeed, it was

employed by some of the greatest jazz composers: Charles Mingus showcased his band members in his compositions, as did Duke Ellington ("Concerto for Cootie," for example, honors trumpeter Cootie Williams). The new element Bynum inserts is the unexpected degree of autonomy he grants the players to choose which bits of the music with which they wish to engage, and how. Ultimately, it raises the question of how much of it is his, how much is theirs and how much is Music itself, speaking through them all.

Essential Listening

Taylor Ho Bynum Sextet, *The Middle Picture* (Firehouse 12, 2007)
Stephen Haynes/Taylor Ho Bynum, *The Double Trio — Live at the Festival of New Trumpet Music* (Engine Studios, 2008)
Bill Dixon, *Tapestries for Small Orchestra* (Firehouse 12, 2009)
Taylor Ho Bynum Sextet, *Navigation* (Firehouse 12, 2013)
Taylor Ho Bynum 9-Tette, *The Ambiguity Manifesto* (Firehouse 12, 2019)
Taylor Ho Bynum, *Enter the PlusTet* (Firehouse 12, 2016)

Tomeka Reid & Nicole Mitchell: The Importance of Radical Imagination

The cello hasn't got an especially high profile in jazz. Although legendary bassists like Ron Carter and Oscar Pettiford have doubled on the instrument here and there, it's mostly been heard on avant-garde or Third Stream-leaning records. During the late 70s and early 80s, cellist Abdul Wadud made a string of thrilling appearances on albums by saxophonists Arthur Blythe and Julius Hemphill, among others, and performed in a broad range of contexts on the loft jazz scene, but he was just one man.

In 2014, Tomeka Reid and filmmaker/journalist Joel Wanek traveled to Cleveland, Ohio to interview Wadud. It was obvious from the piece, which was published on the website Point of Departure, that she viewed him as a major inspiration for her own work. Reid had grown up in Washington, DC, but at that point, she was living and working in Chicago, and playing in various groups led by flautist Nicole Mitchell and drummer Mike Reed.

"When I think back on it, we didn't listen to any jazz in my house," she told me in 2018:

> but I remember my mom really liking...20th century classical music, or new music, and they would have shows on [Washington, DC radio station] WPFW that we would listen to sometimes. So I guess I must have had those sounds in my ear...and then I was also into a lot of punk rock bands that used a lot of distortion, so I feel like a lot of people that listen to that kind of music have also gravitated toward avant-garde music because there's a lot of [those] sounds being made as well.

Indeed, the Chicago underground scene has long been a crossroads where punk, noise, jazz and free improvisation meet and interbreed. Players like Ken Vandermark, Jeb Bishop and Matana Roberts are just a few of a whole generation of musicians who reject boundaries between genres, if they even see them at all, and cellist Fred Lonberg-Holm was an important figure in the city's improvised music community beginning in the 1990s. "Moving to Chicago and being around that environment — it wasn't a conscious choice, it was just that those were the settings I kept finding myself in," Reid said. "At first I was like, 'What is this?' But then I started to enjoy it."

Reid's style can be quite forceful. She doesn't play her instrument like a bass, as some jazz cellists do; indeed, she frequently appears in groups where there is a bassist, like her own quartet and Jaimie Branch's Fly Or Die, the violin/cello/bass trio Hear In Now, Taylor Ho Bynum's 9-Tette and the Art Ensemble of Chicago. This frees her up to make a space for herself more akin to a lead instrument. Still, the cello can be fairly easily drowned out or swallowed in a crowded mix; its virtues are subtle ones.

Reid is aware of the problem. "I think that's why I often play in string-focused contexts," she told me, "because it's hard when you have lots of horns and drums to kind of come out of that sound, but you just go for it and try to be a part of what's happening." I mentioned to her that at the Art Ensemble performance in 2017, I had been able to see her playing more often than I could hear her, something that had also happened when I saw Okkyung Lee play with Cecil Taylor at the Whitney Museum the year before.

"I think if they're gonna be out there like that," she said of bandmates in various overpowering situations,

> then I'm just gonna say, how out there can I get on my own instrument, you know? It just pushes me to play stronger, or

> figure out ways to get more sound out of my instrument. It makes me think about what things are gonna cut [through], so I'll have to play in my upper register or maybe I have to do different length notes, or be more percussive, or something, so that it can cut through.

Reid's own quartet, and Hear In Now, are exactly the kind of "string-focused contexts" she was talking about. The quartet, which made a self-titled album in 2015 for the Thirsty Ear label, then returned in 2019 with *Old New*, on Cuneiform, is a striking and unique ensemble. Reid and guitarist Mary Halvorson are the front line, with Jason Roebke on bass and Tomas Fujiwara on drums. The music they make together is a kind of hillbilly bebop — Reid saws at her cello, taking fierce, powerful solos and leaving Roebke and Fujiwara alone to keep the bottom end throbbing as she and Halvorson dance through clipped, speedy unison melody lines before throwing stinging outbursts back and forth. Halvorson's guitar frequently sounds like it's sliding out of her control thanks to her mastery of her relatively simple battery of effects, and Reid's cello groans and screams. Some tracks carry dedications — "Niki's Bop" is for Nicole Mitchell, "Billy Bang's Bounce" is for the late jazz violinist, "Samo Swing" is for the late painter Jean-Michel Basquiat — while others bear simple, declarative titles like "Ballad" or "Improv #1." On "Wabash Blues," from *Old New*, the rhythm section is allowed to take over two-thirds of the way through the piece, and Fujiwara's solo is like a series of exponentially growing explosions.

Hear In Now is a string trio, albeit one more focused on the low end than is typical. Mazz Swift is on violin, Reid on cello and Silvia Bolognesi on bass. Their music is harsh and unforgiving, with a concentrated energy, free of discursive or foggy passages. Every note counts, and there's no true leader. Each woman takes the lead role at times, with the others providing countermelodies or percussive sounds as needed. On "Transiti," from their second album, 2017's *Not Living in Fear*, Bolognesi slaps the strings of her bass to create a sound like a rat-trap snapping shut, as Swift and Reid make their instruments zing and cry. And when the bass comes in at full strength, it's a massive boom that nearly overpowers the other two. Melodically, the music pulls from modern classical, free jazz, folk, blues and hard-to-define zones in between. It rarely swings, but it always has a pulse.

One of Reid's most adventurous projects is a quartet with vocalist Kiyoko Kitamura, Taylor Ho Bynum and guitarist Joe Morris. As might be expected from that lineup, it's highly abstract improvised music, rough going for all but the most committed listeners. Kitamura is a vocalist who, here at least, specializes in extremely fast, staccato phrases almost like scat singing, and a kind of caterwauling somewhere between free jazz singers like Jeanne Lee and Linda Sharrock and the extremes reached by Diamanda Galás. Morris is a guitarist and bassist who can play pretty much anything; on this group's two albums, *Geometry of Caves* and *Geometry of Distance*, he's mostly going for tightly constrained pings and scrapes, somewhere between Django Reinhardt and Derek Bailey. The guitar's strings sound so sharp and wiry you worry that he's slicing his fingers open with every note. Reid plays her cello like a bass here, albeit a high-tuned one. Bynum displays a dizzying variety of techniques and tones on the cornet, going from an ultra-low, almost tuba-like drone to hyper-quick, busted squiggles, hissing kissy noises and even more indescribable sounds. There's no conventional song form present in their work, but each piece has consistency of mood, so there's logic, if you listen carefully and let it explain itself to you.

Working with Nicole Mitchell undoubtedly taught Reid a lot about how to support vocalists. Texts are hugely important to the flautist/composer, and she frequently creates multimedia works that involve drama, dance, video and more.

Mitchell is originally from Syracuse, New York, but she grew up in California and eventually went to college in the Midwest, and moved to Chicago in 1990. There, she began working for Third World Press, the largest independent Black-owned publishing house in the United States. She formed a crucial relationship with author and poet Haki Madhubuti, and met a great many musicians, quickly becoming an important figure on the Chicago jazz scene. At the turn of the century, she founded her long-running group the Black Earth Ensemble; Reid joined their ranks in 2002.

In addition to Black Earth, Mitchell has led a lot of one-off groups of various sizes and instrumentations, and been a part of other people's projects as well — she's in some of Anthony Braxton's large ensembles, and has recorded and performed with several of cornet player Rob Mazurek's groups, including the Exploding Star Orchestra and its offshoot projects. But her primary impact has been as a leader and an organizer. As a composer, she has created music that covers an extraordinarily broad spectrum, from jazz to modern composition, incorporating instruments, sounds and rhythms from across the planet.

Her 2017 album *Mandorla Awakening II: Emerging Worlds* featured an incarnation of Black Earth that included Kojiro Umezakin on shakuhachi (a Japanese wooden flute), Renée Baker on violin, Reid on cello and banjo, Alex Wing on electric guitar and oud, Tatsu Aoki on bass, shamisen (a three-stringed Japanese instrument) and taiko percussion, and Jovia Armstrong on percussion. Two tracks, "Staircase Struggle" and "Timewrap," had vocals from poet avery r young. Mitchell is an avowed sci-fi fan, citing the late Octavia Butler as a particularly strong influence, and that fact, combined with the album's title, made it easy to throw the "Afro-futurist" tag around. But the music had almost no sci-fi elements, even if it did occasionally build up to a churning groove that recalled the Exploding Star

Orchestra or Sun Ra's Arkestra.

The way the flute, shakuhachi and shamisen interacted on a track like "Sub-Mission," though, seemed more tied to the past than the future. And when the entire ensemble came into full bloom on "Dance of Many Hands," the combination of Baker's violin and Wing's guitar, and the flutes and percussion, gave it a genuinely otherworldly sound. This was music that couldn't be tied to any one tradition or territory. It implied that Mitchell's vision of the future was philosophically egalitarian and culturally omnivorous, with none of the paranoia that gives rise to charges of "appropriation."

In 2018, I met up with Mitchell at the New School, where she was curating a series of events at John Zorn's performance space The Stone. Her relatively small stature and squeaky, girlish voice make her intelligence that much more imposing, but she's friendly — she'll laugh at a dumb question, then pick apart its faulty premises and take her interlocutor somewhere entirely new. She knows what she believes and what she's after, and thus it's no surprise that she was the chair of the Chicago chapter of the AACM for several years, the first woman to hold that role. Her tenure overlapped with the group's forty-fifth anniversary, and included the organization of a lavish tribute concert in Chicago, partnerships with European festivals, raising money, working with the New York chapter, and recruiting and orienting new members.

"I think there's a lot of issues that come up in any organization," she says, when asked if the AACM struck her as a boys' club, or an environment where gender issues took a back seat to other political goals, as has often happened in all sorts of organizations.

> Gender issues come up, but also sometimes, especially when you have people that are very passionate, they've created something on their own and they've put their whole

> life into it, you also have challenges with generational communication, between the founding generation and the younger generation, because there's kind of a fear that maybe the younger people won't pass it on in the same way, or maybe they don't care about it as much...and so I feel that any of these organizations that have been around as long as the AACM, those are some of the challenges you're gonna deal with, and they definitely have been there.

In fact, she found the AACM's collective structure — and its insistence that members must write their own music — liberating, and encouraging.

> It makes it hard to institutionalize how the relations [among members] are gonna be...I wouldn't say there was an idea like 'Women need to take a back seat' or anything like that. Looking at some of the other women and the things that they've done...they had the opportunity to find out what they wanted to do and be pushed to go beyond their own boundaries and design their own music and stuff like that.

Asked to explain the compositional principles that guide her work, Mitchell cites "density" and "layers moving around, sometimes independently of each other," and "dealing with sound as color and energy." She also seeks a certain organic rhythmic tension that she ties to drummer Milford Graves' idea that the human heartbeat, not a metronome, should guide one's sense of rhythm. "How did we decide that we want things so regimented?"

Texts are key to Mitchell's work; many of her pieces have lyrics or spoken passages, and even her instrumental works have a detailed backstory, whether the listener is made aware of it in the notes or not. She's also interested in creating music that will manifest specific emotions or feelings in the listener:

> I'm very fascinated with the idea of music being powerful, and having an impact on us psychologically and physically — can I make certain sounds that can induce certain feelings? How do you reflect all the different things that nature can do, in music? How can you take the vast different expressions of the weather, for example, and be able to express that through sound?

Mitchell's creative drive makes her omnivorous. She draws from African and Asian music as much as from jazz, and employs traditional notation, graphic notation, guided improvisation or whatever combination of those techniques will work best for a given piece. She describes attempting to express meteorological sensations with instruments, which brings to mind the program music of the nineteenth-century Romantic era, when composers would write suites that attempted to render extra-musical narratives through music. To her, it's all one thing, and it's for whoever wants to listen:

> My aesthetics are not based on trying to entertain a certain specific audience; they're more internal, in terms of what I feel connected to. I identify with the idea of contributing to contemporary African-American culture, and Black experimentalism is something that I think is really important. I think that radical imagination is something that's important. So I project that in order to encourage it, in order to turn other people on to it.

Essential Listening

Nicole Mitchell's Black Earth Ensemble, *Xenogenesis Suite: A Tribute to Octavia Butler* (Firehouse 12, 2008)

Nicole Mitchell's Black Earth Strings, *Renegades* (Denmark, 2009)

Nicole Mitchell's Ice Crystal, *Aquarius* (Delmark, 2013)
Tomeka Reid Quartet, *Tomeka Reid Quartet* (Thirsty Ear, 2015)
Hear In Now, *Not Living In Fear* (International Anthem, 2017)
Nick Mazzarella/Tomeka Reid, *Signaling* (Nessa, 2017)
Nicole Mitchell, *Mandorla Awakening II: Emerging Worlds* (FPE, 2017)
Nicole Mitchell, *Maroon Cloud* (FPE, 2018)
Tomeka Reid Quartet, *Old New* (Cuneiform, 2019)
Nicole Mitchell/Lisa E. Harris, *EarthSeed* (FPE, 2020)

Mary Halvorson: How Can I Create Something New?

When I arrived at the Waverly Diner in downtown Manhattan, where I was to meet guitarist Mary Halvorson for lunch on a sunny Thursday afternoon in February 2018, I didn't see her outside. This was not a surprise; musicians are almost always late for everything but gigs. So I waited a few minutes, watching people come up out of the subway or exit taxis or just walk by. Finally, about 5 minutes after our appointment, I called her to see where she was and how much longer she might be. "Oh, I'm inside already," was not the answer I was expecting.

Slightly embarrassed, I ducked inside. We ordered and ate, and talked about the things people involved with underground and avant-garde music talk about: day jobs past and present, record stores that don't exist anymore and the few that still do, encounters with Ornette Coleman. (I traveled to his midtown loft apartment once to interview him for *The Wire*; Halvorson got to play with him there, once, an occasion she recalled with a kind of disbelieving joy.)

Halvorson is short and slight enough that she can almost hide behind the large Guild Artist Award hollow-body guitar she plays, but in conversation as onstage, she captures and holds one's attention through striking intelligence and unexpected but apposite ideas. She's friendly in the manner of a bookstore clerk, or the kind of co-worker whose competence quietly anchors an entire office.

Her music has grown slowly and organically over the course of about 15 years, like a tree branching. On 2008's *Dragon's Head*, her first album as a leader, she fronted a trio featuring bassist John Hebert and drummer Ches Smith. That group also made a live album, *Ghost Loop*. Two years later, it expanded to a quintet with the addition of trumpeter Jonathan Finlayson and saxophonist Jon Irabagon; *Saturn Sings* was followed by 2012's *Bending Bridges*, the first album in her career to have the same personnel as its predecessor. On 2013's *Illusionary Sea*, tenor saxophonist Ingrid Laubrock and trombonist Jacob Garchik joined, making the group a septet. And in 2016, she added pedal steel guitarist Susan Alcorn and released *Away With You*. Alcorn's singing drones allowed the group to display a beautiful side of otherwise thorny compositions. On "The Absolute Almost," the long pedal steel notes were like prairie winds vibrating Halvorson's barbed-wire strings.

The compositions featured on this string of albums had parenthetical numbers at the end of their titles; these indicated the order in which Halvorson wrote them, and there are only a few gaps. The albums are best heard as a multi-part suite, so that the group's evolution — and her growth as a composer — can be heard clearly.

"I didn't think tangibly about it, that they've all been different personnel...but I do, in my head, think I don't want to make the same record twice," she told me:

> So it's definitely something I think about — what am I interested in now, and how can I try something different or create something new? And it's not like I'm trying to do something different to make a point. I think I just want to keep trying to challenge myself and grow by doing something different and not being like, well, it worked last time, so let me do it again.

Halvorson is also a member of the collective trio Thumbscrew with bassist Michael Formanek and drummer Tomas Fujiwara. That group has been recording since 2014, and has made five albums for the Cuneiform label. In 2018, they released two albums simultaneously, *Ours* and *Theirs*. The former was a collection of new compositions, while the latter was a set of covers. They followed that in 2020 with *The Anthony Braxton Project*, a collection of his compositions, radically rearranged.

Whether playing their own tunes or others', the strength of their own personalities (individual and collective) comes through. Formanek's bass sound is massive, like he carved the instrument out of one of those redwood trees you can drive through. Halvorson, on the other hand, frequently does something to her guitar to make it sound like it's coming from underwater, or being beamed down from orbit, and Fujiwara's drums have a martial crispness. As with a lot of modern Brooklyn jazz, there's an element of simultaneity, as opposed to togetherness, to the music, which makes Formanek's count-off at the beginning of the standard "East of the Sun" weirdly hilarious. But when they lock in, they create a unique blend of jazz, twanging post-rock and high-energy improvisation.

Also in 2018, Halvorson's urge to expand bubbled up again, and she turned Thumbscrew into the foundation of a new group, Code Girl, by adding trumpeter Ambrose Akinmusire and vocalist Amirtha Kidambi.

Code Girl debuted with a self-titled two-CD set of 14 songs. The band name comes from Braxton; it was a phrase he said one day while they were on tour together, and it caught her attention. "I have no idea what he was referring to or why he said it, but I wrote it down, and I was just joking around — I said 'What's the code?' and he said '5-5-5-5.' So I wrote that down." On the album's stark white cover, the words *Code Girl* are written in block letters formed by patterns of 5s.

Kidambi sings Halvorson's words — which read on the page like collections of evocative phrases, arranged in attractive patterns — in a mannered, theatrical fashion, sometimes evoking singers from the softer side of the folk-country spectrum like Gillian Welch, and other times adopting a heart-on-sleeve style that's almost Morrissey-esque. Behind her, Akinmusire takes solos that dip and dive like murmurations of birds; Formanek's bass bounces with enough force to jostle a speaker off a shelf; and Fujiwara is a soft but emphatic voice, his drums massive and martial but somehow never overpowering.

In 2020, Code Girl returned with a few membership changes — Akinmusire was replaced by Adam O'Farrill, and tenor saxophonist María Grand joined — and a guest vocalist. British art-rock legend Robert Wyatt sings on three of the eight tracks on the group's second album, *Artlessly Falling*.

No matter the ensemble, Halvorson leads by disappearing into the middle of the music. Her playing is sharp and clean, every note sprung precisely from the strings, with only minimal effects: a dash of shimmering reverb here, a sudden buzz of distortion there. And regardless of context, she is recognizable in seconds. Consistency of technique and equipment helps; she's been using the same small set of effects for nearly 2 decades.

"I really enjoy a strong attack, and I want to hear the acoustic quality of the instrument," she said. "And I've always played this way. From the second I picked up guitar, I was hitting the strings really hard. And I use really heavy strings, a big hollow-body guitar, and a heavy pick also, so that attack is really there." In the studio, she mikes the strings and the amplifier separately, to create what she describes as "this sort of dual sound," which can be startling. She'll be picking out a melody and suddenly a wave of distortion will appear, like a malevolent ghost.

"I can create a delay so I hit a note, you hear the attack and then half a second later you hear the sound out of the amp. But I like, even if something is loud and distorted, to be able to hear the natural sound like the picking, even if it's faint."

The effect she's best known for is her Line 6 DL4 delay pedal, which she uses to create a squiggling sound like rapidly unspooling tape. She'll do it in the middle of a solo, even in the middle of a phrase, giving the impression that the music has slipped out of her control:

> It was just something I discovered by accident; I was turning a knob and it made that sound and I thought, 'Oh wow, that was cool.' It's sort of an expressive thing to me; it almost sounds like a human voice, so it's just a way to add a little something just slightly strange to what could otherwise be a super clear line.

Controlling the effect via a foot pedal gives her the ability "to play a line and just have it go off in the middle of it really quickly, which is nice."

Halvorson's relationship with Anthony Braxton goes back to college; she studied with him for 3 years at Wesleyan University in Connecticut. Over time, she became a crucial element of his music, playing in trio, septet and 12+1tet contexts, and joining the ensembles that performed his Trillium operas. Before her, he had rarely worked with guitarists; the main exceptions were some duos with Derek Bailey and Joe Morris. When asked about the artistic ground on which they meet, she takes a long pause.

"Anthony...is someone I've always found incredibly open-minded about music," she says:

> I mean, people might assume that he only likes stuff that's similar to his world, but he's into everything and that was actually an early lesson, something I learned from him. I see this a lot with students that are college-age, is they get pretty narrow...you're like, 'This is the shit, this is what I do and I only like this little thing.' And I think having a teacher at that age that had this really expansive concept of really drawing from everything...allowed me to stay out of a box.

Halvorson also studied with Morris, a free music veteran/legend who was equally insistent that she refine her own aesthetic and approach rather than follow in someone else's footsteps. When they played together, he would never pick up his own guitar;

instead, he would play bass. Morris, who published the book *Perpetual Frontier: The Properties of Free Music* in 2012, operated as more of a sounding board and source of encouragement than an instructor. "We would improvise and talk about it...like, 'OK, I hear you doing this, how can you develop that thing further?'"

In addition to the groups she leads or co-leads, Halvorson is a member of projects including saxophonist Ingrid Laubrock's Anti-House with pianist Kris Davis, bassist John Hebert and drummer Tom Rainey; various groups led by Fujiwara; and, as mentioned earlier, Tomeka Reid's quartet. The two first played together in the collective Living By Lanterns, interpreting never-recorded themes by Sun Ra on 2012's *New Myth/Old Science*. They're highly complementary creative spirits, each one an excellent listener who strives to hold the ensemble together while still making an individual statement. "I think when you have people that are real improvisers and real listeners, and you have compositions which I think have pretty distinct characters — each [Reid Quartet] song has a pretty clear identity, and we're all just trying to do the best we can to honor that particular piece of music."

In 2019, Halvorson was awarded a MacArthur Fellowship, the so-called "Genius Grant." She routinely wins critics' polls, and is generally regarded by the jazz press as one of the most important guitarists around. But she's still out there on her own in one important respect: it's impossible to hear people imitating her in the way they imitate, say, Pat Metheny or Kurt Rosenwinkel. Perhaps that will come in a few years.

Essential Listening

Anthony Braxton, *Trio (Victoriaville) 2007* (Les Disques Victo, 2007)

Mary Halvorson Trio, *Dragon's Head* (Firehouse 12, 2008)

Mary Halvorson Quintet, *Saturn Sings* (Firehouse 12, 2010)

Mary Halvorson, *Meltframe* (Firehouse 12, 2015)
Mary Halvorson Octet, *Away With You* (Firehouse 12, 2016)
Tomas Fujiwara, *Triple Double* (Firehouse 12, 2017)
Thumbscrew, *The Anthony Braxton Project* (Cuneiform, 2020)

Linda May Han Oh: Ebb and Flow

The day after Thanksgiving 2016, I headed to the Jazz Gallery to see bassist Linda May Han Oh premiere a set of music by a double quartet — specifically, a jazz quartet paired with a string quartet.

The Jazz Gallery's stage, small at the best of times, was crowded with instruments. Matt Mitchell was at the piano, at stage right; Oh was tucked into the back, between him and drummer Ches Smith; and alto saxophonist Greg Ward was at far stage left. In front sat violinists Sara Caswell and Fung Chern Hwei, violist Benni Von Gutzeit and cellist Jeremy Harman.

The Jazz Gallery had awarded Oh a commission in 2012, and this project was the result. The music was a stunning vision of chamber jazz, or more accurately chamber music with saxophone and drum kit. It was like a tornado striking a flowerbed — a mosaic of colors seemed to rise into the air, spinning wildly and swirling around and around in a way that was mildly disorienting, utterly captivating and at times swooningly romantic. The melodies were carefully assembled, but lived-in as well, and the best way to experience the pieces was to close your eyes and let the soft, swaying strings drift past, as though you were stepping from rock to rock across a stream. Oh's own sound was thick and insistent, unmistakable but never overpowering. She was the beating heart of the music, always allowing the lush melodies to lead while serving as both foundation and mortar.

The ensemble recorded the music nearly 9 months later, in late August 2017, and it was finally released in May 2019 as the album *Aventurine*. On record, it became even more lush and baroque, as the eight musicians were joined on several tracks by the vocal ensemble Invenio — singers Louisa Rankin, Josh Kyle, Andrew Murray and Jonathan Skovron.

Aventurine came out on Biophilia, a label run by Oh's husband, pianist Fabian Almazan. Their model wrestles with the environmental concerns raised by the music industry's reliance on plastic and aluminum as storage media. The releases, known as Biopholios, are elaborate, 20-panel posters printed using plant-based ink on paper harvested in a responsible manner according to standards set by the Forest Stewardship Council and folded in an origami-like fashion. There is no actual CD, only photographs, liner notes, recording information, etc, and a unique code which permits the listener to download the music in any format they desire. This was Oh's second album to appear in this format, following 2017's *Walk Against Wind,* and her fourth album overall.

The daughter of Malaysian immigrants, Oh grew up in Perth, Australia, which she described to me on the phone one afternoon in early 2019 as, "one of the most isolated major cities in the world." But she recalled seeing the Mingus Big Band, saxophonists Gary Bartz and Jim Snidero, and pianist Andy Milne come to town, and there was a local jazz scene that captured her attention and interest. She played piano and bassoon at first, before switching to bass as a teenager. She graduated from the Western Australia Academy of Performing Arts, and received her masters degree at the Manhattan School of Music.

"My mum did say at one point, when I was in high school, 'Why do you want to play jazz? There's just too many boys.' That was her perception: there aren't too many girls there — why would you want to do that?"

Oh retains an immigrant's, outsider's perspective at all times, and it seems to be at least partly by choice. She's an Asian woman, from not-America, in a genre dominated by white and Black American men, and a bassist to boot. But she insists on the validity of her own perspective, and thus comes up with ideas no one else would. On her second album, 2012's *Initial Here,* an album she described as "generally about identity," the piece

"Thicker Than Water" is a duo on which Oh overdubs herself multiple times on bowed bass, backing vocalist Jen Shyu. "That was written specifically for her, because I knew that she could sing in Mandarin and in English — she's also just an incredible musician, she can sing anything that you give her, and I was a big fan of hers." On the rest of the tracks, she leads a quartet featuring saxophonist Dayna Stephens, Almazan on piano and Rudy Royston on drums.

She has developed a specific compositional language, one which is directly traceable through her discography, as she's happy to point out. "If I were to show you the sheet music, or talk you through some of the forms, you might find that they're generally just short vehicles," she said of the music on *Walk Against Wind*. Most of that album was written for and performed by a quartet with tenor saxophonist Ben Wendel and electric guitarist Matthew Stevens up front, and Justin Brown on drums. Almazan appears on three tracks, and Minji Park plays traditional Korean percussion — the janggu (a drum) and the kkwaenggwari, a type of gong — on one.

She added that:

> quite a few of them have signifying themes, and some of them are like sister songs, related to other ones either throughout the album, or...to other albums that I've recorded. 'Yoda' from *Sun Pictures* is kind of a sister song related to 'Deeper Than Happy' from *Initial Here*, and kind of carrying on in that vein of major lydian-sounding chords, with lows and highs of ones and sevens outlining those chords — that kind of carries on through to 'Ikan Bilis' which is on *Walk Against Wind*.

Not long after the recording of *Initial Here*, Oh and Royston both joined trumpeter Dave Douglas's new quintet, which also featured saxophonist Jon Irabagon and Mitchell at the piano.

That group made three studio albums — 2012's *Be Still*, which also featured vocalist and guitarist Aoife O'Donovan, 2013's *Time Travel*, and 2015's *Brazen Heart*. Douglas has always possessed the ability to shift back and forth between traditional, melodic post-bop and avant-garde exploration without blinking; he was a prominent figure on New York's downtown scene beginning in the 1980s, and in the 90s joined John Zorn's quartet Masada, which performed compositions that blended Ornette Coleman-style figures with Jewish scales.

The members of Douglas's quintet all shared his open ears and adventurous spirit. The music on *Be Still* was frequently soft and hushed; six of the nine tracks were interpretations of hymns and folk songs that Douglas's mother, who died in 2011, had asked him to perform at her funeral. O'Donovan sang in a near-whisper, even on more uptempo pieces like the bluegrass piece "High On a Mountain." Hearing Irabagon (whose playing in other contexts has a gleeful virtuosity that frequently feels almost smirking) and Royston digging into such back-country material was fascinating.

A year later, the group returned with a more swinging and hard-boppish album. They were stretching out more, really exploring the music and letting it carry them away. Where *Be Still* had featured 9 tracks in 43 minutes, *Time Travel* offered only 7 in 54, the longest of which, "The Pigeon and the Pie," ran past the 10-minute mark. There was still a meditative quality to the compositions and the various players' improvizations, but the pieces built to strong crescendos, and Mitchell, Oh and Royston were a tightly bonded team.

Brazen Heart, which had 11 tracks and ran for 65 minutes, was another conventionally "jazzy" record, but one which maintained a connection to traditional folk and gospel music with versions of "Deep River" and "There is a Balm in Gilead."

To celebrate the release of *Brazen Heart*, Douglas booked a long weekend of gigs at the Jazz Standard, playing two sets a night from Thursday through Sunday just before Thanksgiving 2015. Over the course of those eight sets, all of which were recorded and released as four two-CD sets and a complete package, the band performed every piece from *Brazen Heart* and *Time Travel*, and seven of nine from *Be Still*.

Live, the pieces remained recognizable — the group didn't take the melodies apart, turning phrases into oblique hints, the way the Miles Davis quintet of the 1960s did with the standards and other pieces they performed. Instead, they radically extended them, allowing solos to go as long as they needed to. "Going Somewhere With You," a 5-minute piece on *Be Still*, was performed twice, and the shorter of the two versions was nearly 15 minutes long. Similarly, "Bridge to Nowhere," the opening track on *Time Travel*, expanded from 8 minutes to nearly 24 at the beginning of the final Sunday-night set.

In 2015, Oh also began working with Japanese-American pianist Art Hirahara, whom I first heard in Australian alto saxophonist Nick Hempton's band. While his own early releases were just okay, his contributions to Hempton's albums *The Business* and *Odd Man Out* were creative and focused, giving the quirky, bouncing melodies some necessary gravitas.

Oh first appeared on Hirahara's *Libations & Meditations*, a conventionally swinging trio date with John Davis on drums. Then, on 2017's *Central Line* and 2018's *Sunward Bound*, he underwent a sudden creative evolution following the death of his father, and made the best work of his career. The group also included saxophonist Donny McCaslin, and Rudy Royston was on drums, and the music was a blend of uptempo hard bop, lush ballads and radical, non-kitsch interpretations of some traditional Japanese melodies. The first album closed with "Yuyake Koyake," a song played to let schoolchildren know the day is over, and the second included another children's song, "Akatombo," and a 1950s pop hit, "Ringo Oiwake."

"I've never really asked Art what he needs or wants from

me," Oh told me,

> 'cause I feel like he's so open to my interpretation of things and he kind of lets me do what I feel, so he'll be totally cool with me doubling the melody at times, and hinting at certain things — that's something that he's open to and perhaps likes about what I do. It's kind of an ebb and flow, of voices that are in the foreground and voices that are in the background.

"He's got such a beautiful touch," she adds. "To me it's very crisp and clear, and the ideas he plays kind of carry along with that. There's a conviction and a crispness that I really appreciate."

Easily Oh's most high-profile situation, for the past few years, has been her membership in guitarist Pat Metheny's quartet, with Gwilym Simcock on piano and Antonio Sanchez on drums. They released their first studio album, *From This Place,* in 2020, and it was a massive, highly ambitious effort on which they were backed by a full orchestra. The strings were more than just a swaying, swooning backdrop, too. They took a dominant role at times, while at other moments they accentuated what the quartet members were doing in a deep and considered way, like the orchestrations on classic CTI albums from the 1970s.

The 13-minute album opener, "America Undefined," set the parameters for the whole project. Metheny and Simcock took lyrical, tale-spinning solos, which were followed by a short but beautiful piano-bass duet passage. Then, 8 minutes in, Metheny vanished, and the trio, the orchestra and some very subtle electronics, likely added in post-production, created what amounted to a whole second piece full of atmospheric washes of sound and gentle melancholy.

That kind of swooning effect is uncommon in Oh's own music. Though she has a facility for ballads and string writing, there's a toughness at the core of her sound and her compositions that's impossible to overlook or discount.

Essential Listening

Linda May Han Oh, *Initial Here* (Greenleaf Music, 2012)
Dave Douglas, *Time Travel* (Greenleaf Music, 2013)
Linda May Han Oh, *Walk Against Wind* (Biophilia, 2017)
Art Hirahara, *Sunward Bound* (Posh-Tone, 2018)
Linda May Han Oh, *Aventurine* (Biophilia, 2019)
Pat Metheny, *From This Place* (Nonesuch, 2020)

Tyshawn Sorey: Write It Out and Believe in It

I've only ever seen Tyshawn Sorey perform as a jazz drummer. He's stunningly effective in that role. He's a big guy, tall and heavy, and like many big drummers I've seen — Johnathan Blake, George Coleman Jr. and the death metal drummer Gene "the Atomic Clock" Hoglan — he sits perfectly upright, head centered and back, looking down at the drums before him with something like disdain.

He wears black clothes, and dark sunglasses. There is no perceptible eye contact between him and the musicians with whom he's playing. He hits everything in front of him with astonishing precision, but equally decisive force. There are times when his solos have the explosive power of death metal, displaying more thundering energy than any other jazz drummer I've ever heard, and his snare rolls are crisper than anyone this side of Billy Cobham. He'll take your breath away.

Sorey fascinates me. He's a living example of how seeming multifaceted is in fact a form of unification. He is wholly himself: a drummer, but also a composer; a highly educated academic professional who presents his music at workshops and in concert halls across the globe, but also a guy from Newark, New Jersey with a raucous sense of humor who takes real joy in making and listening to music. He studies the work and methods of Roscoe Mitchell and Anthony Braxton, but is just as conversant in Iannis Xenakis and Charles Wuorinen.

One Monday afternoon in October 2017, Sorey and I were sitting in a theater inside the Guggenheim Museum in New York. He was going to be performing with John Zorn later, but in the meantime I was there to play records for him — Autechre, Metallica, Redman, Zorn's project Painkiller, Eric Dolphy and more — and capture his responses, and the broader discussion that inevitably followed. There was a subject we returned to again and again in our conversation, one I'd previously discussed with elder statesmen and masters of this music — with Roscoe Mitchell and Cecil Taylor, with Wadada Leo Smith and Ornette Coleman and Bill Dixon. That was the question of composition and improvisation, and where those lines were to be drawn and how, and perhaps most importantly of all, by whom.

Jazz musicians who write music that's not immediately recognizable as "jazz," however the listener chooses to define that term, generally hate being asked "So, how much of this is scored and how much of it is improvised?", as though there's a golden ratio — a Goldilocks zone — that will make it not so composed that it loses its "soul" but not so improvised that they're "just making it up as you go along." Unless it's asked from a literally methodological perspective — from a fellow musician, or fellow composer, seeking to analyze and understand the work — the question is freighted with a range of assumptions and aesthetic priorities, none of which are particularly flattering to the questioner.

"To me, that's a question that's kind of irrelevant, in terms of what we're dealing with now and also what we've been dealing with for maybe 80 years," Sorey told me with a laugh. "It's kind of ridiculous...that we're still trying to sort of hear the seams, as it were...in one sense, you could say that the listener wants to know how involved you are when it comes to making music with your collaborators."

To him, the apposite question is, "why not listen to the entire work and experience the nature of the work as it is?" He sees fully improvised music, completely through-composed music and every zone in between as equally valid. "To blur out the distinction is what I'm after."

In his 2002 essay *Improvised Music After 1950: Afrological and Eurological Perspectives*, trombonist and composer George Lewis, who also wrote the 2008 book *A Power Stronger Than Itself: The*

AACM and American Experimental Music, asserted fundamental and culturally rooted differences in musical practice, but maintained that all options were open to all players. "African-American music, like any music, can be performed by a person of any 'race' without losing its character as historically Afrological," he wrote, and don't overlook those scare quotes. "My constructions make no attempt to delineate ethnicity or race, although they are designed to ensure that the reality of the ethnic or racial component of a historically emergent sociomusical group must be faced squarely and honestly."

Sorey accepts Lewis's framing, but takes it further, refusing to recognize any limitations on his own creativity. He cites Anthony Braxton and Roscoe Mitchell, naming the former man's *The Complete Braxton 1971, Creative Orchestra Music 1976, Quintet (Basel) 1977,* and 1969's *3 Compositions of New Jazz* as particularly inspiring. "He taught me through these records to really, no matter what it is, write it out and believe in it...there's no such thing as 'traditional' or 'avant-garde' or anything like that. You write what you write...and try to get it played, and see if you can get people to come to the concert and check it out." Further, he praises Braxton for his efforts at self-definition.

Aware that his music was sure to be mischaracterized by critics and overlooked by historians and scholars – perhaps because of the sheer volume of his output – Braxton self-published in 1985 the *Tri-Axium Writings,* a three-volume set of books that attempted to explain and contextualize his creative philosophy and methodology as he saw it, while also offering notes on his compositions. "He sought to really define his terms in a way that was clear for everybody to understand," Sorey said. "I understand exactly what he's after in terms of his placement within music as just one who's wanting to learn," and he added Mitchell, Lewis, trumpeter Bill Dixon, and pianist and AACM co-founder Muhal Richard Abrams to that list.

Sorey's music doesn't cover as broad a range as Braxton's

— yet — but he gives the impression that it could, and likely will one day. His listening is so omnivorous, and his range of compositional interests so wide-ranging, that almost nothing seems beyond him. In recent years, his catalog has metastasized with remarkable speed. He has made one album after another, each of which would be seen as a career-defining opus in the life of a lesser player.

In 2016, he released *The Inner Spectrum of Variables*, a two-CD set composed for piano trio — Cory Smythe on piano, Chris Tordini on bass — and string trio (Fung Chern Hwei on violin, Kyle Armbrust on viola, Rubin Kodheli on cello). It's a marathon, multi-movement work that blends classical and jazz and veers from thunderous bombast to near-silent meditativeness. The first disc begins with solo piano from Cory Smythe and moves through passages of solo cello and piano-and-strings, before ending with an ominous, elegiac soundscape. The second disc is just as dark and harsh, but beams of light break through here and there.

A year later, he returned with *Verisimilitude*, recorded with just Smythe and Tordini. The music this time seemed to owe as much to composer Morton Feldman as to the traditional jazz piano trio. Sorey added subtle electronics to create atmospheric effects, and on pieces like "Obsidian" he limited himself to soft tom rolls like distant thunder, and small percussive sounds like objects shifting in the next room. About 12 minutes into the 18-minute piece, he seemed to suddenly erupt, but as with all his work, it was in fact precisely thought-out and expertly controlled. The album's centerpiece was the nearly 31-minute "Algid November," which traveled through several movements without delineating them as such. It swung sometimes, but just as often, Sorey and Tordini would leave Smythe twirling in the air, virtually alone.

In 2018, he released a truly massive project. *Pillars* was a three-CD set, with each disc containing a single track running between 75 and 78 minutes, performed by a nine-member ensemble that included as many as four basses, and allowed many of the players to switch instruments as it progressed.

He told me:

> I'm not too into orchestras but that's how I envisioned *Pillars*, as this small orchestra of musicians who have an arsenal of instruments to work from, because I feel like if everybody's on one instrument all the time, you can't really get to all of the sonic spaces that I was interested in exploring on that record. So, Stephen Haynes has this arsenal of brass instruments, and I have this whole array of percussion instruments that filled up half the room when we did the recording.

The full ensemble features Haynes on various members of the trumpet family; Ben Gerstein on trombone and melodica; Todd Neufeld on electric and acoustic guitar; Joe Morris on electric guitar and upright bass; Carl Testa on bass and electronics; Mark Helias and Zach Rowden on additional basses; and Sorey on drums, percussion and trombone. The piece itself is hard to describe without taking detailed notes about the sequence of events and simply listing them, and to do so would diminish its impact, because as with any work of such extended duration, it's more like installation art. You should just put it on and walk around in it, let different parts catch your ear, and absorb what you can. It begins with a drum solo, but after that it's the closest thing to that overused term, a "sound world," that I can imagine. Forcefully bowed basses create gigantic drones as electric guitars clang and zing, and Haynes' horns recall Lester Bowie's work with the Art Ensemble of Chicago, shifting between murmurs and shouts. The electronics surge and pulsate, feeding back and emitting almost tectonic roars. It's uncategorizable music, sharing as much with the work of Bill Dixon as with that of Sunn O))) or Icelandic composer Anna Thorvaldsdottir.

Sorey also works in smaller, more intimate contexts. In 2019, he held a residency at the long-running New York avant-garde space The Kitchen. One of the performances was a duo with pianist Marilyn Crispell. The 65-minute encounter took place in a nearly pitch-dark room; Crispell told me, by phone from her home in upstate New York, that the two of them could barely see each other. "I'm sure that had an effect on the music we played. It was very conducive to a dreamlike state."

The performance, as preserved on the CD *The Adornment of Time,* is remarkably cohesive. It travels through several distinct phases, but neither player ever seems to catch the other off guard. This may be because they come from similar places as composers who improvise, and who are deeply attuned to the creative and philosophical principles of the AACM, Sorey as a student and Crispell as a peer.

"Tyshawn gives me a lot of space — in a way, a lot more space to introduce things than I'm used to," she told me, admiringly. "Often, someone will just put something down and I'll react to it, which became a way of operating for me. And so, I suddenly felt that I was not in that kind of comfort zone anymore, that I had a different kind of responsibility for the direction of the music."

At the beginning of 2020, Sorey released *Invisible Ritual*, a series of eight linked improvizations with violinist Jennifer Curtis, on the classical label New Focus. There have been violin-drums duos before in the out-jazz realm, most notably Rashied Ali and Leroy Jenkins' *Swift are the Winds of Life* and Billy Bang and Dennis Charles' *Bangception*. This was not that. On this album, Sorey switched at will between drums and piano while Curtis played in a hushed, starkly minimal style drawn from modern composition and chamber music. Eventually, she did erupt, on the fourth movement, taking a sawing approach somewhere between a Bartók string quartet and Michael Sampson's rawboned fiddling with Albert Ayler's mid-60s sextet. When she went out, Sorey followed in full doom metal mode, demolishing the kit with apocalyptic hammer blows.

In March 2020, Sorey offered *Unfiltered*, a digital-only album that would have been a two-CD set. Like *The Inner Spectrum of Variables* and *Pillars*, it was a multi-part suite; the shortest of its three segments lasted 30 minutes, the longest 55. It was recorded with an ensemble of musicians a decade or more younger than himself: alto saxophonist Nathan Reising, tenor saxophonist Morgan Guerin, pianist Lex Korten, vibraphonist Sasha Berliner and bassist Nick Dunston. It had more of a "free jazz" feel than those other releases, though. The solos could get raucous and raw, and Sorey's drumming was a tumbling wave of rhythm, as if a "pulse" player like Rashied Ali or Milford Graves had chosen to limit himself almost entirely to toms and cymbals.

He had been working on the music, with that ensemble, off and on for 2 years, and premiered it with a week-long stand at the Jazz Gallery, five nights during which they performed one long set per night. In an interview for the club's blog, conducted by Noah Fishman, he contrasted the studio and live versions by saying:

> The record we made is but a snapshot of what we're able to do...of what happened on that day in the studio. Recordings are good. They get the music out there for all to hear, and having these documents for perusal is a very nice thing. But I'm not at all married to recordings...the music we make on a given night is designed only for the audience who shows up, and who decides to stay there with us.

Essential Listening

Tyshawn Sorey, *Koan* (482 Music, 2009)
Steve Lehman Octet, *Mise en Abîme* (Pi Recordings, 2014)
John Zorn, *In the Hall of Mirrors* (Tzadik, 2014)

Tyshawn Sorey, *The Inner Spectrum of Variables* (Pi Recordings, 2016)

Tyshawn Sorey, *Verisimilitude* (Pi Recordings, 2017)

Tyshawn Sorey, *Pillars* (Firehouse 12, 2018)

Tyshawn Sorey/Marilyn Crispell, *The Adornment of Time* (Pi Recordings, 2019)

Jennifer Curtis/Tyshawn Sorey, *Invisible Ritual* (Tundra, 2020)

PART III

Shabaka Hutchings; Yazz Ahmed; Nubya Garcia; Shirley Tetteh; Brandee Younger; Makaya McCraven; Nduduzo Makhathini; Siya Makuzeni; Thandi Ntuli; Linda Sikhakhane; Ndabo Zulu; Kamasi Washington, Ryan Porter, Cameron Graves, Miles Mosley, Thundercat; Dwight Trible; Darius Jones

Introduction

The term "spiritual jazz" is so broad that it's effectively meaningless. What does "spiritual" even mean in this context? Does it refer to one particular religious tradition? Both Wayne Shorter and Herbie Hancock are Buddhists; can anyone point to a particularly "Buddhist" tone or melodic structure in their compositions or improvizations? I can't. Art Blakey was a Muslim, but as far as I can tell his faith never bled into what he played when he sat behind the kit. Chick Corea is one of several prominent jazz musicians who are dedicated Scientologists; is his music "spiritual"? So it's clear that a musician can be deeply spiritual without playing "spiritual" music.

That said, there are many jazz musicians whose work *is* explicitly informed by their beliefs, whatever form the latter may take. Saxophonist Albert Ayler, for example, gave his early compositions titles like "Holy Ghost," "Angels" and "Spirits Rejoice," and in his final years embraced an overtly gospel-ized sound while making albums with titles like *Music is the Healing Force of the Universe*. Latter-day free jazz saxophonist Charles Gayle is even more directly Biblical in his references. In a 2013 interview with *Cadence* magazine, he said, "I want the people to enjoy the music and if it in any way can suggest something about the Lord, for their benefit, that would be first in my mind."

Alice Coltrane famously abandoned commercial music-making entirely in the mid-70s, retiring to California to run a spiritual center. In the years after her death, the devotional music she made as Swamini Turiyasangitananda and distributed only to members of her ashram has been reissued and compiled for mainstream releases.

But what does music made for spiritual reasons mean to a listener who approaches it without understanding of or interest in the faith that inspired it? If an atheist listens to a gospel choir and takes pleasure from the rhythm and the sound of the voices, or if someone who is not a Sufi Muslim listens to the Qawwali music of Nusrat Fateh Ali Khan, their pleasure is legitimate and appropriate, even if they do not share all the feelings made by the music's creators.

Alice Coltrane, along with her husband John, Pharoah Sanders, Sun Ra and a few others, are the artists most closely identified with so-called "spiritual jazz." Some, like saxophonists Gary Bartz and Azar Lawrence, have been brought back to prominence in recent years through association with younger players. Lawrence has performed with Kamasi Washington and South African pianist Nduduzo Makhathini, while Bartz has recorded an entire album with the young British septet Maisha. The Sun Ra Arkestra, despite the death of its founder in 1993, soldiers on.

This section will inevitably raise the questions that surround spiritual jazz in the twenty-first century. The first wave, in the early 70s, arose out of a particular set of sociopolitical conditions that don't exist in the same way they once did, even though the core issues remain. Therefore, it can seem like putting on African-inspired clothing, chanting and shaking bells and borrowing all the other trappings of the original spiritual jazz era is nothing more than costumery. But Shabaka Hutchings, Nubya Garcia, Yazz Ahmed, Nduduzo Makhathini, Kamasi Washington and the other artists discussed in this section have serious messages to impart, addressing a broad range of issues from racism to impending environmental catastrophe, so the issue of image versus reality must be considered. As with the traditional suit-and-tie jazz musicians discussed in the first section of this book, the visual presentation of the spiritual jazz musician is crucial, for them and their audience. The wrapping tells you what to expect from the package.

But each of these players comes from a different background. Ahmed is from Bahrain, and Muslim, while Makhathini is both a Christian and an actual spiritual healer in his community. Some of them are exploring more expansive, cosmic zones of thought, as in the apocalyptic sci-fi imagery of Hutchings' group The Comet Is Coming or Darius Jones' densely metaphorical narratives. Still others, like Garcia, Shirley Tetteh and Makaya McCraven, display little overt spirituality, but track titles like "Boundless Beings" and "Source" (Garcia) or "Traveling Space" and "Inner Flight" (McCraven) hint at something nonetheless. And all of them are keenly aware of the world they live in day-to-day, whatever their ideas may be about realms beyond.

Shabaka Hutchings: I Guess He Can Play...

I have always had the odd if innocuous expectation that every man I meet will be my height. Since I am 6′2″ (188 cm), this is frequently not the case. However, when I met Shabaka Hutchings, I was surprised to find myself looking up. He is very tall, at least 6′5″ and maybe 6′6″, and thin, if well-built. Like many extraordinarily tall men, he is extremely gentle and friendly in person. We met in a rehearsal room at the New School's Mannes School of Music in January 2018, joined by Yazz Ahmed and Nubya Garcia, and he towered over all of us.

He somehow seemed even taller the night I saw him perform at New York's Mercury Lounge with his electronic trio The Comet Is Coming; his bandmates, keyboardist Dan "Danalogue" Leavers and drummer Max "Betamax" Hallett, set up at far stage left and far back, respectively, giving him plenty of room to roam. (With TCIC, he calls himself King Shabaka, by the way.)

It was March 2019, and the group had just released their second full-length album, *Trust in the Lifeforce of the Deep Mystery*, when I saw them. An EP, *The Afterlife*, would follow later in the year. They are a true collaboration — he's not in charge. Leavers and Hallett were a duo called Soccer96 first, and Hutchings proposed a collaboration after seeing them live. During a phone conversation with all three members, he told me he wanted to see "how far I could push that energy before it breaks — and it hasn't broken yet."

The trio's early material (the album *Channel the Spirits* and the *Prophecy* and *Death to the Planet* EPs) was less focused, more about vibe than compositions, but their more recent work is both viscerally exciting and beautiful. Hallett is a ferocious drummer, and Leavers' Roland synths and pedal boards are almost defiantly retro. There wasn't a laptop to be seen anywhere onstage — he was playing it all, live and in the moment.

Their melodies often have a synthwave feel, with some improvisatory flourishes that recall Alice Coltrane's devotional music of the 1980s. Hallett played a small kit but created a big, powerful sound, cranking the beat up to at times astonishing tempos.

Hutchings, born in London but raised in his parents' native Barbados from age 9 to 16, is a classically trained reeds player who started out on clarinet — he occasionally posts videos on Instagram of himself playing Bach and the like. Onstage, though, he's almost anti-virtuosic in his approach. The first time we spoke, he talked about playing what he called "stupid sax." He explained:

> You go through college and there's all these things in the air, in the zeitgeist that says, "You need to be better." And it's come from working in the capitalist system. We need to accumulate more jazz chops. We need more information, we need more facility, we need more everything. But what about if we don't need any more anything? What if we need to go back to a place where we just have our creativity, and a piece of metal? And I call that stupid sax. You take the saxophone and you just get ignorant. I practice — I'll transcribe and I'll practice out of étude books, but the real thing is when I'm onstage trying to actually approach the instrument from a point of unknowing, trying to unlearn all that stuff. I really don't want to sound like Mark Turner or Joe Lovano, 'cause they just sound too good. They sound like they know what they're doing. I'd rather be that guy in the corner with people going, "Uhhh...I *guess* he can play."

Hutchings can definitely play. He's not a big-voiced, resonant player like John Coltrane or Sonny Rollins or JD Allen, and he doesn't construct elaborate solos. He has a hoarse, crying sound rooted in R&B honking and West Indian parade music, with a little bit of reverb and distortion added with a pedal, and he grabs onto phrases and digs in, turning them into something mantra-like, driving the audience wild with pure repetition and force. He took an unaccompanied solo at the Mercury Lounge that consisted of a single riff, ground into the stage until the audience was all but screaming.

There's a gentle side to his playing, too, of course. On bass clarinet, his repetitive phrases have a moody but soothing effect, like Eric Dolphy singing a nursery rhyme to a drowsy child. But at the Mercury Lounge, it was the fast, stomping performances of pieces like "Summon the Fire" and "Super Zodiac," which blended together seamlessly into one long stretch of jackhammer drumming, pulsing synths and fierce sax, that set the tone. The room was packed, and people were bouncing around, nodding their heads and jumping in place; a woman at the lip of the stage danced furiously throughout the set.

Hutchings' other primary group, Sons of Kemet, is just as energetic; they draw explicitly on a Caribbean party vibe, mixing it with raucous free jazz blowing. The lineup has changed from album to album, and guests are frequent, but the primary instrumentation is always the same: saxophone, tuba and two drummers. They create a pounding ocean of rhythm, and tuba player Theon Cross, who replaced Oren Marshall after their debut, is both bassist and co-lead voice.

The tuba isn't a common instrument in jazz. Alto saxophonist Arthur Blythe partnered with Bob Stewart for several albums in the late 70s and early 80s, creating a unique sound that blended old-timey jazz with pumping urban funk, and Bill Lowe occasionally plays it with Taylor Ho Bynum's 9-Tette. But Cross, with Sons of Kemet and on his own releases, has brought the instrument to a new prominence. The two drummers — mainly Tom Skinner and Sebastian Rochford, though Moses Boyd, Eddie Hick and Max Hallett all appear on the group's third album *Your Queen is a Reptile* — are positively thunderous. This is music to march to, or to jump up and down to.

Poet Joshua Idehen, who's also recorded with The Comet Is Coming, and jungle vocalist Congo Natty make appearances on *Your Queen is a Reptile*. Each track is called "My Queen is..." and pays tribute to a figure from Black history. Many of them are relatively obscure — Harriet Tubman and Angela Davis were the only two I recognized right away, but a quick search taught me about most of the others. On "My Queen is Yaa Asantewaa," named for an Ashanti warrior queen who lived from 1840 to 1921 and led a rebellion against the British occupying forces in what is now Ghana, Hutchings and guest saxophonist Nubya Garcia trade off phrases, but they also wind their lines together like they're dancing. Behind them, the percussion clatters and booms, as the tuba maintains a steady, throbbing pulse.

Though Hutchings is one of the leaders of the current London jazz scene, which has often been portrayed as something rising up unbidden, almost an insurgency, he has deep ties to the music's history. He worked with Courtney Pine, one of British jazz's breakout stars in the 80s and 90s, and with Evan Parker, a legend in the world of free improvisation since the 1960s.

Hutchings told me Parker advised him to leave it all on the stage, to give his all every time out, and he's taken that advice to heart. "When I'm playing, I'll get into this space of almost playing as if it's the last notes that we are going to play," he explained. "Part of the ethos of The Comet is Coming is, you have to live as if the comet is coming — and environmentally, I guess, that is particularly pertinent at the moment."

Hutchings leads a third ensemble, Shabaka and the Ancestors, which arose from repeated trips to Cape Town to visit a now-ex-partner. After going back and forth for 4 years, and playing with a crew of local musicians every time he was there, he decided to document those relationships on record in 2016. He spent a month slowly writing tunes, booked a studio and made the album *Wisdom of Elders*. One day of rehearsal, one live performance, one day in the studio, and done.

The band consisted of alto saxophonist Mthunzi Mvubu, trumpeter Mandla Mlangeni, keyboardist Nduduzo Makhathini, bassist Ariel Zamonsky, drummer Tumi Mogorosi, percussionist Gontse Makhene and vocalist Siyabonga Mthembu. Interestingly, Hutchings kept Makhathini out of the rehearsal and the live gig; he wanted him to come to the material as fresh as possible in the studio, and determine for himself what he could add in the moment. The resulting music is softer than either of Hutchings' other groups; it has a gentle African pulse, with tinges of reggae and gospel at times, and Mthembu's poetic lyrics, delivered in a keening, almost hymn-like cadence, give it an additional layer of depth.

Because of the geographical separation between Hutchings and his bandmates, Shabaka and the Ancestors initially felt like a one-off. But when we met in 2018, he told me that there were plans for a second record, and 2 years later, *We Were Sent Here by History* materialized. Everyone from the first session returned, though Makhathini only played on two tracks (a different pianist, Thandi Ntuli, also appeared) and Mlangeni on just one. It's basically a concept album; all the track titles come from a poem by Mthembu, and the music is even deeper and more introspective than before. "The Coming of the Strange Ones" is a particular highlight, a pulsing, shuffling vamp that feels like dancing barefoot in the dust, as the stars whirl above you.

In 2017, just as awareness of the London jazz scene was beginning to percolate, Hutchings curated a compilation, *We Out Here*, for DJ and producer Gilles Peterson's Brownswood label. It was recorded over 3 days of studio sessions, with nine ensembles in total, many of which shared members. Nubya Garcia was in some ways the center of the project; she plays on five of the nine tracks. Hutchings' own track, "Black Skin, Black Masks," features clarinet (by George Crowley) and bass clarinet winding around each other, as haunted-sounding piano, deeply throbbing bass and frantic drums keep the music churning like a cross between Charles Mingus and the debut of some new post-drum 'n' bass subgenre. Other tracks are led by Theon Cross, Moses Boyd, keyboardist Joe Arnon-Jones, Garcia and the ensembles Maisha, Ezra Collective, Triforce and Kokoroko. Almost all of these folks — and more — have made albums in the last few years, and every one has been worth hearing. The best have brought something entirely new to the table, making music that combines classic and modern jazz while incorporating the sounds of London nightclubs and the Afro-Caribbean diaspora, and making it all into a seamless whole.

Essential Listening

Sons of Kemet, *Lest We Forget What We Came Here to Do* (Naim Jazz, 2015)

Shabaka and the Ancestors, *Wisdom of Elders* (Brownswood, 2016)

Various Artists, *We Out Here* (Brownswood, 2017)

Sons of Kemet, *Your Queen is a Reptile* (Impulse!, 2018)

The Comet is Coming, *Trust in the Lifeforce of the Deep Mystery* (Impulse!, 2019)

The Comet is Coming, *The Afterlife* (Impulse!, 2019)

Shabaka and the Ancestors, *We are Sent Here by History* (Impulse!, 2020)

Yazz Ahmed: Becoming Whole

Trumpeter Yazz Ahmed's second album, 2017's *La Saboteuse,* seemed to come out of nowhere. It first took the form of four digital EPs of three or four tracks each, and was finally issued as a full-length CD in May 2017. The music blended jazz and Middle Eastern/North African desert music, layers of ringing and clattering percussion supporting vibraphone, multiple electric pianos, guitar and two horn players: Ahmed herself on trumpet and flugelhorn, and Shabaka Hutchings on bass clarinet.

The way the multiple keyboards and the deep, dubby bass intertwined and layered themselves over and under and around each other recalled Miles Davis's electric music of the early 1970s, somewhere between the zap and rattle of 1972's *On the Corner* and the mantra-like, infinitely patient pulse of "Ife," from 1974's *Big Fun*. But there was a sense of spiritual solitude and intimacy in the music, too, as on "Misophonia," where Ahmed's heavily reverbed trumpet was heard in duet with what sounds like glass bottles being tapped together.

Ahmed was also in communication with the jazz tradition throughout the album. Her horn playing was lush and lovely, particularly on the flugelhorn, where she has a tender tone ideally suited to ballads. "The Space Between the Fish and the Moon," despite its title and the glitchy electronics popping and humming behind her, was a romantic flugelhorn-and-vibes showcase that if played on purely acoustic instruments, could please any old-school jazz fan.

Though "la saboteuse" was the name Ahmed gave the inner voice of doubt that all creative people must wrestle with in order to do their work, the album was an extraordinarily confident and pathbreaking artistic statement.

I met Ahmed along with Shabaka Hutchings and Nubya

Garcia in January 2018, when she was in New York to perform at Winter Jazzfest. We all sat in a rehearsal room at the Mannes School of Music, with a student band playing somewhere down the hall, and discussed her background, how she'd come to jazz, and how she was able to reshape the music in her own image, taking what she wanted from its history while moving forward into twenty-first century (immediately pre-Brexit) England.

Born in Bahrain, she moved to England at 9, where she met her maternal grandfather, Terry Brown, a trumpeter who had played with saxophonist Tubby Hayes and produced records for the Pye and Philips labels in the 1950s.

"I used to listen to Dizzy Gillespie a lot," she told me. "He was the first trumpet player I was introduced to by my grandfather... he would share with me all these old bebop records, and that's kind of where my education started. I used to play along with these records and not really understand what was going on, but enjoy the spirit of it."

Ahmed came to jazz as she came to England, as an outsider, someone walking between worlds. She says:

> I felt like there was something missing and so when it came to my jazz studies, I was studying American jazz, British jazz, but it took a while, till my late twenties, that I started to rediscover my roots. I started listening to Rabih Abou-Khalil, an oud player, and it struck a chord with me inside and I felt that I became whole again, reconnecting with this very spiritual, heartfelt music.

Ahmed's first album, 2011's *Finding My Way Home*, reflected the beginnings of her journey toward establishing her own musical personality, a journey she says she's still on. It was primarily built around duets for flugelhorn and electric bass, three composed and four improvised. The compositions included a version of British jazz saxophonist Stan Sulzmann's

"Birthdays, Birthdays" and a take on Miles Davis's "So What," plus one Ahmed original, "Affirmation," which drew on classic jazz as well. The four improvised pieces, on the other hand, incorporated Arabic scales, swaddling the music in a fog of reverb as though it's drifting in from a half-remembered past. Still other pieces, like "Flip Flop," were modern but traditionalist hard bop and could have been written and performed at any time post-1964.

Six years passed between *Finding My Way Home* and *La Saboteuse*. Ahmed was busy, though, navigating the increasingly challenging landscape of the twenty-first century music business. "I funded the first and second albums on my own, really, so I had to take on any tours or gigs that I got to pay the bills. Everything was sort of done on mates' rates, stealing studio time, that kind of thing." She got three large commissions, though, which raised her profile significantly in 2015 and 2016. The first was the *Women of the World Suite*, performed with an all-female ensemble on International Women's Day 2015 and including pieces dedicated to Rosa Parks, Malala Yousafzai and other influential women. The second, *Alhaan Al Saduri*, was created with a fellowship from Birmingham Jazzlines and inspired by work songs of Bahraini pearl divers and wedding songs of all-female drumming groups from that country. It was a collaboration with the London Symphony Orchestra, as part of their Soundhub program.

In addition to this work, she was a touring member of the art-rock band These New Puritans, and performed on Radiohead's album *The King of Limbs*. She and her partner, Noel Langley, can be heard on the songs "Bloom" and "Codex."

"We visited the studio and they played us some of the stuff they'd been inspired by," she recalled:

> They played us some Alice Coltrane, you know, and it was quite surprising. I didn't realize they were into that kind of

> music. And so we did a bit of experimenting with some of the written parts that they'd already prepared, and some improvising, and they just took it away and sort of made their own thing of what we did on the sessions.

For Ahmed, observing Radiohead's process, and their willingness — in partnership with producer Nigel Godrich — to use the studio as a compositional tool was a learning experience.

> You know, there are so many possibilities that you don't have with live music...I really took that to heart and I used a lot of those techniques in recording *La Saboteuse*. I love the way they work; they're incredibly serious, they're very focused. When we did the live session, they were like, three takes and that's it, move on to the next one. They're brilliant to work with, and I love the use of electronics; that's where I became curious about the Kaoss Pad and stuff like that, creating new sound worlds.

Onstage at Le Poisson Rouge in Greenwich Village, she wore a multicolored satin robe that looked like it might have belonged to a member of Sun Ra's Arkestra. Her quartet included vibraphone, electric bass and drums, and they created a shimmering cloud of notes, with a surprisingly hard backbeat underneath. The exoticism of *La Saboteuse* was mostly absent, as the limited instrumental palette only allowed for relatively traditional rhythms. However, even in this more conventional context, the murmuring intimacy of her voice came through, and influenced the others' contributions as well. She nodded and bobbed her head as she played, counting off the groove and occasionally conducting the other three with a quick, subtle hand gesture.

Ahmed is an extremely generous collaborator, always giving

as much credit as possible to her fellow musicians. The booklet that accompanies *La Saboteuse* devotes two full pages to each member of the ensemble, including a photo, a quote from them and her thoughts on their contribution — and this goes not only for the musicians, but the mixing and mastering engineers who worked on the project, as well.

Her third album, *Polyhymnia,* was released in early 2020. It features a reworked version of the music she'd written and performed on International Women's Day in 2015; its six tracks are dedicated to Saudi film director Haifaa Al-Mansour, civil rights activist Ruby Bridges, Pakistani advocate for female education Malala Yousafzai, Rosa Parks, the British voting rights advocates known as the Suffragettes, and UK saxophonist and bandleader Barbara Thompson.

Polyhymnia is the ancient Greek muse of music, poetry and dance, and the music on the CD is performed by an ensemble that's two dozen strong at times, and includes many prominent female players from the London jazz scene, including saxophonists Camilla George and Nubya Garcia, guitarist Shirley Tetteh and pianist Sarah Tandy. It begins with the nearly 10-minute "Lahan Al-Mansour," a surging big band piece that combines Arabic tonalities with the panoramic scope of a movie score. The music rises and falls in thrilling waves of sound, individual instrumentalists drifting out of the ensemble charts for solos, then sinking back into the whole. Other tracks like "Barbara" and "Ruby Bridges" draw elements from soul, New Orleans funk and even Afrobeat. Ahmed has moved far beyond blending traditional hard bop with Arabic melodies. She has become a synthesist of discernment and power, to the point where questions of influence and inspiration become moot, even pedantic. As she told me in 2018, "I just take bits from everyone — whoever I feel close to emotionally." In the process, she creates music that is uniquely hers, but with universal appeal.

Essential Listening

Yazz Ahmed, *Finding My Way Home* (Suntara, 2011)
Yazz Ahmed, *La Saboteuse* (Naim Jazz, 2017)
Toshio Matsuura Group, *LOVEPLAYDANCE – 8 Scenes From the Floor* (Brownswood, 2018)
Yazz Ahmed, *La Saboteuse Remixed* (Naim Jazz, 2019)
Yazz Ahmed, *Polyhymnia* (Ropeadope, 2019)

Nubya Garcia & Shirley Tetteh: We're Not Americans

Born in London to Trinidadian and Guyanese parents, Nubya Garcia began playing piano at 5, eventually moving to saxophone — first alto, then tenor and baritone, with a dash of flute, clarinet and bass clarinet here and there. She's primarily drawn to the low end of the horn spectrum, and that manifests in her music, which features straight-ahead sax playing with a clearly audible Sonny Rollins/Dexter Gordon influence laid over rhythms that blend jazz, hip-hop, funk and Caribbean street rhythms.

Onstage at Le Poisson Rouge in 2018, she led a quartet populated by friends she'd known for years: keyboardist Joe Armon-Jones, bassist Daniel Casimir and drummer Femi Koleoso. She gave them plenty of room to run; they set up the groove of "Lost Kingdoms," from her debut EP, 2017's *Nubya's 5ive*, and she was dancing across the stage before she'd even got her horn strapped on. After playing the head, she let Armon-Jones take the first solo, a wild eruption halfway between the ornate salsa of Larry Harlow and the pounding chords of Matthew Shipp.

Garcia herself took only a brief moment in the spotlight before yielding it again, this time to let Koleoso go off in a way that mixed the militaristic precision of Billy Cobham with the unstoppable swing of Art Blakey. She went back to dancing to his beat at first, but eventually stood aside in awe, listening like everyone else. It wasn't until the performance's final third that she seized the spotlight, taking a solo that was more about energy and impact — short, punchy phrases slightly warped by a distortion pedal — than bebop virtuosity.

"Influence-wise, I think when I was starting out I listened to a lot of piano players and trumpet players, and then later on I kinda got into Bird — I was still playing alto at that time," she told me at the New School:

> Coltrane and Sonny [Rollins] and Dexter [Gordon] were a huge influence on my younger self...trying to digest "Giant Steps" at the age of thirteen, I was like, "I don't know what's going on, I'm going to put this down for a second," and came back to it and it was a completely different experience however many years later. I believe in listening to and absorbing things at the right time.

Nubya's 5ive actually featured six tracks; she recorded two versions of "Hold" and was unable to choose between them. The first take was set to a relaxed hip-hop beat with a foundation of electric piano, like something you might hear on a Roots or DJ Krush album. The second was more uptempo, a kind of street parade music with a thick bounce. On both versions, there were two drummers, Koleoso and Moses Boyd (the primary timekeeper throughout), and Theon Cross guested on tuba. The drummers created a dense clatter, but the groove stayed locked-in and rock-steady. On the studio version of "Lost Kingdoms," which opens the EP, Sheila Maurice-Grey played trumpet, and the two women traded ideas back and forth in a mutually inspiring but non-competitive way.

Garcia's full-length debut, *Source*, was released in late summer 2020. The core band consisted of Armon-Jones, Casimir and drummer Sam Jones, but numerous guests appeared, notably Maurice-Grey and alto saxophonist Cassie Kinoshi. Once again, the album demonstrated that she's a melody-minded player who enjoys exploring a tune's possibilities, rather than going for extreme effects. She almost never screams, though she'll wander around in the tenor's lower reaches, a choice that's only augmented by the dubby, bass-heavy production. The title piece runs nearly 12 minutes, and she's joined by Maurice-

Grey, Kinoshi and trombonist Richie Seivwright. In addition to the thick groove, it features wordless backing vocals by all three women and tight horn section charts, all swathed in echo and reverb. The solos arise organically out of the rock-steady rhythm, and the feeling is like floating forever on a softly rising and falling tide.

Maurice-Grey and Garcia are both members of Nérija, a septet that was all-female on its self-titled debut EP. On the group's 2019 album, *Blume*, though, original bassist Inga Eichler had been replaced by Rio Kai. Garcia is just one of four horn players — in addition to Maurice-Grey, the band also includes Kinoshi and trombonist Rosie Turton, as well as guitarist Shirley Tetteh, Kai on bass and drummer Lizzy Exell. The compositions on *Blume*, many of which were written collectively (on the debut EP, individual members brought in tunes), had a dreamy quality, occasionally nodding to classic 60s jazz. On "Last Straw," Garcia dropped short, introspective phrases over a skipping beat and Tetteh's almost West African-sounding guitar, leaving space for thought between each burst of notes and letting intensity build gradually. As she wound down, her horn was first bounced sharply from the left to the right speaker and back, then washed away like a cloud drifting out of view.

Garcia is also a member of Cross's trio, along with Moses Boyd — they recorded the 2015 *Aspirations* EP and 2019's *Fyah* together. His tuba playing is as thick and deep as it is on Sons of Kemet's albums, and sometimes he feeds the instrument through reverb and subtle effects to act almost as a dub bass line underneath Boyd's loose-but-tight drum patterns and Garcia's hypnotic, mantra-like sax lines. For her part, she loops phrases over and over, only occasionally cutting loose. It's a collective music, more about groove than solo statements.

Garcia's other major project is Maisha, another septet, this one led by drummer Jake Long. Their music is blatantly indebted to early 70s spiritual jazz, particularly the work of Alice Coltrane and Pharoah Sanders. Their debut EP was recorded live, but their 2018 album *There is a Place* was very much a studio creation. In the opening moments of the first track, the nearly 12-minute "Osiris," Garcia can be heard on both tenor saxophone and flute, and eventually she solos on tenor for nearly half the track, with a pulsing, shaking Afrobeat rhythm behind her, courtesy of Tetteh, bassist Twm Dylan, Long and percussionists Tim Doyle and Yahael Camara-Onono. There's an additional layer of lushness added, though, courtesy of a string quartet whose playing is somewhere between the soaring orchestrations of Coltrane and the slick arrangements on early 70s albums by Stanley Turrentine or Grover Washington Jr.

"There's no hierarchy in the bands that I'm a part of, other than my own," Garcia told me:

> They've kind of been building for a few years now, so the way that I like to do things is just treat them with the same importance, because that's what they are to me and I value everyone I play with and it's not like I've chosen one higher than the other. It hasn't really worked that way for me, which I think is really good.

In the second half of "Osiris," Shirley Tetteh took over, vaulting the music into an entirely different realm. Her extended solo was like a cross between Grant Green in 1962 and Phelps Collins with James Brown's band in 1969; her lines came incredibly fast, with bite like she was whipping strands of barbed wire at your face, and even the rising strings couldn't contain her. It was almost like they were trying to play her off at an awards ceremony, but she wasn't going anywhere until she'd said what she meant to say.

Since 2017, Tetteh has been featured on a string of the most exciting recordings to come out of the London scene, including vocalist Zara MacFarlane's *Arise,* alto saxophonist Camilla

George's *The People Could Fly* and bassist Daniel Casimir's *Escapee*. In addition to her work with Maisha and Nérija, she's also a member of alto saxophonist Cassie Kinoshi's SEED Ensemble.

She grew up listening to a vast array of sounds, including the Ghanaian music of her parents' generation, radio pop, grime and UK garage, and even bluegrass, and eventually developed a taste for shreddy prog and fusion guitarists like Steve Lukather, of the 80s pop band Toto. "I saw him do the craziest things with a whammy bar, making it sound like a slide guitar, and he always had these really cool tricks up his sleeve and insane technique," she told me over the phone from London. She also expressed a love for Jeff Beck, Jimmy Page and Allan Holdsworth.

Her own playing betrays little of this style. She's a chameleon, who can strum out gentle jazz chords behind George, or tear into a Grant Green-esque solo with Maisha. She uses relatively few effects, at least in part because, as she confesses, "I've lost two batches of pedals on the train," and plays a Cort Yorktown, a Korean-made hollow-body guitar that looks a little like a Gibson, if you squint. "There are guitars that are amazing, that are really well made and stuff — this might not be that kind of guitar, but I just happen to really like it."

Tetteh's career, like that of many young London players, began with Tomorrow's Warriors, a program founded by bassist Gary Crosby that provides musical education and artistic development. "The first time I went to their sessions I met Moses Boyd, Theon and Nat Cross, Tyrone Isaac-Stuart who's a great alto player, Jared Boswell, Sheila Maurice-Grey, Nubya..."

According to Tetteh, Nérija's *Blume* is a showcase for the increasingly collaborative nature of the group's music:

> For the first EP, everyone just brought tunes to the band and we played them. On this album, we wrote three songs completely together, and there's little bits and pieces where

> maybe one or two people wrote more than others. There's two tunes that were brought in fairly complete, and then for others people brought in ideas and we helped flesh them out. And then there's maybe three tunes where we all had a fairly equal stake.

Kinoshi's SEED Ensemble, whose debut *Driftglass* was released in February 2019, shares four members with Nérija: Kinoshi, who writes all the material, Maurice-Grey, Tetteh and Kai. The band numbers ten in all, and Kinoshi's compositions are complex and tightly arranged, frequently serving as a backdrop for poetry or spoken word expression. Unlike with Nérija, where she solos on the majority of tracks, Tetteh serves mostly as a member of the rhythm section along with Kai, drummer Patrick Boyle and either Joe Arnon-Jones or Sarah Tandy on keyboards.

According to her, Kai and Boyle bring tricks they learned with Tomorrow's Warriors, studying the music of Steve Lehman, Steve Coleman and Andrew Hill:

> They'll play all of that stuff on Cassie's music, which none of it's in four anyway, and they'll throw a lot of challenging things your way. So that's the major challenge, is listening to everything that everyone's doing and playing something creative over the top of it and keeping your place 'cause Patrick and Rio are always fucking with you, in the best way.

Because of its players' backgrounds and the cultural environment they came up in, the music of the London scene sounds completely different from American jazz — or anything else. Tetteh told me her uniquely expressive sound "was just kind of something that happened once I accepted that I could allow all parts of me to exist. We're not Americans, and we couldn't try to be."

Similarly, Nubya Garcia said:

> Other genres that have inspired you, they're always gonna come out in your music, so I think for me definitely all of the sounds that I'm trying to include in what I'm doing, or what we're creating together onstage and in the studio — there's such a range, and they all have equal weight, you know. We all met playing traditional jazz, swing and bebop, but along that route, we started hanging out, we started going to other gigs, many of us were at college together, we lived together, blah blah blah. When you go to nights that aren't specifically jazz nights but you're taking so much from that and then bringing it back to the colleges and the Tomorrow's Warriors and the other jam sessions...yeah, I think it's very true that you create what you've been listening to, an amalgamation of it. So I think that's why you're hearing such a range of influences in our music.

At the same time, the polyglot cosmopolitanism, the embrace of sounds from across the Afro-Caribbean diaspora, the Middle East and beyond is very much a London thing, as the violent parochialism of Brexit has proved. That's something Garcia was keenly aware of, even if some of her peers may not have been back in 2018, when we spoke.

"I think in London we live in a massive bubble of what the UK is actually like in terms of its opinions to ethnicity and immigrants, basically," she told me.

> In the run-up to Brexit, I was convinced, 'Oh, there's no way this is gonna go ahead' and as it got closer and closer, I left London to do a gig in the north, in Huddersfield or something, and that was the first time I'd seen firsthand that most of the banners around the town were Vote Leave. I think I saw one out of over a hundred that was Vote Remain. That was when I knew. I was just like, 'Oh, goddamn,' firsthand, you know? Because London is a multicultural city — it's not

perfect, like, in that respect, but it's nowhere near on the same level as other parts of the UK, and you don't realize that, but the second you leave the M25 — when you're on the road, and you're doing all the venues in London or the festival circuit or whatever, and you step into service stations and you actually see what the UK's like — it's unforgiving. I will be watching very carefully to how the UK changes over the next decade.

Essential Listening

Nubya Garcia, *Nubya's 5ive* (Jazz Re:freshed, 2017)
Maisha, *There is a Place* (Brownswood, 2018)
Theon Cross, *Fyah* (Gearbox, 2019)
Nérija, *Blume* (Domino, 2019)
SEED Ensemble, *Driftglass* (Jazz Re:freshed, 2019)
Gary Bartz & Maisha, *Night Dreamer Direct-to-Disc Sessions* (Night Dreamer, 2020)
Nubya Garcia, *Source* (Concord, 2020)

Brandee Younger & Makaya McCraven: Making Connections, Shining a Light

In the summer of 1989, between my junior and senior years of high school, I traveled to Los Angeles and while I was there, I saw Fela Kuti live at the Universal Amphitheater, an outdoor venue. He had long since swapped out the band that made his best and best-known albums, in the 1970s, but it was still an amazing show. He had what seemed like an army of dancers and backup singers, in addition to his vast musical ensemble, and the songs — I swear they only played three, maybe four, in 2 hours — were like an endless sea of rhythm and taut Afrobeat funk.

Almost exactly 30 years later, I got to see Fela's legendary drummer, Tony Allen. He'd invented Afrobeat in that killer Seventies band; it was his approach to rhythm — a light, dancing groove that layered polyrhythms in a way that didn't seem physically possible, since human bodies still only have four limbs — that was the root of the entire sound. Fela himself said "Without Tony Allen, there would be no Afrobeat."

Allen knew what he could do; he claimed to be able to play a different time signature with each limb. But as he told me by phone from Paris:

> I can't explain it to you with my mouth; it's not possible. You have to see it in action. Because I never preview what I'm going to play — it comes according to my wavelength. So, it's impossible for me to explain what I'm playing. You want to know it? I'll show you how it's done, and if you can handle it, that's it.

That night in August 2018, I saw it in action. In the last few years of his life, Allen turned his mastery of groove into a mastery of swing. He signed to Blue Note, and released an EP of tunes made popular by Art Blakey and the Jazz Messengers, followed by a full-length album, *The Source*, that was one of the best jazz albums of 2017. Then he brought that band to Le Poisson Rouge, performing to a packed house.

The group included a trumpeter, a saxophonist, a pianist who doubled on organ, and an upright bassist. They focused on material from *The Source*, playing a kind of patient, bouncing-in-place hard bop. While the trumpeter and saxophonist took fierce, high-flying solos, Allen and the others settled into a swinging but at times almost dub-like groove. He stayed silent, wearing a hat and sunglasses behind the kit and barely seeming to move as he played, but between songs he broke into a wide grin that showed just how much fun he was having playing this music. The crowd was shuffling to the rhythm from first note to last, swaying back and forth almost as one throughout the set.

The opening act was a surprise — a harp-bass duo. Brandee Younger and Dezron Douglas performed a short but captivating set of compositions by Alice Coltrane and Dorothy Ashby, as well as original material.

Younger studied at the University of Hartford in Connecticut, then earned a graduate degree at New York University's Steinhardt School. Her early background was in classical music, but she eventually gravitated toward jazz. "My parents met a woman who played harp and thought that it would be interesting for me to learn about, since I was already involved in music. Then they learned that it was a scholarship instrument. End of story," she told me via email. She found herself inspired by Coltrane and Ashby, the two most prominent jazz harpists, just as much as by legendary classical players like Carlos Salzedo and Marcel Grandjany.

Younger released a short album — seven tracks in under a half hour — called *Wax & Wane* in 2016, featuring flautist Anne Drummond, saxophonist Chelsea Baratz, guitarist Mark

Whitfield, Douglas (on electric bass) and drummer Dana Hawkins. The music was more funk than jazz. The opening track, "Soul Vibrations," was built on a groove reminiscent of Sly and the Family Stone, and Younger didn't immediately seize the lead, choosing to blend into the ensemble at first. But when she started her solo, her sound was otherworldly, and her ability to pluck single notes at high speed was closer to the work of a fusion-era guitarist than the shimmering glissandos typical of the harp.

"Soul Vibrations," "Afro Harping" and the title track were all Ashby compositions, but the lushness of Younger's arrangements differentiated them from the earlier recordings, and her originals, like "Essence of Ruby" and "Black Gold," were the best tracks on the record.

I spoke to Younger before and after her set at Le Poisson Rouge, and she told me that she was working on releasing a new album. *Soul Awakening*, an album that had been recorded in 2012 but never released, arrived in June 2019. The core band included Douglas and drummer E.J. Strickland, plus saxophonists Stacy Dillard and Chelsea Baratz. A wide array of guests appeared on one track or another: saxophonists Antoine Roney and Ravi Coltrane, trumpeters Freddie Hendrix and Sean Jones, trombonist Corey Wilcox, flautist Nicole Camacho and vocalist Niia. The album included one track each by Dorothy Ashby and Alice Coltrane – "Games" and "Blue Nile," respectively. But again, it was Younger's original material that was the draw. The combination of her shimmering harp and Baratz's soul jazz saxophone (and Hendrix's subtle trumpet contributions) on "Linda Lee," a dedication to her mother, gave it a surging, emotive quality reminiscent of Kamasi Washington's work.

As one might imagine, it's not easy lugging a harp to gigs, especially in New York. "Harpists in the city either drive a large vehicle or use a trained harp mover," Younger told me. "If it's an especially difficult situation, I minimize what I have to bring and take a van taxi. You need a few muscles."

There's also the issue of maintenance:

> Harps have to be kept at a consistent temperature with the right amount of humidity. String upkeep has been tough as of late [in 2016], due to an inconsistency in the gut supply. You're looking at about $500 for a full set of strings (a concert grand harp has 47 strings) so when they're breaking at record rates due to bad gut supply, it really grinds your gears! The harp has to be tuned daily...the more it is tuned, the better it holds its pitch. Harpists carry tuning keys, so we tune it ourselves.

Thanks to her skill on her uncommon instrument, Younger is an in-demand guest who's appeared on albums by saxophonists Lakecia Benjamin (interpreting the music of John and Alice Coltrane), Ravi Coltrane and Camille Thurman; bassist Christian McBride's big band; pop-R&B singer John Legend; trumpeter Taylor Haskins and others. "Everyone wants something different," she told me. "I'd say that most musicians want 'colors' that can be achieved through swift arpeggios. Also, some folks favor the Alice Coltrane-esque glissandi, while others want the harp as a melody or rhythm instrument, because they want a lighter texture than what the piano offers." In 2020, she signed a contract with Impulse! Records — Alice Coltrane's former label — to release music as a leader.

One of the musicians who's brought Younger in for multiple projects is drummer and producer Makaya McCraven, whose unusual working methods have yielded a string of albums and mixtapes that sound like nothing else out there, and have created a sensation within and outside the jazz world. I first encountered him at Winter Jazzfest in 2018, drumming for Chicago trumpeter Marquis Hill's Blacktet. He was already well known, though. He had signed with the upstart Chicago label International Anthem, and released his second album, *In the Moment*, in 2015.

He'd spent a full year hosting a residency at the Bedford, a former bank vault converted into a restaurant/club, with guests including Hill, tenor saxophonists Tony Barba and De'Sean Jones, guitarist Jeff Parker, vibraphonist Justefan and bassists Joshua Abrams, Matt Ulery and Junius Paul. At the end, McCraven went through tapes of all 28 performances, slicing it up, looping the strongest sections and shuffling the music around until he'd come up with a double LP of vamps, moments of wild expressiveness and mesmerizing, trance-like passages. It wasn't seamless — the tracks had beginnings and ends, and that was by design. "I'm chopping stuff up in a way that I want it to still resemble the original music," he told me by phone. "I still want it to sound live, like a band."

It did, but not all the time. It also sounded like a DJ mix or a beat tape, and McCraven believes that was what caught the attention of the music press and listeners who would never have made time for jazz with a capital J. "We played a local gig at this little bar for a year, struggling to build a network and build a scene, and once I recontextualized it within this beat parameter, all of a sudden I could make way more connections with people and shine a light on my local community, on myself, and on music in general."

He employed a similar working method for each of his subsequent releases, with varying degrees of sophistication. *Highly Rare* was much more musically aggressive and free, and it was sourced from a cassette recording of a single gig, so it sounded rough, too, but it had a visceral impact. *Where We Come From*, subtitled *ChicagoxLondon Mixtape*, similarly documented a single performance: a first-time collaboration between McCraven, saxophonists Nubya Garcia and Soweto Kinch, tuba player Theon Cross, and keyboardists Joe Armon-Jones and Kamaal Williams.

"Great groups of musicians come up together in communities," says McCraven, who was born in Paris and raised in western Massachusetts, but found his musical tribe when he moved to Chicago. "The London scene, they came up together, they play with each other."

The gig documented on *Where We Come From* was one of a series of one-off performances that ultimately yielded his 2019 album, *Universal Beings*. He traveled to New York, London, Los Angeles and back to Chicago, collaborating with local musicians in each place in order to sample the flavors of "different centers of different movements in jazz that are happening right now." The music wasn't recorded in studios, but rather at pop-up gigs in unorthodox venues, and the pool of collaborators included some longtime running partners like Parker, Paul and Ross, but also included Garcia, Younger, Tomeka Reid and Shabaka Hutchings. It's a double LP, and each side is devoted to recordings from a single city. But the goal is to reveal each one as facets of a whole, to "improvise with some musicians I've never even met, and do it in non-traditional spaces — not a proper concert, but something more underground and community-oriented, and try to have this narrative that we are part of a larger music community than just our respective local scenes."

At the 2020 edition of Winter Jazzfest, McCraven mixed players from New York and Chicago for two nights at Webster Hall. On Friday, January 10, he presented a set called *In These Times* with a seven-piece band including Hill on trumpet, Greg Ward on alto sax, Irvin Pierce on tenor sax, Matt Gold on guitar, Ross on vibraphone, Younger on harp and Paul on bass. The following night, Younger's own band opened the show, playing music from *Soul Awakening*, and then McCraven's group reappeared, to interpret the music of Gil Scott-Heron, as they had done on *We're New Again*, a reworking of the singer and poet's final release, *I'm New Here*, from 2010.

For the album, McCraven took Scott-Heron's vocals and

created entirely new musical backdrops using Younger, Parker, Paul and others. The fragmentary nature of the original album — it was recorded over a long period of time, a track here, a track there, and assembled by the label — lent itself to his production techniques, and he created something arguably better than the original. Onstage, Scott-Heron's recorded vocals were played back as the band explored the arrangements, but were not the dominant element; in fact, they were often submerged beneath the music. It was as if McCraven was inviting the late singer to be part of the musical community he was building.

Essential Listening

Makaya McCraven, *In the Moment* (International Anthem, 2015)

Brandee Younger, *Wax & Wane* (Independent/Self-Released, 2016)

Makaya McCraven, *Where We Come From: ChicagoxLondon Mixtape* (International Anthem, 2017)

Makaya McCraven, *Universal Beings* (International Anthem, 2019)

Brandee Younger, *Soul Awakening* (Independent/Self-Released, 2019)

Gil Scott-Heron, *We're New Again: A Reimagining by Makaya McCraven* (XL Recordings, 2020)

Nduduzo Makhathini, Siya Makuzeni, Thandi Ntuli, Linda Sikhakhane & Ndabo Zulu: Recovering Indigenous Knowledge

I had never heard of the Zürcher Gallery on Bleecker Street until the night I went there to see pianist/composer Nduduzo Makhathini and his group perform in January 2020. It was the single Winter Jazzfest performance I was most excited to see, and I ducked out of a set by the all-star band the Cookers early, in order to run down the block and make sure I got a spot.

I needn't have worried; the gallery was half empty when I arrived. I saw Makhathini sitting in a folding chair, his wife beside him, and walked over to introduce myself. We'd conducted a lengthy interview the previous October, and exchanged several emails before that, as I had become enraptured by his music and made a few overtures to US labels on his behalf, in a thoroughly unofficial, friend-to-friend, "you've gotta hear this guy" capacity. I had nothing to do with his eventual signing to Blue Note – the first South African artist to do so in the label's 80-year history.

He stood up and swept me into an embrace, and introduced me to his wife, Omagugu, who was seated beside him. We talked for a moment, and then they had to prepare for their set.

I had come across Makhathini's 2017 album *Ikhambi* on a blog, and was immediately enraptured. The music was recorded in London, and featured primarily English or European musicians – tenor saxophonist James Allsopp, alto saxophonist James Mainwaring, flautist Eddie Parker, trombonist Dennis Rollins, bassist Magne Thormodsæter – and one South African player, drummer Ayanda Sikade. There were also orchestral instruments (harp and strings) and a vocal chorus, led by Omagugu. The music surged with energy, mixing deep, bluesy vamps from the rhythm section with forceful exhortations from the horns. It had elements of McCoy Tyner's work, as well as influences from Alice Coltrane, Pharoah Sanders and South African players like Hugh Masekela and Abdullah Ibrahim, but he was doing something new with all those ideas, not just imitating his predecessors.

Ikhambi included two three-part suites, "Umthakathi" and "Impande," as well as seven stand-alone tracks; it ran a full 75 minutes, and was clearly intended to be an immersive journey. The first section of "Umthakathi" blended heavy piano blues reminiscent of Coltrane's *Journey in Satchidananda* with passionate, old school-meets-free jazz saxophone that recalled David Murray, as Omagugu offered sardonic-seeming commentary not unlike Jeanne Lee's performance on Archie Shepp's "Blasé." The second movement, by contrast, was a solo piano interlude, with some delicate percussion, while the third was all rhythm, including tablas, handclaps and chanting, with a feeling more North African than South.

"Impande" sounded even more inspired by Shepp's late 60s work, with pounding piano, muscular saxophone and deeply resonant trombone. Some of the other tracks' English-language titles — "Holy, Holy," "Innocent Child," "Windows of Our Hearts" — reflected Makhathini's spirituality, while the title, *Ikhambi,* was a Zulu word used by traditional doctors and herbalists to refer to a blend of healing herbs.

Ikhambi, it turned out, was Makhathini's *eighth* album. I dug into the others and quickly discovered that his work had a startling breadth. One was a solo piano disc, while another featured a trio and a vocal ensemble, but the 90-minute two-CD set *Listening to the Ground* was the most impressive of all. Track titles like "Waltz for Trane," "King Fela," "Lagos Blues" and "We Cry for Peace in Africa" seemed to lay out the parameters of his musical and cultural interests, and the band included Thormodsæter and Sikade, Robin Fassie Kock on trumpet and flugelhorn, Karl-Martin Almqvist on tenor and soprano saxes and flute, Sophie Ribstein on harp, El Hadj Ngari Ndong and Mabaleng Moholo on percussion, and Omagugu and a choir providing vocals.

I learned that Makhathini was also a teacher and producer who seemed to be at the forefront of a group of young musicians. This new South African jazz had a strong spiritual element, but the players — including keyboardist Thandi Ntuli, saxophonist Linda Sikhakhane and trombonist Siya Mazukeni — all had their own identities.

Sikhakhane, who had come to New York to study at the New School, worked with Makhathini on his own self-released debut album, *Two Sides, One Mirror*. In an email, he wrote, "Beyond being one of the greatest pianists of our time, he deliberately uses his gift of divination and healing through music...Makhathini's contribution plays a big role in decolonization and the recovery of indigenous knowledge."

South Africa has long been recognized as the continent's primary home for adventurous, forward-looking jazz, beginning in the 1950s with the Blue Notes, led by pianist Chris McGregor. That band included trumpeter Mongezi Feza, alto saxophonist Dudu Pukwana, bassist Johnny Dyani and drummer Louis Moholo-Moholo, all of whom achieved individual success in Europe after leaving South Africa in 1964. Meanwhile, the Jazz Epistles — whose 1959 album *Jazz Epistle, Verse 1* was the first by a black South African jazz band — included pianist Abdullah Ibrahim, then known as Dollar Brand, and trumpeter Hugh Masekela. The latter man has been called "the father of South African jazz," and his decades-long career included crossover hits and years of work as a human rights activist.

Thandi Ntuli's second album, *Exiled*, is a double CD that features gently grooving compositions with frequently wordless vocals, atop modernistic piano and lush arrangements. When she writes lyrics, they have real bite, dealing with African and diaspora identity in the modern world. One track, "The Void," features a recitation by poet Lebo Mashile, who was born in the US. "I reached out to a few poets that I respect and admire to write something, because I don't consider myself a poet, so I felt it really needed the artistic flair of someone who has worked on that craft," Ntuli told me. "I eventually came across a TED Talk on YouTube called 'Memory Matters' that Lebo gave, and many of the sentiments...really touched on some of what I felt the essence of 'The Void' was."

In 2019, Ntuli traveled to Bern to present some of the music from *Exiled* with an expanded ensemble that included a four-piece horn section and a string quintet.

Two members of the band on *Exiled*, saxophonist Sisonke Xonti and bassist Benjamin Jephta, are also present on Makuzeni's 2016 debut, *Out of This World*. "The scene is quite small in South Africa so a lot of us use similar personnel on our projects," Ntuli acknowledged. Similarly, trumpeter Sakhile Simani is on *Out of This World* and Sikhakhane's *Two Sides, One Mirror*, as well as Makhathini's *Sketches of Tomorrow* and *Mother Tongue*.

Makuzeni is both a trombonist and a vocalist, who sings and scats in English and isiXhosa. "I always say the trombone chose me," she said:

> I played recorder at school until my music teacher suggested I should pick up another instrument. There was a big band program at the school, and my audition process involved me trying out all the instruments in the room — to no avail — until I got to the trombone. I took it home that afternoon and have not looked back since.

Her voice is full, but with a barbed edge, somewhere between Miriam Makeba and Erykah Badu, and her music combines jazz, funk and hip-hop beats into an organic, swirling sound fueled by thick electric piano, booming bass and crisp drums, with taut but soulful horn arrangements. She thinks of herself as an instrumentalist, and describes singing as "essentially playing another instrument, though I do feel technically I have fewer boundaries when I sing. Scatting allows me to tap into a space where I can push the possibilities of my voice, create spontaneously, and explore new textures and sounds."

Linda Sikhakhane also plays on Ntuli's *Exiled*. She told me, "Linda's sound on the tenor saxophone is incredible. Rich, sultry and I can identify it in an instant. I loved how his sound was very fitting for what I was reaching for in terms of production..."

To a Western ear, Sikhakhane's spiritual, questing style and deep tone may seem inspired by John Coltrane and Pharoah Sanders, but it's got deep African roots, too. "As a Zulu South African growing up in KwaZulu-Natal, which is a culturally rich province, modal music has always been the core of my upbringing and being exposed to different types of ceremonies which exercised this music helped me relate to the likes of bra Winston 'Mankunku' Ngozi, a legendary South African saxophonist whose sound introduced me to Coltrane," he said. "I'm more of a receiver than a composer, and my ambitions are to execute life experiences and heal the world through music." The centerpiece of *Two Sides, One Mirror* is a nearly 11-minute piece, "Ibuzwa Kwabaphambili," which showcases Sanele Phakathi's McCoy Tyner-esque piano, the leader's crying horn and vocals from Omagugu Makhathini.

Though Sikhakhane enjoyed his time studying in New York (he graduated from the New School in 2019), he told me, "Home is where I'll end up for sure, I really love South Africa."

Ntuli described the scene there as small, but vibrant. "We don't consume as much in terms of live shows as the scenes that are well located such as the Europe/US markets, but there are incredibly talented musicians and unique composers." And jazz is beginning to take root in other parts of Africa; she described performing to welcoming audiences in Mozambique, Swaziland

and Kenya.

Makuzeni, too, asserted that contemporary South African jazz had real power and potential. "We have a lot of instrumentalists and session musicians, and most of them are also composers. There are some dedicated jazz clubs to perform [in], but I think like anywhere, more would be beneficial. Our audiences are incredible as it's a mix of young and old." She's performed even more broadly than Ntuli, describing gigs in Algeria, Sengal, Kenya, Cameroon, Mozambique, Namibia, Zimbabwe, Lesotho and Swaziland.

During the apartheid era, all aspects of South African culture were politicized, none more than music. Thus, being a jazz musician in South Africa today can carry a burden of social responsibility. Ntuli says it's up to each person to choose whether or not to take on the mantle of activism:

> I do know that because our past still has a very heavy presence in the current state of South Africa that sometimes, these political overtones inevitably come through, and it may not even necessarily be lyrically but in the artistic pursuits of the different individuals. Our generation seems to definitely be tackling the idea of identity a lot, and I've seen that come across in many people's music, however subtly.

For Nduduzo Makhathini, it's not about politics as much as spiritual communication between generations and manifesting an awareness of history. He told me that when he was in school, South African jazz was not part of the curriculum; the focus was on American musicians, and he had to learn about Masekela, Ibrahim, Chris McGregor and Bheki Mseleku on his own.

> You would encounter some of their music through...we had these, like, ensemble groups, and there was a lady called Susan Berry — she was my first piano teacher, and she really

> had an interest in African music that was obvious. So in her ensemble you would get pieces from the history of South African jazz, but she also dealt with the more modern kind of South African jazz...but other than that, there wasn't any kind of juxtapositions in terms of saying, 'Well, when Coltrane dies in '67, 'Mankunku' Ngozi records "Yakhal'Inkomo" in '68.' Those kind of linkages were not explored. Even just resonances were not explored. I only got to know about South African jazz history when I finished studying and I was just looking for something. But I must say, with that being said, I was fortunate enough to have Bheki Mseleku, who was there when I was starting — it made it easy for me at least to gravitate toward someone like McCoy Tyner, but coming from Mseleku, I needed some kind of close reference to the music, a kind of deeper connection. And Mseleku was really instrumental even for me to get into Coltrane.

Makhathini's latest album, *Modes of Communication: Letters from the Underworlds,* has a churning energy that brings to mind the gospel-charged free jazz of Don Pullen, while remaining consistent with his own previous work. The band includes trumpeter Ndabo Zulu, Sikhakhane on tenor saxophone, Logan Richardson — the only non-African — on alto saxophone, bassist Zwelakhe-Duma Bell Le Pere, Sikade on drums and Omagugu on vocals. As always, he's got a lot to say; the disc has 11 tracks and runs 75 minutes. The longest track, "Umlotha," comes right in the middle. It's an instrumental driven by forceful piano, but showcasing raucous, almost free jazz interaction among all three horns, and wave upon wave of percussion.

At the Zürcher Gallery, people flowed in in larger and larger numbers the closer the hour drew for his performance. Many of them were African and knew his work, while others were critics and journalists and still others were the tourists and fans Winter Jazzfest draws in every year. The group was a mix of Africans and Americans, featuring Omagugu, Richardson (beginning with the second number — he was late) on alto, Rashaan Carter on bass, Damion Reid on drums and a percussionist whose name I didn't catch. The pieces they performed, including "Yehlisan'uMoya," the opening track from *Modes of Communication*, all had a swelling, passionate quality, exploratory but never losing an essential earthbound feeling. From the piano bench, Makhathini conducted the band with head nods and glances, but more often than not he was as transported by the music as the most rapt audience member, a broad grin splitting his face. And afterward, he was mobbed by well-wishers and new fans.

Some months later, in summer 2020, I found myself talking to Makhathini again, along with trumpeter Ndabo Zulu and vocalist Mbuso Khoza. We were discussing Zulu's album *Queen Nandi: The African Symphony*, but our Zoom conversation lasted nearly an hour and covered a broad range of subjects.

The album is a two-disc set running over 100 minutes and featuring two keyboardists (Makhathini and Africa Mkhize), bassists Shane Cooper and Derrick Hodge (who also co-produced), two drummers (Sikade and Sphelelo Mazibuko), two percussionists (Njabulo Shabalala and El Hadj Ngari Ndong), trombonist Siya Charles and both Khoza and Zoë Modiga on vocals. Not everyone plays on every track; the ensemble frequently splits into smaller sub-groups. The last song, "Nandi (Ukukhothama)," is a duet for trumpet and Fender Rhodes.

The music mixes conventional jazz orchestration with South African rhythms and percussive techniques, including the use of traditional Zulu drums. Within the context of South African jazz, this is a somewhat radical move, since the country's music scene is mostly centered around Johannesburg and Cape Town, and the KwaZulu-Natal region has not been given its moment in the spotlight yet.

Each disc begins with an epic, 17-minute track. "Umgidi,"

which opens the second disc, features a call-and-response between Khoza's hoarse, incantatory lead vocals and a male chorus, with clattering percussion in back and pulsing, fanfare-like horn lines, bolstered by heavy, McCoy Tyner-esque piano. Sikhakhane's tenor sax solo builds from a forceful cry to reed-splitting shrieks worthy of Pharoah Sanders. Zulu's own sound is bitten-off, and frequently smeary in the manner of Ambrose Akinmusire. Even though his phrases have punch, he sounds like you're eavesdropping on him talking through a tricky philosophical concept.

Mbuso Khoza is a singer, songwriter, historian and public intellectual who works to preserve and honor Zulu culture. He has been collaborating with Makhathini for several years, having appeared on the pianist's 2014 album *Sketches of Tomorrow* in addition to making his own music. His broad goal is to overcome the psychic legacy of colonialism and raise South Africans' consciousness about their own history and culture — not in some hokey, ultimately ahistorical "we were kings" way, or telling a simplified story for tourists, but re-forging a genuine link to the past, where one had been severed for centuries. He leads the Afrikan Heritage Ensemble, a vocal group, and his lyrics on *Queen Nandi* are improvised amahubo (praise songs) telling the story of the titular figure, who was the mother of the famous Zulu king Shaka. He sounds like a preacher, or a bard; he could as easily be reciting the *Iliad* or *Beowulf*.

Even if one takes *Queen Nandi* as "just" a musical work (if, for example, one is ignorant of the relevant history and unable to understand the language), it's impressive as hell. But it's part of a broader cultural project arising from the current generation(s) of South African musicians. While previous generations were animated and fueled by the struggle against apartheid, a new struggle has begun — to explore, understand and synthesize a present-day identity that ties up the dangling threads of history. Zulu, Makhathini and Khoza are working together and separately to achieve this, and nobody knows yet what the results will be, but attention must be paid. First, because the art itself is stunning, and second, because it is one facet of a broader humanist vision that is both admirable and a model to be emulated elsewhere.

Essential Listening

Nduduzo Makhathini, *Listening to the Ground* (Gundu, 2015)

Benjamin Jephta, *Homecoming* (Independent/Self-Released, 2015)

Siya Makuzeni, *Out of This World* (Independent/Self-Released, 2016)

Nduduzo Makhathini, *Ikhambi* (Universal South Africa, 2017)

Linda Sikhakhane, *Two Sides, One Mirror* (Independent/Self-Released, 2018)

Thandi Ntuli, *Exiled* (Independent/Self-Released, 2018)

Nduduzo Makhathini, *Modes of Communication: Letters From the Underworlds* (Blue Note, 2020)

Thandi Ntuli, *Live at Jazzwerkstaat* (Independent/Self-Released, 2020)

Ndabo Zulu, *Queen Nandi: The African Suite* (Mageba Music, 2020)

Kamasi Washington, Ryan Porter, Cameron Graves, Miles Mosley, Thundercat & Dwight Trible: A Force to Be Reckoned With

August in New York is grotesque, even in the evening. It's like walking around in a steam bath. The night of August 24, 2015, it was roughly 80 degrees Fahrenheit on the street as I walked the short distance from the A train to the Blue Note Jazz Club on West Third Street in lower Manhattan. When I arrived, the line at the door stretched down the block, and the last available seat was between two of the club's tiny tables. My back was wedged against the wall, and my knees were pressed so tightly together I might have been in a subway car at rush hour. Still, I was too excited to be uncomfortable, as I waited to see saxophonist Kamasi Washington make his New York debut.

He'd traveled across the country from his hometown, Los Angeles, performing in large theaters to enthusiastic crowds charged up by his aptly titled three-CD manifesto, *The Epic*, which had been out since mid-May. He was to perform four sets over two nights at the Blue Note, a prestigious venue but one that only held 150 people, tops. I craned my neck to get a sense of the crowd, and a sense of shock built gradually. I'd been attending jazz shows since the mid-1990s, and had never been one of the oldest people in the audience until that night.

The audience were almost uniformly in their twenties and thirties. Here and there, couples went through dating rituals, the men earnestly infodumping everything they'd learned about Washington from Pitchfork and Twitter, the women smiling and nodding. Others were discussing the fact that listening to jazz, never mind coming to a jazz club, was a new experience for them, and they weren't sure they were doing it right. Should they order dinner, or just drinks? Were they expected to clap after every song, after solos or just at the end?

Fortunately, Washington made it easy to appreciate his music, and to feel at home at his show. He smiled at the crowd, genuinely thrilled to be there and to receive such a warm reception. He'd brought a six-piece band that included 17-year-old pianist Jamael Dean, trombonist Ryan Porter, singer Patrice Quinn, upright bassist Miles Mosley and two drummers, Tony Austin and Ronald Bruner Jr. In New York, the lineup was augmented by electric bassist Stephen Bruner (aka Thundercat), trumpeter Igmar Thomas and alto saxophonist Terrace Martin. The combination of booming upright and liquid, almost psychedelic electric bass, and the thunder of the two drummers, who combined forceful swing with driving rock and hip-hop backbeats, built the platform atop which Washington, Porter and Dean danced.

On the cover of *The Epic*, and on the T-shirt I bought after the show, Washington looked like a free jazz prophet wandering in from the wilderness, wearing a flowing robe, his Afro and beard bristling and wild. But his actual sound ran the gamut from voluble, high-speed hard bop lines to fierce screams, combining multiple approaches into a sort of postmodern collage of 5 decades of jazz technique. Porter took only one solo the entire night, preferring to harmonize with Washington or Quinn. Dean's playing was lyrical and speedy, when he could be heard; when the group was in full collective cry, though, he was buried in the mix. Mosley's turn in the spotlight came with a jokey introduction from Washington, who pointed out that it was "a regulation bass – no motors or buttons"; the resulting solo employed echo and electronic distortion to fantastically creative effect, building to a bowed passage of near noise-rock intensity. Toward the end of the night, the drummers launched a raucous percussion duel that would have brought the crowd to its feet had the tables not been too close together to permit any movement beyond impassioned rocking back and forth.

The Epic — 17 tracks, 172 minutes of music spread across three CDs — was grandiose in every respect. In addition to Washington and his coterie of collaborators, it featured a 32-piece orchestra and a 20-voice choir who sang mostly wordless syllables, rising and falling and setting a heroic tone. On disc, Washington sounded like a Pharoah Sanders acolyte; he'd chew on a few notes like a mantra, then erupt in fierce shrieks. Pianist Cameron Graves, who got the first solo of the set, came across like a disciple of McCoy Tyner, but with the fervor of Don Pullen.

Despite its side trips into funk, reggae and R&B, *The Epic* was a spiritual jazz album at its core. Had Impulse! Records given Sanders the budget for an orchestra and choir in 1972, he might have come up with something very much like it. Songs were built on throbbing, vamping bass lines, played on acoustic and electric at once, and they went on at great length. The first piece, "Change of the Guard," ran more than 12 minutes. At times, when the music moved closer to R&B, it recalled the instrumental tracks from Earth, Wind & Fire albums. Far too much to take in at one sitting, it was an album to dip into over and over again.

The next time Washington played New York, 6 months later, he headlined Webster Hall, which held 1500 people — more than the ten most famous jazz clubs in the city put together. I didn't go. And in the 3 years after the Blue Note performances, he and his band toured the US and Europe, playing theaters and festivals to crowds plenty of pop and rock acts would envy. He played both Coachella and Bonnaroo. And in June 2018, the week before his album *Heaven and Earth* was released, I finally saw him for a second time, at Forest Hills Stadium in Queens, opening for the electronic-rock band Alt-J.

The sun was still out when the band took the stage, with almost the same lineup as in 2015: Washington, Porter and

Quinn up front, with new keyboardist Brandon Coleman at stage left and Mosley and the two drummers in back. With only 40 minutes to play, they stacked the set with new and newish music, performing "Fists of Fury" and "Street Fighter Mas" from *Heaven and Earth*, and "Truth" from the previous year's *Harmony of Difference* EP. And the audience, which was again overwhelmingly young, at least down on the ground where I was, was absolutely into it. They were dancing, cheering, shouting and occasionally singing along with Quinn's often-wordless vocals.

The fact that Washington and crew hit hard certainly helped them get across to rock audiences. He wore a football player's mouth guard to play, removing it to address the audience between tunes. As always, Mosley used pedals to crank his bass up to a skull-vibrating roar. Coleman soloed like a cross between Tyner and Keith Emerson, switching between piano and synthesizer at a moment's notice, and the double drummers were positively apocalyptic. As I walked out of the outdoor stadium on that summer evening, the weather much milder than the night I'd first seen this band perform, my head was swimming as I considered what I had been thinking about for 3 years already. What did it mean that Kamasi Washington had so thoroughly broken out of jazz's tiny corner of the music world? Was this a sign of a broader movement, or was he a one-off? I decided that it was mostly just him. He had that something that made people want to watch, and listen. And a big part of it was that he didn't act like a star with backing musicians. He was there representing a group. Indeed, at the Blue Note, he'd mentioned that one of the pieces, "Oscalypso," was written by Porter. (It would later appear on the trombonist's album *Force for Good*.)

Heaven and Earth presented a more grounded and even autobiographical version of Washington than *The Epic*. Through track titles and his choice of covers, he allowed listeners a few glimpses into his childhood and upbringing. The album opened with "Fists of Fury," a radically expanded version of the theme from a 1972 Bruce Lee movie, with dual lead vocals from Patrice Quinn and Dwight Trible. "Street Fighter Mas" was an imagined soundtrack to playing arcade games as a kid, with oozing funk bass from Miles Mosley and snapping drums from Snarky Puppy's Robert "Sput" Searight. "Vi Lua Vi Sol" featured a Vocodered vocal from Brandon Coleman, shadowed by Porter and periodically dive-bombed by swooping prog-rock synths. One of the biggest surprises, though, was "The Invincible Youth," which began with an eruption from all three horns over thunderous drums and clanging piano. It was as close as the band had ever come to free jazz. But it was just a fanfare; when the music restarted, it slid into a loping jazz-funk groove, over an almost go-go beat, and the saxophone solo was more Grover Washington Jr. than Kamasi Washington.

In January 2020, I was in a hotel room in lower Manhattan, talking to Thundercat, and he told me that the tight-knit crew dynamic I'd noticed at Washington's shows had always been there. He and his brother Ronald Jr. were part of a group of childhood friends that included Washington, Martin and pianist Cameron Graves. "We would spend a lot of time at Cameron's house," he recalled. "Mr Graves was really gracious to let a bunch of crazy-ass ratchet kids stay in his garage and try to learn 'Giant Steps' and all these different things, blasting music all day and acting all weird and hormonal and being real suspect...if it wasn't for Carl Graves, we wouldn't be the people we are today."

Thundercat's parents, and the Washingtons and the Graves, all trusted each other and their sons enough to let them disappear into a world of adolescent music-making. California is a sprawling state where very little is walkable and almost everything requires a drive, and Graves' house was an hour or so away from South Central Los Angeles, where the rest of what would become the Young Jazz Giants, and later the West Coast Get Down, lived. But they hung out, and made it work. "I had this ponytail," he told me with a laugh, "and Cameron used to wear muscle shirts 'cause he'd be working out and doing kung fu, Ronald was this real prima donna, Kamasi looked fifty — he always had a suit on. We're going to the store? He had a suit for the store. But that was life. We really were friends, and a band."

Ryan Porter grew up in Compton, a separate suburb of Los Angeles, and came into the circle through a multi-school band assembled by Reggie Andrews. "Where I grew up, I couldn't hang out in the front yard and ride my bike like most kids," he told me by phone from Virginia. But every Tuesday and Thursday, he would play in Andrews' multi-school band at Locke High School in Watts:

> That would help us get acquainted with more of the students that weren't going to our high school at the time. I met Kamasi before then, at Jazz America, which was another program for kids who wanted to learn improvisation from the wide range of jazz educators that we have in Los Angeles...[the multi-school band] played Gerald Wilson charts, we played Horace Tapscott charts, a lot of different arrangements from the community of musicians that were contributing to the program.

As time went on, Washington and his cohorts became part of the Leimert Park scene. That neighborhood, long the artistic hub of Black Los Angeles, was the home of World Stage, a performance space and community center formed in 1989 by pianist/composer Horace Tapscott, leader of the Pan Afrikan Peoples Arkestra, and drummer Billy Higgins, along with poet and activist Kamau Daáood. It's still there, under singer Dwight Trible's stewardship. "I'm a World Stage baby," Thundercat told me with pride. "My parents live in Leimert Park now."

Trible, who moved to Los Angeles from Cincinnati, Ohio in 1971, has been one of a group of LA-based musicians who have dedicated themselves not only to keeping Horace Tapscott's musical legacy alive since his death in February 1999, but to preserving the communitarian spirit that he brought to that city's jazz scene "I think this is the fourth generation of the Arkestra," he told me by phone in 2019.

> After Horace passed, [saxophonist] Michael Session took over and was leading the group for several years, and now his son, who's a drummer named Mekala Session, is leading the Ark and he's bringing in a lot of his friends from UCLA and Cal Arts and all that stuff...you've got these young people that are still excited about this music and see the importance of this organization. So now the Ark is probably as vibrant as it has ever been. It's a beautiful thing.

Trible's theatrical, Broadway-meets-gospel baritone can be heard prominently on Washington's albums *The Epic* and *Heaven and Earth*. "You never know what effect you're having on people," he told me:

> I've known Kamasi since he was a young kid, and you see [people] around, and you try to be nice, and you never know what it is that they are formulating and putting together. All of those guys that are with the West Coast Get Down were always around the Leimert Park thing...I just used to see Kamasi and the Bruner brothers around, and they were always very respectful and all that, and now...the guy is a force to be reckoned with.

Washington self-released his first album, *Live at 5th Street Dick's*, in 2005. It consisted of two CD-Rs, and the lineup included Porter, Terrace Martin, Graves, Brandon Coleman on keyboards, Mosley on upright bass, Thundercat (then simply Stephen Bruner) on electric, Robert Miller — who'd later join Snarky Puppy — on drums, and his father Rickey Washington on soprano saxophone. The band was called the Next Step; they hadn't become the West Coast Get Down yet. Three of the tracks, "Changing of the Guard," "The Next Step" and "Askim," would later appear on *The Epic*.

In 2007, he released *The Proclamation* with most of the same crew, except that Ronald Bruner Jr. and Tony Austin were on drums, and vocalist Patrice Quinn had entered the picture. Another track that would later appear on *The Epic*, "The Rhythm Changes" debuted here, along with versions of Ornette Coleman's "Lonely Woman" and the standard "Like Someone in Love."

The following year, he changed things up with *Light of the World*, an overtly Christian album made with a smaller group: just Porter, Coleman, Jae Deal on bass, Miller on drums and a singer identified as Manhi-Xan. They played gospel tunes like "The Lord's Prayer," "Amazing Grace," "Going Up Yonder" and "When I Think About Jesus."

Mosley, too, was self-releasing music at this time. First came 2005's *Sicaceremony*, followed by 2006's *Taming the Proud*, and finally 2007's *Bear*, all of which featured Washington and Porter. And the trombonist's first album, *Anaya*, was made with the same crew and self-released in 2008.

Over the next few years, each player went his own way, landing the kind of gigs that establish someone as a professional musician who can be relied on. Mosley worked with Korn vocalist Jonathan Davis and Soundgarden singer Chris Cornell on their solo projects; Graves joined actress Jada Pinkett Smith's metal band Wicked Wisdom; each of the Bruner brothers took a turn in the thrash-punk band Suicidal Tendencies, Ronald for a year or two and Stephen for nearly a decade; and Washington and Porter, along with Thundercat and Terrace Martin, became members of Snoop Dogg's touring band beginning in 2011. The trombonist told me that traveling with Snoop and seeing the level of organization that went into large-scale touring impressed him and showed him a level of professionalism to aspire to.

In December 2011, they all regrouped back in LA, spending the entire month at the Kingsize Soundlabs studio. "We recorded something north of 170 songs in 30 days," Mosley told me by phone from LA. The marathon session yielded Washington's triple CD *The Epic,* Mosley's *Uprising* and other albums that have yet to be released.

In addition to Washington, Porter, Graves, Coleman and Tony Austin, *Uprising* featured trumpeter Dontae Winslow and saxophonist Zane Musa, and like *The Epic,* multiple songs were augmented by an orchestra and a choir. But it wasn't a jazz album; it was a 70s-style soul record. Mosley sang on every track, and the arrangements had more in common with Earth, Wind & Fire than Pharoah Sanders. But in the middle of its organic, strutting grooves, tight horn charts and lush orchestrations, he took bass solos that sounded more like a distorted, overdriven electric guitar. Mosley explained that he and Austin came up with the idea that "in order to get the bass to really, really shine, it could be the only thing that was effected. So everything else had to be as real as possible...whatever was in the room was in the room. It's a really modern, forward-thinking upright bass sound slapped on top of honest-to-God arranging and songwriting."

Graves' debut album, *Planetary Prince,* was also released in 2017. It was not tracked during the Kingsize Soundlabs session, though. "I went back in about three or four months later, because I wasn't too happy with some of the recordings...so I booked another session with the players that I wanted to be on it," which included Washington, Porter and both Bruner brothers, as well as trumpeter Philip Dizack and bassist Hadrien Feraud.

They tracked the album in a day; as Graves explained to me, "All the cats have played my tunes over and over again for like five years, so there was no rehearsal. It was so easy to go in and do one or two takes of every single song...it was great."

Most of the material had been workshopped at an LA club called the Piano Bar, where the West Coast Get Down performed for years on Wednesdays and Fridays. This allowed each member to write tunes and bring them to the others, who would essentially workshop the material onstage, and as Graves explained, "the ones that really stuck, we would keep...that's how Kamasi came up with *The Epic*, all those songs, and now my record."

Graves' music is the most florid of any of the West Coast Get Down composers. Where Porter is focused on hard bop grooves, and Washington paints on broad canvases with strings and choirs, and Thundercat and Mosley explore different types of funk, the pianist blends classical and prog-rock complexity, coming up with something almost Chick Corea-esque in its ornate over-the-topness. He told me that he hears jazz harmony when writing or playing classical music, and that he's equally drawn to drop-tuned sections derived from death metal and fractured piano chords like those deployed by hip-hop producers like DJ Premier or J Dilla. When he's not making his own music, he's a member of fusion bassist Stanley Clarke's band, a meeting of musical minds that makes perfect sense.

Each member of the West Coast Get Down has particular musical strengths, and it's a testament to their friendship and artistic open-mindedness that they can each fit so seamlessly into any context, no matter who's nominally in charge on a given recording. A tight-knit crew, they seem destined to reshape Los Angeles jazz in their own image.

Essential Listening

Young Jazz Giants, *Young Jazz Giants* (Birdman, 2004)
Kamasi Washington, *The Epic* (Brainfeeder, 2015)
Cameron Graves, *Planetary Prince* (Mack Avenue, 2017)
Miles Mosley, *Uprising* (Verve, 2017)
Kamasi Washington, *Harmony of Difference* (Young Turks, 2017)
Cameron Graves, *Planetary Prince: The Eternal Survival EP* (Mack Avenue, 2018)
Ryan Porter, *The Optimist* (World Galaxy, 2018)
Kamasi Washington, *Heaven and Earth* (Young Turks, 2018)
Ryan Porter, *Force for Good* (World Galaxy, 2019)
Dwight Trible, *Mothership* (Gearbox, 2019)
Ryan Porter, *Live in Paris at New Morning* (World Galaxy, 2020)

Darius Jones: It's About Connections

In 2009, alto saxophonist Darius Jones was the man of the moment, flying across the New York avant-jazz scene like a comet. Late of Richmond, Virginia, he came to New York in 2005 and played in a variety of contexts, including the sax-electronics duo Birds in the Meadow and the quartet Little Women, a two saxes/electric guitar/drums outfit whose music owed as much to No Wave as free jazz. But in 2009, he released his debut as a leader, and heads whipped around.

Man'ish Boy (A Raw & Beautiful Thing) was recorded with avant-garde legends Cooper-Moore on piano and diddley-bow (a one-stringed instrument like a droning bass) and Rakalam Bob Moses on drums. The music was part jazz, part gospel and part avant-garde exploration in pursuit of pure sound, uniting at least two generations of free jazz players in collective spiritual exultation.

Jones had the richest, fullest alto saxophone sound since Arthur Blythe, but he eschewed the Pentecostal fire and fury of churchified (tenor) players like Albert Ayler or David Murray. His tone cut like a bandsaw. He could play fast, but he knew when to let a phrase ring out or dissolve into overtones; his sound pierced the listener with blunt force, like a chisel to the sternum.

In January 2011, I saw him perform with his regular trio — bassist Adam Lane and drummer Jason Nazary (also a member of Little Women) — at the University of the Streets on 7th Street and Avenue A in Manhattan. They were premiering music that would ultimately be part of his second album, *Big Gurl (Smell My Dream)*. The hour-long set began with a murmured "Okay" from Jones, who raised the horn to his lips and launched into a slow, John Coltrane-esque melody which was not so much supported as challenged by Nazary. The drummer was working his hi-hat and floor tom with sticks, one held backward for greater impact, thumping the kick drum almost as an afterthought and keeping time in a way that suggested the eccentric rhythms of John Lee Hooker's 1940s and 50s sides as much as the free work of Milford Graves or Rashied Ali in the 1960s. It felt ancient. Jones simmered without ever boiling over, offering fierce but controlled shrieks as the intensity of the piece built. He stepped away at one point, and Lane took a hypnotic, repetitive solo with Nazary tap-tap-tapping on the snare behind him.

Jones is a thoughtful player, never abandoning himself to wild squalls of sound. He picks out notes one by one, like someone selecting the ripest berries from an overflowing basket. In some important ways, he seems closer in spirit to swing-era saxophonists than free players. This was proved when the trio tackled Duke Ellington's "Take the 'A' Train." His solo was somewhere between Ornette Coleman and Charles Gayle, full of fast, distorted flurries at the bottom of the alto's range, but after another bass solo from Lane, he closed things out with a thick, lurching blues groove.

Late in the set, they performed a ballad called "I Wish I Had a Choice," which Jones introduced with a short monologue about the sacrifices required to make a living in the arts. The piece itself was romantic and delicate. He had returned to his method of playing individual notes, rather than phrases, and there was a palpable suspense. But then Nazary took a solo that was all crashing cymbals, as if trying to wash away everything Jones had just finished painting. The piece's mood hung on by a thread. Somehow, though, it never slipped entirely away.

On his third studio album, *Book of Mae'bul (Another Kind of Sunrise)*, Jones assembled an entirely different band with pianist Matt Mitchell, bassist Trevor Dunn and drummer Ches Smith. At that time I was familiar with Dunn from groups like Mike Patton's Fantômas and John Zorn's Moonchild, and Smith from ensembles led by Marc Ribot, Mary Halvorson and Tim

Berne, among others. I *also* remembered that he'd been in the noise-rock trio Theory of Ruin, led by former Fudge Tunnel guitarist Alex Newport. The combination of that rhythm section and Jones, who was coming out of an entirely different context, was immediately interesting, and the album lived up to my expectations.

It began with "The Enjoli Moon," a tender ballad that allowed him to roll out its melody with great care. The notes flowed through the horn as if escaping a deflating balloon. He never hurried, wringing all the harmonic energy he could out of each sound before proceeding. At the piano, Mitchell followed his example, and Dunn was a subdued presence, taking only the briefest of solos. Smith, while energetic to the point of aggressiveness, never overpowered the ensemble.

Over the course of the seven tracks that followed, though, that tenderness faded, replaced by a muscular tension — *Book of Mae'bul* demanded that you engage with it. It could not be heard passively in the background. At the same time, nobody was interested in stereotypical "free jazz" blare. There was a moment toward the end of "Be Patient With Me" where Smith delivered a tom roll that was a stunningly direct imitation of Elvin Jones, but otherwise he seemed determined to do the unexpected, to react in ways that a typical "jazz drummer" would not, even as the music remained firmly rooted in jazz vernacular.

At the same time that he was putting his own spin on the avant-garde jazz tradition, Jones was making fascinatingly uncategorizable music with Little Women. The two projects existed in parallel, never touching each other's territory even though they had drummer Nazary in common.

The other members of the group were tenor saxophonist Travis Laplante, a rigorous conceptualist, and guitarist Andrew Smiley, whose command of noise was as fierce and unrelenting as anyone since Shellac's Steve Albini. They released their debut

EP, *Teeth,* in 2009, and their first of two full-length albums, *Throat*, the following year.

Talking to Jones about Little Women in 2010 was fascinating. He said:

> Playing with another horn player, I guess I feel more like there's this front line, so we have a function, and then the rhythm section has a function as well, and then we can all blur this together and become one whole thing. Also, when I'm playing with another horn player, I'm trying to really connect with him or her so we can have synergy as a front line, playing lines together, making sure my voice and his voice are creating a singular voice that's the combination of us both. Like in Little Women, a lot of times I'm really surrendering to what Travis is playing, his ideas and stuff like that, and he would say the same thing. It's a give-and-take. Sometimes he wants to do something, and I'll go there with him. Sometimes I'll say I don't wanna go there, I wanna do this more accompanying thing, or play on top of what he's playing, making what he does accompaniment. It's just about connections.

Those connections, which run between all four members, were more than sonic; they were organic and physical. Laplante's and Jones's horns would twine together, repeating incantatory phrases in high, squealing registers, as Smiley's guitar and Nazary's drums rang and clattered. There was almost no low end to Little Women's music. It stung and jabbed, like Ornette Coleman's Prime Time band covering Teenage Jesus and the Jerks. The high frequencies and pitiless repetition could be cathartic or torturous, depending on your mood.

Teeth and *Throat* were exciting enough, in a rolling-tinfoil-into-a-spike-and-jabbing-at-your-fillings sort of way, but Little Women's third and final release, 2013's *Lung*, was their masterpiece. Was *a* masterpiece. It was a single extended piece, some 42 minutes long, that traveled through multiple movements. Sometimes it was murmuringly quiet, other times blisteringly loud and shrill. There were passages of intensely rhythmic, focused aggressiveness, and stretches of seemingly formless, questing exploration. At times, it passed out of the realm of music entirely.

As the titles of their releases implied, the members of Little Women were as fascinated by sound's effects on the body, and the body's ability to produce sound, as by conventional concepts of melody, harmony and rhythm. A crucial part of their methodology, even on *Teeth*, was the use of extremely close microphones, in order that Laplante and Jones might capture the sound of breath leaving their lungs. The last 2 minutes of that EP featured the group members chanting, jabbering and even sobbing in a pre-linguistic manner, as though their music had reduced them to some atavistic state.

Lung began with almost 2 minutes of just the sound of slow respiration. Breath going in, breath coming out. It was synchronized, but not perfectly so, and it was far from effortless. It recalled the labored breathing that accompanies the practice of yoga; it reminded the listener that meditation — the attempt to achieve transcendence — is hard work.

The first instruments heard were Nazary's sticks dancing across the cymbals. Not a "drum solo" so much as a quiet summoning. It wasn't until the 4-minute mark that the horns and guitar entered, each man playing a hypnotic yet somehow pastoral melody that wound in and around the others' contributions. Then Jones and Laplante lowered their instruments and began singing long, monkishly droning notes. Their voices wavered and went off-pitch; they sucked in breaths, then resumed.

The piece passed through one "movement" after another, but there were no breaks. It was a continuous performance, and one totally lacking in "free jazz" fervor, no matter how intense the music got. *Lung* was a work of steely collective discipline, recorded in pristine detail because capturing the sounds of the men making the music was every bit as important as preserving the notes they played. It was a document of men at work, creating something larger than themselves — it was hard to think of another piece of music to compare it to. It had more in common with Sebastião Salgado's massive photos of miners and shipbreakers, or movies like *Sorcerer* and *Fitzcarraldo*. I hadn't listened to it in years, but when I pulled it out in 2020, it was if anything even more stunning than I remembered. And yet, Darius Jones would go even further.

One of the things I discussed with Jones the first time I interviewed him was his obsession with sound. He was fascinated by the sounds of the universe, perceptible even in so-called silence. The experience of entering an anechoic chamber, a totally soundproofed room, has been described by those who've done it as both exhilarating and terrifying, but not silent; the sounds of one's own body become overwhelmingly loud. Jones recalled having seizures as a child, triggered by sounds, and told me that he could induce a kind of intoxication or euphoria by lingering over a single note on his horn until it began to affect his mind.

He also viewed himself as a storyteller, at least on the albums released under his own name. Man'ish Boy was the central character in a series of connected tales. The album *Man'ish Boy (A Raw & Beautiful Thing)* was a metaphoric translation of his rural Virginia childhood into music; *Big Gurl (Smell My Dream)* was an interpretation of his college years; and *Book of Mae'bul (Another Kind of Sunrise)* was a tribute to the women in his life. But the question of whether Man'ish Boy was even human — was he, in fact, a visitor to Earth? — was left open. On 2014's *The Oversoul Manual*, the implicit became explicit.

The liner notes explained that the album took place on the

planet Or'gen, and that the music was "a sacred text meant to guide a Unit [three or more humanoids] toward the required connection that will manifest their child. For this connection to reach the level of power necessary to create another soul, the Unit must perform these 15 songs, which gives each mother the opportunity to impart her wisdom, experience, and deepest desires for the child." This drew it into the same Afro-futurist pantheon as the works of Nicole Mitchell, inspired by the writings of Octavia Butler. However, this was in no sense a jazz album.

There were no instruments. *The Oversoul Manual* was an album of a cappella vocals, arranged for four female voices, collectively known as the Elizabeth-Caroline Unit, and sung in a language of Jones' invention. The singers — Amirtha Kidambi, Sarah Martin, Jean Carla Rodea and Kristin Slipp — didn't come from jazz backgrounds, though Kidambi has also sung with Mary Halvorson's group Code Girl. There was no blues feeling or soulful melisma in their delivery. It was pure and clear, free of almost all adornment, even vibrato. Occasionally, one of them would allow her voice to drop into a growl, but for the most part their singing was choral, and at times piercingly loud. The tones they struck occasionally reverberated not just in the room, but also within the resonant chambers of the singers' heads and bodies, in exactly the ways Jones had discussed with me, as though he was trying to induce out-of-body experiences in both performer and listener.

The 15 pieces bore titles made up of circles, dots and triangles ("o o o o o," "•••," "Δ•••••Δ"), and didn't blend seamlessly together, but the pauses between them were short. Some flew by in less than a minute, while others passed the 7-minute mark.

The language Jones had devised for the piece was unprecedented. Many rock groups and musicians have sung in made-up languages, and scat singing, of course, attempts unsuccessfully to wordlessly imitate the sound of instruments.

This was something else. It didn't have words, only phonemes akin to solfège tones: single syllables, many of them from the do, re, mi, fa, sol, la, ti scale taught to children, with numbers intermingled.

As the voices rose, harmonized and overlapped, it was possible to think of the recitations of numbers in Philip Glass's *Einstein on the Beach*. But it was just as easy to imagine yourself eavesdropping on a religious rite, the procedures and meaning of which you were not privy to. This was music to be sung by people wearing robes. The closest analog would be the sound of a Roman Catholic choir, and like high mass, it was possible to close your eyes, let your attention wander and feel the voices course around you until a tingle of not-quite-ecstasy took over.

Despite the science-fiction liner notes, the naked voices and sacramental tonalities of *The Oversoul Manual* made it feel ancient rather than futuristic. Jones' instrumental music may have drawn at times from his experience in the Black church, but this felt closer to the work of Arvo Pärt or Luigi Nono. It was deeply affecting on both an emotional and physical level (especially when heard through speakers), and was one of the most surprising releases of 2014.

The Oversoul Manual took Jones 3 years to write, rehearse and record. It was performed at Roulette, in Brooklyn, and then at Carnegie Hall, and the studio version was immaculately recorded. And it was effectively Jones' final statement. He made one more jazz album, *Le Bébé de Brigitte (Lost in Translation)*, and then vanished.

He didn't disappear completely, of course. He was still playing live, here and there, in a variety of interesting contexts. But he had stepped off the album-cycle music-business treadmill. The last time I saw him in person was at the Art Ensemble of Chicago performance at Columbia University. When I asked him that night what he was up to, he said that he just didn't feel like he had anything to say on an album right then.

I called him up in June 2020, to check in and see how he was doing, and his feelings had not changed. He expressed the belief that the work required to write and rehearse and record an album was too often a discouraging rather than an inspiring process, and we discussed the fact that so much of the most impressive and memorable jazz is never captured on tape — it happens in front of a crowd, and if you're not there, you're out of luck.

He told me about the years of rehearsals and rewrites that had gone into *The Oversoul Manual*, only to have critics respond with somewhat hostile puzzlement. "Why aren't you playing the saxophone? What is this? How am I supposed to categorize it?" On the other hand, he told me that people whose art had inspired him, like Roscoe Mitchell, Henry Threadgill and Wadada Leo Smith, had come to the performance or heard the work, and loved it. So for him, that was enough.

When I asked if he was coming out of retirement anytime soon, he laughed. It turned out that he'd been planning to make three albums in 2020, including a solo disc and one with a group that would have included cellist Tomeka Reid. There's a whole tradition of alto sax and strings that encompasses work by Charlie Parker, Anthony Braxton, Arthur Blythe, Johnny Hodges and others, and he wanted to add himself to that lineage. The solo disc was to have been produced by guitarist David Torn, whose love of technology would doubtless have produced something fascinating. Sadly, all three projects were pushed aside by COVID-19 and quarantine. Whether they will emerge in the future, who can say?

Essential Listening

Darius Jones, *Man'ish Boy (A Raw & Beautiful Thing)* (Aum Fidelity, 2009)

Little Women, *Throat* (Aum Fidelity, 2010)

Darius Jones/Matthew Shipp, *Cosmic Lieder* (Aum Fidelity, 2011)
Darius Jones, *Big Gurl (Smell My Dream)* (Aum Fidelity, 2011)
Darius Jones, *Book of Mae'bul (Another Kind of Sunrise)* (Aum Fidelity, 2012)
Little Women, *Lung* (Aum Fidelity, 2013)
Darius Jones, *The Oversoul Manual* (Aum Fidelity, 2014)

PART IV

Ambrose Akinmusire; Christian Scott aTunde Adjuah; Keyon Harrold; Theo Croker; Marquis Hill

Introduction

This section of the book is different from all the others. Each of the three previous sections has dealt with musicians who play one of a broad range of instruments: trumpet, piano, saxophone, guitar, flute, bass, cello, harp...And while profiling individual players, I have also pointed out the connections between them, as they perform each other's music and support each other in other ways, as members of artistic communities with common creative interests and shared values.

The artists in this section all play the same instrument, the trumpet, and none of them work together. Each is a leader in his own right. Nonetheless, I see connections between them, most notably in the way they incorporate elements of hip-hop into their music.

Almost as soon as hip-hop emerged in the 1980s, jazz artists recognized it as something that had to be reckoned with, for good or ill. The vitriol directed at the music by trumpeter Wynton Marsalis, with support from critic Stanley Crouch, was an outlier position even in his own family — his older brother Branford had a hip-hop/funk project, Buckshot LeFonque, that made two albums, in 1994 and 1997. Other musicians, like saxophonists Steve Coleman and Greg Osby, made their own attempts to grapple with hip-hop, with mixed results. Hip-hop DJs and producers were able to recognize the musical value of jazz, sampling beats and melodies and horn stabs from old Blue Note and CTI albums, but jazz artists seemed unable to understand the new form on its own terms. A rapper might be invited to throw down a verse or two on someone's album, but the words often lacked the pointed specificity that gave the genre its vitality.

One of the most notable attempts at a true fusion of jazz and hip-hop was trumpeter Miles Davis's final album, *Doo-Bop*. It was released posthumously, with production from Easy Mo Bee, who would later work with Notorious BIG, Tupac Shakur, Busta Rhymes, Craig Mack and many others. While critics at the time viewed it as a failure — as much because they didn't think Davis should be associated with such things as due to the project's admittedly mixed quality — when heard now, its best tracks prefigure trip-hop and put his trumpet playing into intriguing new contexts.

The artist who bridged jazz and hip-hop most successfully, though, was trumpeter Roy Hargrove, who maintained two parallel careers during the late 1990s and early 2000s. On the one hand, he played traditional hard bop and Latin jazz, recording standards and proving himself a master of the jazz tradition. On the other, he formed his own funk band, the RH Factor, and became a member of the Soulquarians, a loosely constituted pool of singers and players who worked together to produce albums like D'Angelo's *Voodoo* and *Black Messiah*, Common's *Like Water for Chocolate*, and Erykah Badu's *Mama's Gun* and *Worldwide Underground*, all of which Hargrove played on.

Hargrove, who died in 2018 after a long battle with kidney disease, did more to influence the direction of the music than just record and perform. He was one of the founders of the Jazz Gallery, possibly New York's most important incubator for forward-looking jazz, and he mentored younger players, offering advice and encouragement. Recall that earlier in this book, Jeremy Pelt talked about his admiration for the man, and when Hargrove died, Ambrose Akinmusire tweeted, "I don't think I would be alive if I hadn't met him when I did. I am extremely grateful I got to tell him as a grown man to his face."

The trumpeters in this section are all of the post-Hargrove generation. They were all born in the 1980s, and grew up in a world where hip-hop was not just the dominant form of Black music, but an entire culture unto itself. The idea that they might not engage with it in their own music is absurd. But the ways in which they have done so are fascinating, and unique to each man.

In some ways, a trumpeter is a lot like an MC. The rapper must hold the crowd's attention with nothing but a microphone and his own wit and charisma; a trumpeter can lead a band, obviously, but his instrument is small and relatively underpowered, compared to a tenor saxophone. Saxophonists roar and rumble; trumpeters duck and dart, stick and move. The trumpet players profiled in this section have each developed highly individual approaches, but the element of hip-hop — sometimes dominant, other times a mere tinge — is present in all of their work. They are twenty-first century musicians, after all.

Ambrose Akinmusire: Expressing Complexity

Attending Winter Jazzfest in January 2020, I had the strange but inescapable feeling that the event had peaked. The annual weekend marathon featured 105 performances, spread across 11 venues in Lower Manhattan, and perhaps it was the shows I chose, but when I was exploring, it felt significantly less manic and crowded than it had in previous years. The only room I wanted to get into but couldn't was Zinc Bar on West Third Street. It's a subterranean space, one flight down from the sidewalk, and it was much too small for the crowd drawn by the performers they'd booked.

Shows at the recently renovated Webster Hall, on 11th Street, were busy, but I didn't need to squeeze my way in the way I had when I'd been there to see Cannibal Corpse or the Melvins. I sequestered myself in an upstairs balcony, with plenty of room to sit on a couch or walk around. Other performances I attended at SOBs, Subculture and the Zürcher Gallery were full, but not oppressively so.

On Friday night, January 10, I started my night at SOBs, where the Hypnotic Brass Ensemble were playing. They were preceded by a short performance by a Chicago-based footwork dance crew, which was energetic — they overcame technical difficulties by engaging in audience-participation exercises — but not exactly what I was there for. Neither were HBE, honestly. Once upon a time, these sons of the late trumpeter Philip Cohran, whose own music fell somewhere between the Art Ensemble of Chicago and the Sun Ra Arkestra, had offered a hard-driving, funky, but abstract and spiritual sort of parade jazz. It was possible to hear echoes of Fela Kuti and the Dirty Dozen Brass Band in their romping, stomping, chant-along compositions. At this performance, though, they were wearing slick suits like a "grown and sexy" R&B revue, and the music had a much more commercial bent, including keyboards and electric bass. I half expected them to break out into unison dance steps onstage.

In search of something more thoughtful, I headed to Webster Hall, where trumpeter Ambrose Akinmusire was playing with his long-standing quartet of pianist Sam Harris, bassist Harish Raghavan and drummer Justin Brown. They were positioned fairly close together, with Harris at stage right, Akinmusire and Raghavan slightly off center and Brown in back, his kit on a riser like a rock drummer. They were dressed casually, in subdued tones; the trumpeter wore a black button-down shirt, jeans and a dark baseball cap with an insignia on the front that I couldn't decipher. His short but somewhat unruly locs protruded from the cap, falling around his bearded face as he fit the microphone directly into the trumpet's bell to allow his sound to fully pierce through the room.

Akinmusire has a tone on the trumpet that seems extraordinarily difficult to maintain. He rarely screams, staying more or less in the middle of the horn's range, but his phrases have a loose, baggy quality that keep him forever on the edge of slipping out of tune. He makes a sound like the air coming out of a balloon, as though his emotions are too strong to be contained by melodic precision. It's not unlike what Miles Davis did on the December 1965 recordings at the Plugged Nickel club in Chicago, giving the music a sour edge that simultaneously jars the ear and forces you to stay focused; he won't let you relax.

Brown is a forceful, pummeling drummer who never lets the energy level onstage flag. Raghavan is the perfect fulcrum, bouncing steadily along and rarely drawing attention to himself. Harris, who got almost as much solo space as the leader, takes an approach similar to Akinmusire's. His melodies often seem like they're slipping away from him, but they never are. The music was extraordinarily suspenseful, even at its most subdued, but it exploded more than once.

Months later, talking to Akinmusire by phone, I learned that the tunes I'd heard that night were the ones on his album *On the Tender Spot of Every Calloused Moment*; they'd gone into the studio and recorded them the next day.

"We always try to break some things here and there," he said of the energy they'd summoned onstage that night. "We break some things, and then we sit down and investigate the damage that's been done."

Tender Spot was an extraordinarily introspective, impassioned and beautiful album, a breakthrough in an already impressive career. It began with "Tide of Hyacinth," an 8-minute piece that began with 2 minutes or so of energetic but seemingly directionless meandering, as though all present were clearing their throats and stretching their fingers. But after 2 seconds of silence, Harris picked up the dropped thread and launched into an extended solo that was putatively "free" but extremely disciplined; the florid expressionism was a disguise. Akinmusire was reduced to a voice in the background, a few notes here and there serving as encouragement – he was his pianist's hypeman. Then, at the 5-minute mark, a voice was heard calling out from the middle of the music. Percussionist Jesus Díaz emerged, playing percussion and chanting in Yoruba.

The whole album felt like an exploration of the dynamic between Akinmusire and Harris. The pianist was always a co-lead voice, never an accompanist. On "Mr Roscoe (Consider the Simultaneous)," a piece dedicated to saxophonist and composer Roscoe Mitchell, the trumpeter wandered off mic, continuing his phrase at half its previous volume. Harris, by contrast, was rooted to the spot and never faltered.

Raghavan and Brown got their moments in the spotlight, too. The bassist opened "An Interlude (That Get' More Intense)" with a 2-minute solo that sounded like trees falling in a forest, one booming impact after another. Brown's drumming was as ferocious throughout the record as it had been at Webster Hall; he rarely seemed to even gesture at timekeeping, and the others didn't act like they needed him for that anyway. Consequently, he was free to travel his own path, dropping bomb after bomb and unleashing fast, aggressive rolls across the snare and toms.

Akinmusire viewed *Tender Spot* as a sequel to his first album for Blue Note, 2011's *When the Heart Emerges Glistening*. "The first record starts with a trumpet solo, this record starts with a trumpet solo. And I guess with the exception of Jesus Díaz and Genevieve [Artadi], this is an acoustic record with not too many tricks or overdubs or anything like that, just like the first record. I tried to sequence it like the first record, too."

When the Heart.. was a rapturously received debut. Raghavan and Brown were already in place, but Gerald Clayton was on piano, and tenor saxophonist Walter Smith III was part of the group. Akinmusire and Smith were a tight team in the early 2000s, playing on each other's records and touring together.

I interviewed the saxophonist in 2014, and he told me:

> I am really inspired by [Ambrose's] playing and always feel like he's reinventing his own language and finding different ways to approach music in both his improvisation and composition...from the moment I first heard him play up until now, he has been a constant source of inspiration that has pushed me to practice and write, even when I felt like taking days off. I've played with him more than anyone else in the past 10 years and I have been astounded every time. He has a fearless approach to playing and composing that is very honest, spiritual and human. Personally, he is one of the most moral and genuine people that you will ever meet. I think we've played so much together that we have become very comfortable with how the other phrases melodies and

> builds solos. I feel like even though we play very differently, there is a very common ground where we are able to connect that has become very intuitive and natural.

The interplay between the two men was apparent from the first track on *When the Heart...*, "Confessions to My Unborn Daughter." It began with an extended passage of solo trumpet, but when the piano and then the rhythm section came in after a minute, there was a subtle but stunning production trick: the trumpet slid from the right to left sides of the stereo field, and when it reached the far left, Smith's tenor emerged from there, launching a fresh solo.

Although *When the Heart...*received nearly unanimous critical accolades, and Akinmusire quickly vaulted to the forefront of the jazz scene, it took him close to 4 years to release his third album, *The Imagined Savior is Much Easier to Paint*. Simply put, he had an extremely negative reaction to the acclaim.

"I don't like attention," he explained. "If I didn't have all of these opportunities, which I'm very grateful for, I think I would be playing with the same people, playing the same music. [And] after that first Blue Note record, the attention kinda got to me." He didn't feel comfortable as the hot young trumpet player of the moment:

> So I kinda ran from it. I moved to LA., I started teaching at USC, I said, OK, I'm gonna do this other thing...So that's why it took me so long to come out with that next album, and that's a lot of what the second album is about, from the title and all of these things. So I dealt with some depression and a lot of negative things, but I'm glad I went through it.

Imagined Savior was his first Blue Note record to feature Harris, as well as guitarist Charles Altura, a string quartet and multiple vocalists. It was quite dark at times; the cover depicted

Akinmusire staring into the distance, seemingly lost in thought. But there were moments of exultation, too. The final track, "Richard (Conduit)," was a nearly 17-minute live performance from the Jazz Standard in New York, a demonstration of his quintet in full flight.

Akinmusire took another 3 years to make his next statement; *A Rift in Decorum* was a double CD of all-new compositions recorded live at the Village Vanguard with his quartet, minus Smith. It might have been cheaper to record the new music in a studio; the legendary club charges a lot for the privilege of recording there, and they're selective. "The thing I love about the Vanguard is that they don't do it just for the money," Akinmusire said, laughing. "You can't just have a Vanguard record. When Lorraine [Gordon, widow of club founder Max Gordon] was alive, she didn't care how much money you were willing to spend...if she didn't like you, you were not doing a Vanguard record." The audience wasn't informed that an album was being recorded, and the tunes weren't mixed in with material from previous albums. "I just felt like I was documenting it, and if it came out nice, then I would release it."

Born and raised in Oakland, California, the child of a Nigerian father and a mother from Mississippi, Akinmusire is deeply engaged with social struggle. His parents divorced when he was young, but his childhood was stable; he spent a lot of time in church. "Going to church had a huge impact on who I am today, especially musically," he recalled. "I can remember the first time I heard Art Blakey, I heard 'Moanin,' and it just made sense to me because it sounded like gospel music being played on [jazz] instruments, with a different rhythm. And I think if I hadn't been raised in the church, I wouldn't have heard it that way."

Though it may not immediately register as such to a Western ear, Jesus Díaz's presence on *Tender Spot* is a nod to that religious atmosphere. "This is how I grew up," Akinmusire says. "I'm Nigerian, so I grew up with music that sounded like this in my home and understanding it as — I think a better word is sacred."

All of his albums to date have possessed both explicit and subtle political content; it's essential to his art. He's unlikely to record an album of love ballads, for example:

> Well, I honestly don't think that it would be honest. It's just not a part of my experience...yet. Again, it's all context. I was raised by a woman from the most racist county in the most racist state. My mom used to pick pecans out of Fannie Lou Hamer's yard. I have an uncle that knew Emmett Till, and I'm born and raised in Oakland. My mentors were Black Panthers — my first trumpet teacher was a Black Panther. So this is how I grew up. And that's my experience. Even now, living in Oakland, when I walk out, it's hard to even explain — it's a whole other thing. So I don't have — my life just isn't that. My life isn't a bunch of love ballads. It's difficult. It's beautiful. It's beautifully complicated, and I think if I am about expressing my life and expressing the world as I, Ambrose Akinmusire, see it, then I have to find a way of expressing this complexity.

Essential Listening

Walter Smith III, *Casually Introducing* (Fresh Sound New Talent, 2006)

Walter Smith III, *III* (Criss Cross Jazz, 2010)

Ambrose Akinmusire, *When the Heart Emerges Glistening* (Blue Note, 2010)

Archie Shepp, *Attica Blues Orchestra — I Hear the Sound* (ArchieBall, 2013)

Ambrose Akinmusire, *The Imagined Savior is Far Easier to Paint* (Blue Note, 2014)

Ambrose Akinmusire, *A Rift in Decorum: Live at the Village Vanguard* (Blue Note, 2017)
Ambrose Akinmusire, *On the Tender Spot of Every Calloused Moment* (Blue Note, 2020)

Christian Scott aTunde Adjuah: Where the Power Rests

I've never seen Christian Scott aTunde Adjuah perform live. I had intended to see him for the first time on Friday, March 13, 2020; he was appearing for a week at the Blue Note, in New York. But venues were already being reduced to half capacity due to the expanding COVID-19 pandemic, and I emailed the publicist to say, "Thanks for your help in getting me on the list, but there's no way I'm coming into NYC this weekend."

I was really excited to see that show, too. I'd been listening to Scott's music for about 5 years at that point, and had become convinced that whatever jazz's future looked like, he was going to play a major role in it.

Scott's work blends old and new in unprecedented and riveting ways. He's a stunning player, capable of screaming high notes and incredible sustain, and he places his ferocious technique into a sonic landscape like nothing else out there. He's also as aware of visual messaging as any artist in jazz history; his clothing and album covers, on which he's frequently covered in gleaming gold chains and jewelry, sporting elaborately braided hair, are brilliant displays of Afro-futurism that both recall and update albums like Pharoah Sanders' *Thembi* and *Black Unity*, and Isaac Hayes' *Black Moses*.

We had a lengthy phone conversation in early 2017, as he was releasing the first volume of *The Centennial Trilogy*, a set of three CDs — *Ruler Rebel, Diaspora* and *The Emancipation Procrastination* — that came out individually at first, and were later bundled.

The first thing we discussed was his horn itself. The bell of his trumpet points skyward, like the late Dizzy Gillespie's did, but there's more to it than that. It's a custom instrument with unique sonic properties.

He told me:

> I have four different prototypes and different models do different things, but with the tilted bell trumpet, it changes a lot...that last angle on the trumpet traditionally is pretty abrasive, so this creates a lot of back pressure; it makes it a little easier to play in the upper register of the horn. But it's very difficult to get a multitude of timbres and textures out of one instrument, so when you make that last angle less abrasive — like, for most of my horns it's between 22 and 27 degrees...I can change the sound and the timbre of instrument from within the horn in a way that's very different from a traditional trumpet. Not just what I'm doing with the traditional ways of being able to change timbre, but also in terms of what I'm doing with the temperature of my breath also affects the instrument greatly...You lose a little in the higher register, but this is something that you can work back up.

It's not just the instrument, though — it's what he does with it, and what he surrounds it with. His fascination with the details of sound is immediately noticeable on record, particularly the albums he's made since 2015 — *Stretch Music*, the trilogy and 2019's *Ancestral Recall*.

Before that, he was evolving, steadily but audibly. Early records like 2007's *Anthem* and 2010's *Yesterday You Said Tomorrow* were made with a crew of peers, including saxophonist Walter Smith III, pianist Aaron Parks, guitarist Matthew Stevens and drummers Jamire Williams and Marcus Gilmore. The music was modern jazz, but electric instruments were welcome and the riffs and rhythms drew from rock and hip-hop whenever that seemed like the right choice. (Brother J, of the '80s Afrocentric hip-hop group X-Clan, appeared on *Anthem*.)

In 2012, he made a broad, expansive statement that synthesized all the sounds he'd been working with into something seamless and entirely his own. A self-titled double

CD featuring Stephens, keyboardist Lawrence Fields, bassist Kristopher Keith Funn and Williams on drums, plus guest horn players here and there, *Christian aTunde Adjuah* was a 2-hour, 23-track valentine to his home city of New Orleans, as well as a statement of political and artistic intentionality. On its cover, he was swathed in peach-colored feathers, recalling the elaborate costumes of the city's Mardi Gras Indians, and track titles referred to landmarks, Black history and events or people of personal significance.

The music was as multifaceted and present-tense as ever, drawing from jazz, hip-hop, funk, New Orleans R&B and rock. The melodies had a melancholy edge, but they'd bite into you and they wouldn't let go. His playing, which always had a gleaming razor's edge, seemed more impassioned and urgent than ever, while retaining the fierce control that had always marked his work.

With *Stretch Music,* though, he moved into a new realm, shedding most of his former collaborators in the process; only Stephens and Fields remained. With his new band, he began shaping a new sound that still contained some of the rock and funk elements from previous albums, but owed much more to Southern hip-hop and dance forms, including trap music and bounce. Drenched in reverb, tracks like "Perspectives" took the synth-heavy sound of Miles Davis's 1980s albums, particularly *You're Under Arrest* and *Tutu,* and moved it into the twenty-first century with crisp, ice-cold beats underpinning swooningly romantic muted horn murmurs.

Stretch Music also marked his move toward artistic independence. *Christian aTunde Adjuah* had been his final release for Concord Records, and he started his own label, also called Stretch Music and distributed through a partnership with Ropeadope. He had no one to answer to but himself, and the time was clearly right for a grand gesture. *The Centennial Trilogy* was it.

Spreading two-and-a-half hours of music across three albums allowed Scott to celebrate jazz's centennial by radically expanding the music's definition. His high-powered horn was surrounded by oceans of live and programmed rhythms, from thundering New Orleans drumming to mechanistic trap beats. He was never just soloing over loops, though. These were fully arranged compositions, with flute, harp and strings appearing at times, and it conjured and sustained a wide range of moods. The music seethed, swooned and became heart-crushingly bleak, depending on the track.

To some, working so extensively with electronics places obstacles in a musician's path. There's not much harmony to a skeletal programmed beat, so perhaps a more linear approach is required, and the element of the blues may not be as immediately accessible. But when I posed this question to Scott, he had a different take.

"There are some songs where obviously, because the palette may be more bare, sometimes less is more, and you're not superimposing too many things and you're just speaking over that environment," he acknowledged:

> But there are other compositions...that take that type of feel, trap and whatever you wanna call that sort of space, but also superimpose more dense harmonic types as the improviser is telling their story or building their story. So you can still take a moment, a trap song or this type of environment that has maybe one or two chords, and you can still imply things with those changes...that help to create a more captivating story type. So it depends on the composition and the story that we're trying to tell. But I don't find it limiting on any level.

His describing tracks as "environments" reminded me of Miles Davis's 1972 album *On the Corner*, on which the trumpet was surrounded by a dense thicket of percussion, handclaps, droning electric pianos and sitars, and the occasional outburst of distorted guitar or squiggling soprano saxophone. It was more like an urban field recording than a "jazz" or even a "funk" album.

Scott told me:

> I guess one of Miles's ideas at one point was, it's actually a lot harder to improvise over a stagnant mode or changes that aren't moving...because once you develop the language you at least have something to say when the changes are moving rapidly. But when the environment doesn't really move much, you actually have to stand there and captivate and the same story type can be a little more challenging. I always thought that was interesting, and kind of like it in this context as well.

Each album in the trilogy was different, though they were all clearly part of a single broad vision. *Ruler Rebel* was stark and spare, the music taking aspects of trap and dub, Scott's trumpet calling out in the almost oppressive darkness. *Diaspora* was lighter, with a lot of space given to female voices — vocalist Sarah Elizabeth Charles and flautist Elena Pinderhughes were featured on six of eleven tracks.

"They're the hardest working people I know on the music side of this business," Scott told me. "They won't yield; neither one of them has any back-down as it relates to the work. I consider myself very fortunate to have these ladies around, and it's really a lot of love, you know? For what it is that they come to do and how hardworking they are."

The final album in the series, *The Emancipation Procrastination*, was the most "organic" of the three. Many tracks sounded more like the product of a live band, with Stevens' guitar prominent and an entire track given over to Ghanaian drummer/

percussionist Weedie Braimah. The nearly 11-minute "New Heroes" was both a conclusion – to the album and the trilogy – and an epic showcase for the entire ensemble.

Scott's follow-up to the trilogy, 2019's *Ancestral Recall*, felt like a gesture of welcoming to people who might be just getting on board with his concept. More tracks than ever before featured vocals, with poet Saul Williams appearing on three and rapper Mike Larry Draw on another. The music, too, was closer to hip-hop than jazz, with tracks built from samples that were joined together roughly, so the seams showed. At the same time, live percussion and multiple wind instruments floated in and out, swathed in echo and reverb, like elements in a dub mix. The combination of breakbeats, congas and sonic murk recalled productions by the UK trip-hop auteur Tricky and reggaeton pioneer Tego Calderón, with of-the-moment technology being turned to the task of maintaining sonic lineages that went back centuries, across the Afro-Caribbean diaspora.

In August 2020, I got to hear what I'd missed by passing on the Blue Note show. Scott had recorded a live album during those five nights – *Axiom*, which featured eight tracks on CD and five more as digital-only bonus tracks, two of them exclusive to Bandcamp. The band at the Blue Note had included Elena Pinderhughes on flute, Alex Han on alto saxophone, Lawrence Fields on keyboards (piano and synths), Kris Funk on bass, Corey Fonville on drums and electronics, and Weedie Braimah on djembe and congas. The set contained tracks from *Stretch Music*, the trilogy and *Ancestral Recall*, plus one new piece, "Incarnation." The performances were fierce, and lengthy – each of two versions of "The Last Chieftain," from *Stretch Music*, was more than 16 minutes long, doubling the length of the studio version and then some.

At the end of the album's opening track, "X. Adjuah (I Own the Night)," Scott delivered a short, biting monologue, addressing coronavirus and issues surrounding his music. He said, "What you're experiencing tonight — what you're gonna experience tonight is the reevaluation. We have just crossed into the second century of creative improvised music, or otherwise, I guess if you prefer belittling and pejorative terms, jazz... we're reevaluating what we're playing and why, we're also reevaluating this relationship," meaning the dynamic between performer and audience.

He continued, "Oftentimes when we come into environments like this to play creative improvised music, someone uses the word jazz and everyone in the room becomes a fuckin' Fulbright scholar. And that's cool, but that has nothing to do with where this music's power rests."

On the most basic level, he was absolutely right. Whether what he and his band played — which included elements of hip-hop, funk, Latin music and sounds from throughout the Afro-Caribbean diaspora, as well as frigid synth atmospheres and his own horn, which was warped by electronics at times and hoarse and brutal other times — was "jazz" meant nothing. It had power and beauty and vitality, and was performed in the moment with a level of organic interaction and collective energy that rendered categorization unnecessary and meaningless.

From my point of view, though, the word "jazz" is not a box or an envelope; it's an umbrella, or a house. All who wish to stand under it, or live within it, are welcome.

Essential Listening

Christian Scott, *Anthem* (Concord Jazz, 2007)

Christian Scott, *Yesterday You Said Tomorrow* (Concord Jazz, 2010)

Christian Scott, *Christian aTunde Adjuah* (Concord Jazz, 2012)

Christian Scott aTunde Adjuah, *Stretch Music* (Stretch Music/Ropeadope, 2015)

Christian Scott aTunde Adjuah, *The Centennial Trilogy* (*Ruler*

Rebel/Diaspora/The Emancipation Procrastination) (Stretch Music/Ropeadope, 2017)

Christian Scott aTunde Adjuah, *Ancestral Recall* (Stretch Music/Ropeadope, 2019)

Christian Scott aTunde Adjuah, *Axiom* (Stretch Music/Ropeadope, 2020)

Keyon Harrold: You Gotta Kill It

Keyon Harrold is from Ferguson, Missouri. He's steeped in the blues and the slow-rolling hip-hop of Atlanta and Houston. He can be heard behind Mississippi rapper Big KRIT on "Drinking Sessions," from his 2017 album *4eva is a Mighty Long Time*. As KRIT raps in an almost panicked, hoarse cry, spitting out his lyrics as though they're burning the inside of his mouth, Harrold's trumpet is a voice in the background, an unceasing alter ego, not unlike guitarist Grant Estes soloing all the way through Suicidal Tendencies' anthemic "Institutionalized," his squealing runs and grinding riffs mirroring vocalist Mike Muir's escalating madness.

That same deep blues feeling and connection to Southern hip-hop came through when Harrold performed in Harlem's Marcus Garvey Park in summer 2019, as part of the "50th Anniversary of Black Woodstock" festival. He was joined by singer Georgia Anne Muldrow for a version of the song "Wayfaring Traveler," from his 2017 album *The Mugician*. On disc, the song was a little over 6 minutes long; live, it nearly reached the 10-minute mark. Guitarist Randy Runyon and drummer George "Spanky" McCurdy set up a deep Mississippi blues groove, which Muldrow scatted along with before launching into the lyrics as the rest of the band — bass, keyboards, background vocalists — came in. By the chorus, her voice had risen to a full soul-gospel wail, but the band kept her grounded, sticking to the blues. Harrold took the same tack with his first of two solos, releasing coiled phrases that clung tightly to the melody. Muldrow began scatting, and Harrold echoed her. Eventually, Runyon's turn to solo came around, and he went full hard rock, emitting piercing screams. On the final chorus, Harrold put down his horn and he and Muldrow sang together. He's got an excellent voice.

The Mugician is a fascinating album. It combines elements

from jazz, funk, soul, blues, rock, hip-hop and even dancehall, but that doesn't make it unique in the twenty-first century. It's the way Harrold combines these elements that makes him worth listening to. The album's title track features hard rock guitars and a gooey synth line pulled straight from an early 70s Herbie Hancock album, laid over a shuffling funk rhythm, but halfway through it transitions seamlessly to reggae so singer Josh David Barrett can take over.

The next track, "MB Lament," is named in tribute to Michael Brown, shot by police in Harrold's hometown in 2014. It features a mournful but passionate horn performance and a ten-piece string section.

"Ferguson — it's home for me. I don't live there now, but growing up, it was beautiful, many great memories, great people, a great sense of community," Harrold told me by phone in 2018.

> Which was fantastic, but outside of that, there's a lot — there's a two-sided coin there that has to do with bias and racial discrimination and systemic issues that were brought to the forefront at the end of the Mike Brown situation and the beginning of the Black Lives Matter movement. A lot of stuff was exposed [for] what it was.

Harrold has 15 siblings, all of whom were involved with music growing up:

> We didn't really have a choice. My father and my mom were in the ministry; my dad was a pastor, my mom was also a minister, so we did a lot of the Levite work in the church, keeping the church going musically. That, plus the idea that my grandfather had a drum and bugle corps and my dad was a teacher, he taught me how to play. All my siblings older than me learned how to play, and one of the things

was my grandfather's grandsons all had to learn how to play the horn.

The horn of which he speaks is a soprano bugle, which is identical to a trumpet, but in a different key. Harrold's grandfather led the drum and bugle corps as a social activity in the St. Louis area, bringing what the trumpeter describes as thousands of people through the organization over the years and in the process keeping them out of trouble and teaching discipline and a collective work ethic. (I encountered a massive drum corps gathering in Bergen, Norway in 2018, and was stunned by the volume, but also by the almost seismic impact of hearing hundreds of boys beating drums in complex patterns, marching through the streets. At the same time, it was fascinating to watch the older players teaching new rhythms to younger ones during rest breaks.) When the corps had enough horn players, Harrold boys were allowed to switch to drums, but Keyon didn't. His brother Emanuel did, and now works with singer Gregory Porter. They played together on Porter's 2012 album *Be Good*.

Harrold came to New York to study at the New School, where he was mentored by fellow trumpeter Charles Tolliver. He became a member of Tolliver's big band, appearing on the 2006 album *With Love* and its follow-up, 2009's *Emperor March: Live at the Blue Note*. In between, he made inroads into R&B and hip-hop, playing on albums by Beyoncé, Jay-Z, Mobb Deep, Mary J. Blige, Maxwell and Joss Stone, and touring with Common.

"Charles, that's my guy, a mentor, a visionary and somebody I looked up to," Harrold told me. "He was telling me, you gotta take no prisoners — any time you get the opportunity, you gotta kill it. You gotta play hard, you gotta go hard."

His first album as a leader, *Introducing Keyon Harrold*, was released on the Criss Cross label in 2009. The band included Marcus Strickland on tenor and soprano saxophones, Danny Grissett on piano, Dezron Douglas on bass and E.J. Strickland

(Marcus's twin brother) on drums. Emanuel Harrold played drums on one track, Jeremy Most contributed guitar to another and Tolliver blew a trumpet solo on the opener, "TMF Nuttz." All the pieces were originals, except for a version of Horace Silver's "Peace" and a medley that combined "Amazing Grace" with Harrold's own "Lord My God."

It was nice enough, but typical of a hundred other debut albums on Criss Cross or Fresh Sound New Talent at the beginning of the twenty-first century. The players were demonstrating their facility with hard bop and modern acoustic jazz, occasionally taking a slight left turn (Harrold's album included a track with the perhaps overly literal title "Hip Hop Joint") but coloring within the lines for the most part. It didn't immediately make me think he was going to be someone to keep an ear out for in the coming years.

In 2016, though, he made a much more interesting move. He was chosen by keyboardist Robert Glasper (a friend and former New School classmate) to perform on the soundtrack to the movie *Miles Ahead*, a fictional story about Miles Davis set in the mid-1970s, when Davis had abandoned music and was living a life of drugged-out debauchery. Most of the music in the movie came from Davis's own back catalog, but four tracks — "Junior's Jam," "Francessence," "What's Wrong With That?" and "Gone 2015" — featured Harrold, Glasper and a rotating cast of sidemen that included Herbie Hancock and Wayne Shorter on "What's Wrong With That?"

The track, which featured dubbed-in crowd noise throughout, was an imitation of Davis's live sound in the mid-1980s, though Shorter left his band in 1970 and Hancock hadn't worked with him since 1972's *On the Corner*, and hadn't toured with him since 1968. Still, Harrold, playing through a Harmon mute to get the pinched-off screaming sound Davis made his own in those years, does a good job of holding his own within the swirl of synths, electric guitar (from Gary Clark Jr.) and Shorter's soprano sax.

"It was an amazing opportunity to record with Herbie and Wayne, and get a chance to stand next to Wayne and actually play and him be like, 'Try this,' or 'Go this way. Think about music in this way.'"

While Harrold cited Davis, Freddie Hubbard and Clifford Brown as crucial early influences when we spoke, he was confident in his own voice on the horn, and his position in the jazz landscape.

> At this point, playing-wise, I don't think I'm really imitating anybody. I'm pretty much focused on my concept and the way I play. I feel like I've developed enough to where it's identifiable. People know that it's me, I can tell that it's myself...I've been playing a long time, I think I'm past the idea of learning how to speak.

Although he never left the scene, 8 years passed between *Introducing Keyon Harrold* and *The Mugician*. In the interval, his music transformed radically, but to him, it was a logical progression, undergone at a necessary pace.

"It took a while to conjure the ideas that I wanted to convey," he explained. "When I did my first album, I was playing tunes that I had already written, and I just wanted to record something. For the second album, as a producer, trumpet player, as an artist, as a writer, as a person who was married, then divorced... it was a long process."

Harrold's greatest challenge on *The Mugician* was finding ways to synthesize all of his inspirations and concepts into one coherent musical vision — to make his love of hip-hop sit comfortably alongside his love of classical and his love of jazz, and to allow each element to work in (literal and figurative) harmony with the others. As he puts it, "It took me a while to grow as an artist. Before, I was just a player."

I asked him about "MB Lament," about whether he knew

Michael Brown's family. He said no, but added:

> My dad still lives very close, like a stone's throw from where it all happened. My connection was...knowing what it was like to grow up in Ferguson, knowing that me being a black man, six foot tall, sometimes I can be looked at as threatening to people, until they get a chance to talk to me and see what I'm really about. The bias, the prejudice, just the idea of what happens by simply walking down the street and being yourself...I had to write that song in homage to his parents, his family, to all of the people who've been killed by police for no valid reason.

He spoke of his own son, and his brothers, and their children, and concluded, "It was basically just giving a vibe and a feeling, without words, to what had happened in Ferguson." And it's the confidence of that gesture – to allow the music to speak, without feeling compelled to bring in a singer or a rapper to make rage and sorrow explicit, to ground it in language – that is what sets Keyon Harrold apart, and makes his music so urgent and beautiful.

Essential Listening

Charles Tolliver Big Band, *With Love* (Blue Note, 2006)
Charles Tolliver Big Band, *Emperor March: Live at the Blue Note* (Half Note, 2009)
Keyon Harrold, *Introducing Keyon Harrold* (Criss Cross Jazz, 2009)
Gregory Porter, *Be Good* (Motéma, 2012)
Marcus Strickland's Twi-Life, *Nihil Novi* (Blue Note, 2016)
Various Artists, *Miles Ahead (Original Motion Picture Soundtrack)* (Sony Music, 2016)
Keyon Harrold, *The Mugician* (Sony Music, 2017)

Theo Croker: This is All Black Music

There are plenty of fathers and sons in jazz. Sometimes the younger generation takes on the older generation's instrument (saxophonist Ravi Coltrane, son of John), but not always — noted cornet player Graham Haynes is the son of legendary drummer Roy Haynes, for example, and alto saxophonist Ornette Coleman's son Denardo became his father's drummer at the age of 11.

It's less common for music to skip a generation. Theo Croker is the grandson of trumpet legend Doc Cheatham, who was born in 1905 and died in 1997, at 91, when Croker was 11. Cheatham, originally from Nashville, Tennessee, played professionally from the 1920s until the end of his life, but didn't break through as a leader until the mid-70s, when he added singing to his repertoire on the 1977 album *Good For What Ails Ya*. For years, he maintained a residency at the New York club Sweet Basil, leading the band every Sunday. Although Cheatham was not from New Orleans, he knew that style of jazz inside and out, and performed it with a sort of dignified verve, shifting back and forth between trumpet and a gentle singing voice that made every love song sound like a lullaby.

Croker's father, William Henry Croker, was a high school principal in Florida, while also running his own father's 80-acre watermelon farm; his mother, Cheatham's daughter, was a guidance counselor. He attended the Oberlin College Conservatory. "I wanted to be in New York and be around Wynton Marsalis at Lincoln Center and things like that. But my father insisted I go to Oberlin, and he took me there to see it," he told me by phone one August afternoon. Once enrolled in what he described as "a very open-minded institution," he studied with trumpeters Donald Byrd and Marcus Belgrave, and saxophonist Gary Bartz, and met drummer Kassa Overall, who became a friend and collaborator; they continue to work together.

Croker found Belgrave, who died in 2015, to be a major influence on his way of thinking about music. "I remember being told by Wynton Marsalis one time that college was pointless," he recalled.

> You know, Wynton's not interested in Donald Byrd and even some of what Gary Bartz does...but when I mentioned Marcus Belgrave, he was like, "That's one of the most brilliant cats ever." Marcus is so original, really original, and he really had the patience to show me and teach me about harmony. And not just show me what everybody did, but show me how to find my own way through it, so that I'm always learning it through my voice. I can check out — I can decipher what other people play, but it's like, how do I use this vocabulary in my own way, arrange the lexicon of it so that it expresses me no matter how I play it? No matter what style or what harmony I'm playing, it's just me.

In a perfect demonstration of that principle, Croker performed at Dizzy's Club Coca-Cola as part of a 2017 tribute to Dizzy Gillespie. The band he led included saxophonist Anthony Ware, pianist Eric Lewis (aka ELEW), bassist Eric Wheeler, Overall on drums and percussionist Luisito Quintero. Slim and colorfully dressed, with long braids dangling well past his shoulders, Croker took fierce solos as the band pounded out "Toccata," from Gillespie's 1960 orchestral album *Gillespiana*, the intricate rhythms honoring his lifelong interest in combining Latin music with bebop. Lewis in particular made much of the repetitive, intense energy of Latin piano styles, hammering away at figures that gradually began to disintegrate beneath his fingers, journeying from precision to expressionistic displays of freedom but never losing the groove laid down by Overall and

Quintero, with Wheeler providing the pulse. At the climax of one piece, when it was the percussionist's turn in the spotlight, all the other musicians downed tools to listen from the wings, as his hands delivered a stunning, hypnotic peroration.

What was obvious, watching that performance, was that Croker was an experienced entertainer. He wasn't onstage just to demonstrate his mastery of his instrument, though that was evident; he meant to give the assembled audience a show, and he and his compatriots did so. They were something to watch, not just something to listen to.

This same quality of showmanship was present on Croker's breakout album, 2014's *AfroPhysicist*. After a 2-minute solo trumpet fanfare, "Alapa (for Doc)," he and his band launched into "Realize," a strutting funk-rock piece with a whomping backbeat and loud electric guitar and organ. There was nothing subtle or diffident about it; the music was intended to get an audience pumped up, if not leaping out of their seats. It could have been the theme to a late-night talk show; no surprise there, since Croker was the musical director and bandleader for *Asia Uncut Star Network*, a Shanghai-based TV show, from 2007 to 2010.

He had begun dividing his time between China and the US almost immediately after graduating from Oberlin. It all started with a 5-month residency at Shanghai's House of Blues, but he soon found that the city's then-booming economy provided many, many opportunities to play in all sorts of contexts. He joined a salsa band, two different big bands and led his own group, the 15-member Afrosonic Orchestra.

It was through that work that he met vocalist Dee Dee Bridgewater, who became his boss, mentor and label head. She hired him to be her musical director, and replaced her previous band with his. "I think I toured once or twice with her band and then she was like, 'All right, I'm gonna bring your band, because people aren't hiring you as a leader, so I'm gonna use your band

and say featuring you.' And she did, for years."

He released three albums — *AfroPhysicist*, 2016's *Escape Velocity* and 2019's *Star People Nation* — through Bridgewater's DDB Productions, in partnership with Sony's revived OKeh label. OKeh, which had existed off and on since the 1920s, released early jazz, blues and "race" records, and was revived with some fanfare in 2013 as a division of Sony Classical. Bridgewater sang on three tracks from *AfroPhysicist*, and one from *Escape Velocity*, but after the first album, she mostly left Croker to make his own luck and become his own man.

Escape Velocity began with "Raise Your Vibrations," a track on which he recited aphorisms like "You were made in the likeness of a peace that nothing can disturb. Reclaim your inner peace so that you may attain your reason for coming into existence — the enjoyment of life." While the music on the album featured a core band (saxophonist Irwin Hall, electric guitarist Ben Munson, keyboardist Michael King and bassist Eric Wheeler), it was co-produced by Croker and Overall, and featured programmed rhythms alongside live kit drumming, and extensive use of samples and electronics.

"Oberlin really taught me who I was," Croker told me. "I stripped away my interest and desire [for] the imagery of what they call jazz, the suit and tie of it, the putting the tradition before the exploration of it, instead of having the tradition as the foundation of your exploration. Oberlin helped me flip that."

Working with Overall there, and afterwards, helped Croker become who he was just as much as working with Bridgewater had. (They were both in her band at the same time.) "I feel like we are kindred creative spirits, and we always have been," he said, his voice filled with almost brotherly affection:

> We're fiercely creative on our own, but when we do something together, it's also unique and it no longer sounds like him or I. He does his thing, it sounds like him, I do my thing and

> it sounds like me, but when we do something together it's something truly special. And we were like that right away, whether we were playing or producing music. Kassa got me into producing music using computers and all that, which I was not — the only thing I used computers for was writing scores, so he got me into a whole other world with that, and of course that started transferring into our playing.

Born in 1985, Croker has never lived in a world without hip-hop. It's not something he has to consciously insert into his musical concept; it's just there, the air he breathes, the water in which he swims. However, he's not interested in being cooler-than-thou or embracing the most cutting-edge beats and rhythms. He wants your attention, and he'll give you a show to get it. And his aesthetic was permanently shaped by working for so long in China, where, in his words, "these people didn't have a concept of what is and isn't jazz — this is all Black music to them."

"By having a show element, you can go deeper into the actual music of it," he explained:

> Duke Ellington, that was show music. That's why his music is so thematic and dramatic. Count Basie is also show music, but I think it was more dance-oriented. When you listen to Ellington's suites...it's like a movie. It's very visual. So that aspect of the tradition is definitely what I was exploring with that, so the material for [*AfroPhysicist*] was just modified and tightened up from what I'd been playing in China.

He also came of age at a very particular moment, which he pointed out. He and the other trumpeters of his generation — Ambrose Akinmusire, Keyon Harrold, Marquis Hill and Christian Scott:

> all come from a time period where the internet wasn't our

> go-to for information. So we had to have a certain vigilance and hunger about getting to the source of this information, and chasing down people like Roy Hargrove or Wynton Marsalis or Gary Bartz or Marcus Belgrave, and creating a bond with them. Not just watching a bunch of videos of them on YouTube, or being able to pull up their full discography. We had to work to get a CD. And because of that, when we get that information, we do a whole other thing with it. Still, to this day. So we have benefited from both. We're not only in the new world. So if all the shit shuts down, if the internet goes down, I can still be an artist and expand.

Expansion is the word that may describe Croker's music best. He works on a broad canvas, and continually finds new ways to combine acoustic and electronic instruments, traditional compositional strategies with present-day production techniques, all the while developing and nurturing a uniquely sensitive, yet brash trumpet voice. He says that on his most recent album, *Star People Nation*:

> I didn't look at any of it as a genre, really. I really let go of that and just implemented it the way I wanted to hear it, and I think that's the formula that works for me, is to have it not matter. When you're in the studio you get to use different keyboards, different electronics, different EQs, all those different types of things to affect the sound, and I think that not having worked this way in acoustic music [before] is sad. And I'm glad it is [being done] now. I think that being some type of no-no is weird, or was weird...it's like, why not? Whatever element you wanna explore, you should be able to explore; that's the whole point.

Essential Listening

Theo Croker, *Afro Physicist* (DDB/OKeh, 2014)
Theo Croker, *Escape Velocity* (DDB/OKeh, 2016)
Nicola Conte & Spiritual Galaxy, *Let Your Light Shine On* (MPS, 2018)
Theo Croker, *Star People Nation* (Sony Masterworks, 2019)

Marquis Hill: Reaching the People

The night I saw Marquis Hill and his Blacktet play, I had spent the afternoon interviewing Shabaka Hutchings, Nubya Garcia and Yazz Ahmed in a rehearsal studio room at the New School. The performance was several hours later, in a different New School building, part of Winter Jazzfest. The room was completely packed: listeners were in every seat, lined up shoulder to shoulder along the walls, and wedged into the doorway. I found a spot against the back wall and watched a few tunes, and when I came out, midway through the set, I spotted Garcia waiting in the hall for space to open up.

The band's music tossed high-flying post-bebop lines from Hill and alto saxophonist Joshua Johnson atop a churning, constantly shifting rhythm from vibraphonist Joel Ross, bassist Junius Paul and McCraven. His beats left me with my mouth open; they were lightning-fast, his stick bouncing sharply off the rim of the snare to create patterns that a drum 'n' bass DJ could have dropped into a set without hesitation. (I had no idea who Ross or Paul were that night, either, but each man has released astonishing work since.)

Hill was born in Chicago in 1987; he's the youngest of his generation of trumpeters, following Keyon Harrold (born 1980), Ambrose Akinmusire (born 1982), Christian Scott (born 1983) and Theo Croker (born 1985). "I love all those guys," he told me by phone. "I listen to their music and check out their videos and when the world was open, pre-corona times...I used to run into these guys and hang out and go to their concerts. To me, it's inspirational."

His first instrument was the drums. He switched to the trumpet in sixth grade, focused on jazz performance in high school, then earned bachelor's and master's degrees in jazz education at Northern Illinois University and DePaul University. His real education, though, came on the bandstand in Chicago, where he played with and learned from that city's veteran musicians like saxophonists Fred Anderson, Ari Brown, Ernest Dawkins and Von Freeman, and trumpeter Art Hoyle. He speaks particularly admiringly of Freeman and Anderson, who hosted regular jam sessions — and Anderson ran the Velvet Lounge, a small jazz bar, for decades, incubating entire generations of players on its cramped stage.

"They kind of ingrained in me the importance of having your original voice," he told me. "You listen to Fred's music and it's very avant-garde and out, people call it free, but he instilled the importance of studying the history of the music, studying what came before you, while at the same time you're trying to find your own thing through the history, and it also becomes your own continuum."

Chicago has always had a fundamentally different attitude toward jazz than New York. The AACM, with its focus on collaboration and collective effort, could have arisen in no other city, and while Hill is not a member of the organization, he shares many of its values.

> All the cats play with one another, support each other's concerts — not to say that doesn't happen in New York, but it's just much more widespread, and I do think there's more of a friendly competition in Chicago, versus the cutthroat thing that sometimes New York gets the rep for. In Chicago, cats are pushing and inspiring each other, feeding off one another, like in a community format.

Over the course of eight albums, beginning with 2011's *New Gospel*, Hill has shaped a sound that has roots in traditional hard bop, but includes melodies, harmonies and rhythms drawn from hip-hop, soul, gospel and more. No sound is off limits. He has done this with the help of a relatively small pool of collaborators. His front-line partners on his first three albums were alto saxophonist Christopher McBride and pianist Joshua Mosier, with various players on bass and drums. McCraven joined the roster on 2013's *The Poet*.

By 2014's *Modern Flows, Vol. I,* the Blacktet had begun to take shape, with McBride on alto, Thomas on vibes, Joshua Ramos (who'd played on *The Poet*) on upright bass and Bryan Doherty on electric, and McCraven behind the kit. That album, which also featured various types of guest vocal performances (sung, rapped and spoken), was the first solid demonstration of what would become Hill's concept: a unique, hip-hop-aware/rhythm-driven but ferociously swinging sound that, thanks to the lack of a piano, could flow as freely as Ornette Coleman's 1959 quartet, with the vibes providing a shimmering cloud of melody on demand.

Thomas, Ramos and McCraven all returned for 2016's *The Way We Play,* joined by Brett Williams on Fender Rhodes. That album was Hill's only release with Concord Jazz, a contract he earned by winning the 2014 Thelonious Monk Institute's International Jazz Competition. Unlike its three predecessors, which had featured almost all original compositions, it included versions of jazz standards like "My Foolish Heart," "Maiden Voyage," "Straight No Chaser" and "Polka Dots and Moonbeams," as well as pieces by Horace Silver, Donald Byrd and Carmell Jones. It was as if, having already demonstrated the breadth of his own musical vision, he was saying, *Yes, we can do that thing, too.*

"I fell in love with jazz, straightahead jazz, at a very young age," Hill says:

> and that sound, that quintet sound, that acoustic bass/ride-cymbal jazz sound, it's always in me, but again, I was born in the '80s, on the South Side of Chicago. I have that influence of hip-hop and the current music of the day. So for me it was a natural progression to incorporate hip-hop and the sounds

> that we hear today into my music. And also, right around the time I started writing music for *Modern Flows, Vol. I,* I don't want to say something clicked, but it became clearer to me that all of these musics that I love and listen to, they're all the same. Jazz, hip-hop, rock 'n' roll, gospel, blues, it's all coming from the same tree. So for me it was easier to erase these genre boundaries in my mind and just write music, create music that I love, create music that I hear in my mind, create music that resonates with me. And now I don't need to think about, *Oh, I need to appease the jazz audience*...it's all Black American music. And for me, I would say that was a bit of a turning point. It freed me, in terms of my compositional style.

Hill's voice on the horn is subtle, but never diffident. He isn't a powerhouse showman like Christian Scott or Theo Croker, but neither does he slur and smear his notes like Ambrose Akinmusire. He's subdued but intense, frequently opting for the lushness of the trumpet's larger sibling, the flugelhorn. If I were to compare him to a player of a previous generation, it would probably be Donald Byrd — ferociously skilled, but willing to apply those skills in almost any context, always making the song the thing.

"I tell my younger students, there's nothing worse than a trumpet player who has beautiful ideas but you can't hear them," he says. And he practices what he preaches, saying that when he picks up the horn each day, "there's lots of technique involved, lots of lip slurs, lots of articulation exercises, but I'm also aware that the music is much more than that. So I kind of separate my practice into two separate entities. I practice the technique things and I also leave space to just create music." He explains something I've heard many times from jazz musicians, including the formidable pianist Cecil Taylor, who was renowned for his mastery of the keyboard and his ability to generate tidal waves of sound. According to Hill, "the goal is to practice those things and get [them] internalized so much that when it is time to step onstage and simply create, the technique is embedded in you. You don't really have to think about it."

Hill's follow-up to *The Way We Play* is easily his most surprising and unique release. In 2017, he, Williams, bassist Junius Paul and McCraven created *Meditation Tape*. From a purely musical standpoint, it's beautiful, featuring muted horn over a bed of keyboards and liquid electric bass that nods to quiet storm R&B. Hill overdubs multiple trumpet voices on tracks, harmonizing with himself. The most surprising aspects, though, are spoken word interludes, most of them of a philosophical and even cosmological bent. These are provided by drummer Marvin "Bugalu" Smith, a legendary player who worked with Archie Shepp and Sun Ra along with numerous other notable figures in jazz, soul, funk and Latin music.

Hill met Smith almost by chance. "I was looking for a place," the trumpeter recalls:

> I moved into a place and Marvin was one of the roommates in the place. So we bonded and connected instantly. Every morning over breakfast, we would just sit and conversate, and he would go into deep thought and meditation and have these deep conversations...and I started to think each morning, *I should start recording this, this is some pretty heavy stuff that's coming out of this man's mouth*. He's experienced, he's been around and played with some of the legends, he's got a lot of life in him and a lot of knowledge, so I started to record these conversations over breakfast and I started to hear music, so I started to compose around these interviews and chop the interviews up...the project just kind of formed really organically.

Hill's go-to rhythm section of Junius Paul and Makaya

McCraven serve his music brilliantly, whether they're pumping out explosive, nearly frantic swing onstage or settling into a smooth R&B groove on record. As leaders, though, they're more associated with the avant-garde and the jazz underground than Hill is, so I was curious whether he saw them as occupying different cultural spaces than himself — and, secondarily, whether he was reaching the audience he wanted to reach.

"The label they're associated with [International Anthem] is more in that scene, so their music and their vision and the way critics see them is gonna be more through that lens," he acknowledged. But when it comes to his own path, he said simply, "I kinda lean on the spiritual thing. I think my music is reaching exactly the people that it's supposed to reach. And expanding more and more...I think us humans, we discover things when we're supposed to discover them, so the people that haven't discovered my music or my impact, I think they will when it's the right time. As an artist, it's my job to continue to explore my art and try to create music that will touch people and heal people, and just put it out into the world, and I think the people that it's meant to connect with, it will."

Essential Listening

Ernest Dawkins' New Horizon Ensemble, *The Prairie Prophet* (Delmark, 2011)

Marquis Hill, *Modern Flows Vol. I* (Black Unlimited Music Group, 2014)

Marquis Hill, *The Way We Play* (Concord Jazz, 2016)

Marquis Hill, *Meditation Tape* (Black Unlimited Music Group, 2017)

Marquis Hill, *Modern Flows Vol. II* (Black Unlimited Music Group, 2018)

Junius Paul, *Ism* (International Anthem, 2019)

Marquis Hill, *Love Tape* (Black Unlimited Music Group, 2019)

PART V

Jaimie Branch; James Brandon Lewis; Matana Roberts; Kassa Overall; Moor Mother; Luke Stewart

Introduction

Let's return to the writer Frank Kogan's concept of Superwords. As I wrote in the introduction to the second section of this book, the two he picked as paradigmatic were "punk" and "metal," words that can be taken as an identity ("I'm a punk") or used as a dismissal ("That's not metal"). And as I said, "jazz" is just as powerful a Superword. In this final section, I'm going to talk about a group of artists who exist mostly separate of one another, and who don't play by the (unwritten) rules of the jazz scene.

These artists have ideas that can't be contained by traditional notions of what is and isn't jazz. This puts them in the company of the composer-performers in the second section of this book, to a degree. But unlike those artists, there's something a little darker, a little angrier, a little more...*punk* about what Jaimie Branch, James Brandon Lewis, Matana Roberts, Kassa Overall, Moor Mother and Luke Stewart (and the other members of Irreversible Entanglements) are doing.

These are musicians who have little interest in gentility or decorum. They're in your face, whether playing in the streets of New York or in art museums. They are confrontational, in the best way, because the issues their art grapples with are some of the most divisive and painful in contemporary American life.

Matana Roberts' ongoing *Coin Coin* series is a massive patchwork quilt of a narrative about her family's history through slavery and Jim Crow and (presumably) up to the present day, which is no picnic itself. Her live performances, meanwhile, can be even more immediately personal, and all the more intimate for being presented solo. Jaimie Branch's *Fly or Die II: Bird Dogs of Paradise* begins with "Prayer for Amerikkka," on which she sings about systemic racism, homegrown fascism and how it all affects American citizens and immigrants alike.

James Brandon Lewis' *Days of FreeMan* and Kassa Overall's *I Think I'm Good* are autobiographical in very different ways, the former cautiously positive and the latter exploring deep and painful emotional issues, but ending on a more hopeful note than might be expected. And Moor Mother's poetry, whether in or outside the context of Irreversible Entanglements, erupts like jets of flame. Her voice is a weapon, and her lyrics are so intense, her delivery so raw and forceful, that you want to shrink away at times. It's too much to take. And the music matches her; they're not "her band," they're a free jazz ensemble with her as a fifth member.

All the music discussed in this section is both demanding and cathartic. It demands to be accepted on its own terms, and respects no sonic boundaries. Some of Lewis' compositions are raw funk grooves, while others are deep, spiritual free jazz and still others are almost hard rock. Moor Mother plays jazz but also creates searing electronic noisescapes. Roberts' albums juxtapose screaming saxophone with dense sonic collages, operatic vocals and string band music. Overall's music borrows from hip-hop, but his compositional strategies are too abstract for almost any MC to hang with...and when he gets behind the kit, he can swing as hard as any drummer around.

Work this earnest, this insistent, finds audiences that will meet it on its terms, and that's exactly what has happened with these artists. They are not the kind of performers who can be presented at the Blue Note or the Jazz Standard, playing tunes as waitresses deliver plates of chicken and ribs to the customers. Their work demands focused attention, so they play art museums, or avant-garde festivals, or theaters, or clubs where the audience is truly there to listen, and engage and be engaged with.

Jaimie Branch: Sometimes I Edit Myself

As you head downtown toward the southern tip of New York City, the numbered, gridded blocks of Midtown fade away, replaced by a maze of narrow, angled, barely-designated streets left over from the horse-and-carriage era. Tucked in between ancient tenements and blind alleys, you never know what you'll find. One warm, sunny afternoon in that blurry zone between late summer and the beginning of autumn, I let my phone's screen lead me to a small empty space between buildings on the Lower East Side. The city had designated it a park, though there was barely a blade of grass to be seen, never mind a tree.

A group of musicians had gathered there to celebrate the lives of trumpeter Roy Campbell Jr., who died in 2014, and poet Steve Dalachinsky, who had died suddenly less than a week earlier, on September 16, 2019. The two men had shared a birthday, September 29. The audience included a few of the old men who have always haunted free jazz shows in this part of the city, and have always been old, but there were many people who looked to be in their twenties and thirties, and several had brought small children.

The third ensemble to perform was a trio led by trumpeter Jaimie Branch, with bassist Luke Stewart and drummer Mike Pride. They were introduced by Patricia Nicholson, a dancer and choreographer and the head of Arts For Art, the organization which had put on the event. Branch murmured a few words about Campbell and Dalachinsky into the microphone, then lifted the horn and played a sharp, fanfare-like melody. Stewart and Pride immediately fell in behind her, swinging loosely while leaving room for frequent rattling outbursts from the drums.

Branch's sound filled the late summer air. She pointed the horn at the sky and emitted short, telegraphic phrases that ended in long, keening notes that wavered and threatened to slide out of tune but always came back around. The trio played a single 35-minute improvised piece, and when Stewart and Pride were soloing, Branch's fingers continued to dance across the trumpet's keys, exploring combinations of notes that she ultimately chose not to blow. By the end, the music had solidified into a bluesy, parade-like groove that felt like it could go on all day, and a number of people who were just walking by had stopped to listen.

Jaimie Branch's work is based in free jazz, a genre with limited crossover appeal, but somehow she's found a way to pull in audiences that would normally ignore music of this degree of rawness and power. After a decade on the scene in Chicago, forming short-lived groups with friends and appearing as a sideman on their albums in turn, she moved to New York and in 2016 assembled a quartet for a monthly performance series in Brooklyn. That group included cellist Tomeka Reid, bassist Jason Ajemian and drummer Chad Taylor, all fellow transplants.

The music was totally improvised at first, but within a few months of semi-regular performances, Branch had developed a clutch of melodic themes which formed the core of her debut album, 2017's *Fly or Die*. Recorded in a day in her sister's apartment, then blended with live takes from the Manhattan club Le Poisson Rouge and acoustic guitar overdubs and additional cornets, the album combined the deep African blues of Julius Hemphill's *Dogon A.D.* with cloudy three-horn passages that recalled the work of Bill Dixon. Ultimately, though, it showed that Jaimie Branch's ideas were entirely her own. Nobody was doing anything that sounded at all like *Fly or Die*, and the album swept many critics' polls, even winning recognition from non-jazz websites like Pitchfork and Stereogum.

Fly or Die II: Bird Dogs of Paradise, released in 2019, was both a sequel and an expansion of its predecessor's musical concepts. Tomeka Reid had been replaced by fellow cellist Lester St. Louis, but Ajemian and Taylor remained, and many of the pieces were structurally similar: vamping themes which the rhythm section stretched and expanded, as Branch soloed or stepped away entirely.

The music was recorded in November 2018, at the end of a European tour. Branch and her band performed for two nights at London's Café OTO, followed by a day of recording and a day of overdubs at Total Refreshment Centre. "I had the recording date before I had the music finished," she told me by phone, a week or two after the trio performance.

> I've been composing and performing for a long time, so writing a set of music is not a new prospect for me, but getting the music that you eventually want to put out, that's a slightly different process. A couple of the tunes had been worked up, but most of them they didn't see until the day before the OTO sets. I wrote out these scores that I gave to everybody that had a lot of information that they had never seen before. And part of the reason for that is a, I write very simple music as far as learning to play and internalizing it, and b, I wanted a fresh take on the issue.

The album flowed like a continuous suite. For example, "Twenty-three n Me, Jupiter Redux," a piece that combined furious free jazz blowing with throbbing synths that nodded to Branch's electronic project Anteloper, led directly into "Whales," a 65-second Ajemian/St. Louis duo that really did sound like whales singing to each other underwater, which became the lilting, almost West African "Simple Silver Surfer."

At the beginning and end of the album, we heard the band live. "Birds of Paradise" and "Nuevo Roquero Estéreo" were taken directly from Café OTO, and though the crowd's enthusiasm gave the music a jolt of energy, that was a secondary consideration at best, according to Branch, who studied audio engineering at Maryland's Towson University and edits her albums herself, in partnership with engineer David Vettraino.

> I'm not putting the track on because you can hear the audience, I'm putting it on because that's the best version we got of that tune. It's not like I'm setting out to have this mix of things, it's just that I'm setting out to capture the best playing that we got going on, and so last time and this time I used both studio and live stuff.

Branch experimented with color as a compositional tool on *Fly or Die II*. "Everybody basically got a flow chart of the way the whole suite of music runs, the whole album, and there are some chord changes in there, some progressions, there are some rhythmic figures written out, but most of the things are instructions," she explained.

> And then when I need something to be notated, I might have an addendum sheet. The last [album], I used traditional notation and scores as well, but this time I didn't — instead, I brought in the use of color, to see what that would do. Can people learn things faster if they're thinking of a section as yellow, or up next is blue? What kind of subconscious things does that do to a musician as you're learning the charts?

There were two other major changes between the first and second albums. One was the replacement of Reid, an artist with a busy career of her own, with St. Louis, a young phenomenon who picked up the cello as a teenager and is a decade younger than anyone else in the band. "Lester, like Tomeka, is a super talented cellist, so anything I throw at him he's gonna be able to dig," Branch said. She took advantage of his skills and imagination when putting the music together:

> I gave him a lot of soloistic space, and I don't know if that has a lot to do with his personality but it definitely has a lot to do with his cello sound. I just know that he can carry

it, whatever it is. He's also super fun — we get along really well, and the hookup he has with Jason is fantastic.

The final change was Branch's decision to sing on two tracks, "Prayer For Amerikkka Pt. 1 & 2" and "Love Song." The latter was a simple vamp over which she chanted "this is a love song, for assholes and clowns" like a mantra, but the former was the most ambitious piece of music she'd released to that point. The first section was a slow, free blues, somewhere between Hemphill and Archie Shepp. Ajemian strummed his bass, then slapped its body in time with Taylor's ominously ticking drums. St. Louis plucked the cello's strings like a guitarist, and Branch's horn emitted piercing cries through a mute. Eventually, she began to murmur, "This is a prayer for America/For the good, the bad, and the rest of ya" as Ben LaMar Gay and Marvin Tate moaned behind her like a ghostly chorus.

She recited a poem about racism, gentrification and capitalist exploitation, while the two men had a conversation behind her about what it meant for them that their city was changing. Seven minutes into the 12-minute piece, though, the tempo doubled, and Branch began singing a different song, telling the story of a refugee from Central America coming to the US, only to be separated from her family and victimized by the government. "This is a warning, honey/They're coming for you," she sang, and her trumpet playing took on an entirely different character, abandoning free jazz for a rippling, brassy tone reminiscent of mariachi music.

Branch said incorporating lyrics and vocals into her work was just "the way the music was headed, you know?" The bluesy first section of "Prayer for Amerikkka" first began to take shape at a live show, and gestated for several weeks on tour, while "Love Song" was "an old song I was trying for the first time with this group. Those lyrics were already written."

The dramatic, narrative-driven, even sardonic tone of

"Prayer for Amerikkka" brings to mind the work of Charles Mingus, as well as Max Roach's *We Insist!* "One of my favorite tunes probably of all time is the *Charles Mingus Presents Charles Mingus* version of 'Fables of Faubus,'" Branch said, "but I wasn't thinking about that super consciously. But it's definitely in my listening bones, you know?"

The second half of the piece was particularly challenging for her. The inspiration came from her mother, who is a social worker in her former hometown of Chicago. "The second half is about a woman she was helping," she said; "it was her daughter, and it was happening while I was working on the record. I felt like that story was important to tell, but also keeping it vague enough because it's so many other people's stories also."

Branch was born in New York, and took up the trumpet at 9. It turned out to be something of a family tradition. "I didn't know both my brothers played the trumpet – they're my half-brothers, and we lived in different houses – and my dad played the trumpet when he was a kid, so as soon as I started playing I learned about this whole family history with it." Her family moved to the Illinois suburb of Wilmette when she was 14, and after high school she attended the New England Conservatory in Boston, then returned to Chicago to find her place within that city's avant-garde jazz scene.

There, she worked at the legendary Jazz Record Mart and forged a number of important friendships with up-and-coming players like cornetist Josh Berman, saxophonist Keefe Jackson, vibraphonist Jason Adasiewicz and drummer Frank Rosaly. Throughout the early to mid-2000s, Branch played on albums led by Jackson, Jason Ajemian, cellist Fred Lonberg-Holm and others, and formed a few groups of her own, including the trio Princess, Princess (with Toby Summerfield on bass and Rosaly on drums) and the septet Musket, which added Ajemian, Lonberg-Holm, baritone guitarist John Paul Glover and second drummer Theo Katsounis. She released music by both ensembles on her own Pionic label.

Branch's command of the trumpet is astonishing. She can be as fierce as Donald Ayler or as introspective as Bill Dixon, and can move beyond notes entirely, into the zone of pure sound inhabited by players like Axel Dörner. And watching her play is fascinating. She tilts the horn skyward, often avoiding the microphone in favor of naked power, and taps the valves almost frantically when not blowing.

"I'm a short person, and if I'm pointing the horn at the ground, good luck," she joked, but there's more to it than that. "The acoustic sound of the trumpet is very different than a mic sound. I like to exist in both spaces." And the phantom notes? "Some of it is editing. I could be playing all of this shit right now but I'm not, so I physically take my head away from the mouthpiece. I'm listening all the time, and I want to be making strong decisions, so sometimes I edit myself."

These days, in addition to leading her trio and quartet, she performs with saxophonist James Brandon Lewis, in a group which also features his regular rhythm section of bassist Luke Stewart and drummer Warren Crudup, and a guitarist (either Anthony Pirog or, on a recent tour, Ava Mendoza). This quintet, with Pirog, made Lewis's most recent album, *An UnRuly Manifesto*, a kind of free funk disc somewhat indebted to Ornette Coleman's Prime Time. "James's trio exists within the quintet, so that's a really cool dynamic...this tight-knit group and kind of two outliers," she said.

Lewis, Branch, Stewart and Crudup joined forces with post-rock trio Harriet Tubman and alto saxophonist Darius Jones to re-imagine Ornette Coleman's piece "Free Jazz" at the 2018 Winter Jazzfest in New York.

"Harriet Tubman, the trio unit, has been playing so long together that we basically did horn rehearsals with Melvin [Gibbs, bassist]," she recalled. "So it was me, Darius and James sitting down with Melvin and working out what the horn arrangements would be, and then we did the gig." The performance was remarkably egalitarian; the three horns seemed to be conducting it, playing the Coleman fanfare in order to signal the end of one solo and the beginning of the next. "It was really a beautiful concept that Melvin wanted to stick to of people really sharing the space," she said. "So we're not gonna do a 15-minute tenor solo and a two-minute trumpet solo and an eight-minute guitar solo...I don't remember exactly what the increment was, but I do remember feeling that it was really cool that the space was going to be shared evenly."

For years, Branch's style has stuck out on the free jazz scene. She's always favored baseball caps, tracksuits and athletic jerseys onstage, but lately she's begun wearing flowing, multicolored robes. "It's a feeling of putting on a robe for this performance, like a boxer puts on a robe to go out and box," she said:

> It's a different dynamic, and I'm exploring that right now. It's part of the way I want to feel when I'm performing. It's also part of getting to that other part of your brain that you need to feel wide open while performing, that is maybe otherwise shut off a little when dealing with the day to day, because it has to be or we'd all be these crazy little sensitive orbs on the floor, crying all the time.

Essential Listening

Jason Ajemian, *The Art of Dying* (Delmark, 2008)
Jaimie Branch, *Fly or Die* (International Anthem, 2017)
Anteloper, *Kudu* (International Anthem, 2018)
Jaimie Branch, *Fly or Die II: Bird Dogs of Paradise* (International Anthem, 2019)
Jeremy Cunningham, *The Weather Up There* (Northern Spy, 2020)

James Brandon Lewis: It Just Depends

The Cell Theatre is a small venue on 23rd Street in Manhattan that typically plays host to plays and other theatrical or multimedia events. The only time I ever went there was on a Wednesday evening in January 2017 to see a triple bill featuring saxophonist James Brandon Lewis's trio, augmented by guitarist Anthony Pirog; an eight-piece band led by soprano saxophonist Rob Reddy; and the post-rock trio Harriet Tubman.

Tubman, a three-way collaboration between guitarist Brandon Ross, bassist Melvin Gibbs and drummer JT Lewis, have been around since the late 1990s. Their music seemed to emerge fully formed on their 1998 debut, *I Am a Man*; it blended blues, dub, funk and art-metal into swirling storms that never quite exploded. They wouldn't make another studio album for almost 20 years; *Araminta*, a collaboration with trumpeter Wadada Leo Smith, appeared in 2017. His mournful, reverbed cries blended seamlessly with the band's moody shuffles and thunderous grooves. Smith wasn't at the Cell Theatre show, though.

Lewis's quartet was up first, celebrating their then-upcoming album *No Filter*. (It would be released that June.) Though he'd been working with bassist Luke Stewart and drummer Warren Trae Crudup III live for several years, the disc was their recorded debut as a unit. Stewart played an electric instrument, rolling out bouncing lines atop Crudup's sharp, insistent drumming. Together, they brought to mind Ornette Coleman's abstract funk band, Prime Time. Pirog, meanwhile, was more interested in creating textures than soloing in the normal sense of that word. Lewis, up front, played with bluster and force, his thick, insistent lines reminiscent of Sonny Rollins in the 1970s, when he was blending jazz with funk and even rock on albums like *Horn Culture*, *Nucleus* and *The Cutting Edge*.

At the time, the show just seemed like a particularly well-chosen bill. (The middle group was a commissioned work by soprano saxophonist Rob Reddy, paying tribute to one of the legends of that instrument, Sidney Bechet; the ensemble included violinist Charlie Burnham, guitarist Marvin Sewell and drummer Pheeroan akLaff, among others. It was interesting, but felt out of place.) But Tubman and Lewis's group would play together again at Le Poisson Rouge at the end of May, and the following year, at Winter Jazzfest 2018, they would join forces for a unique and thrilling concert.

The two trios became a sextet, which then became an octet with the addition of alto saxophonist Darius Jones and trumpeter Jaimie Branch, to perform an interpretation of Ornette Coleman's classic 1961 piece "Free Jazz." As Gibbs explained in a brief introduction, "last year, the universe decided to care" about Tubman, with *Araminta* landing on multiple year-end lists. So they were taking advantage of the moment and doing the kind of once-in-a-lifetime event that makes jazz truly special. Later that year, Gibbs told me, "That traditionally was part of it — if you weren't there, you missed it...I have friends who still talk about gigs that I played that you ain't never gonna hear."

The original version of "Free Jazz," which was recorded in the studio but never performed live, was created by a double quartet. In the left stereo channel, Ornette played alto, Don Cherry played pocket trumpet, Scott Lafaro played bass and Billy Higgins played drums. In the right channel, Eric Dolphy was on bass clarinet, Freddie Hubbard on trumpet, Charlie Haden on bass and Ed Blackwell on drums. After a brief but raucous fanfare by the whole ensemble, each member got a solo (Dolphy, Hubbard, Coleman, Cherry, Haden, LaFaro, Blackwell, Higgins) with other players commenting as they went, and the original theme serving as a bridge between solos.

The Tubman-led version used more or less the same structure, with Branch soloing first, followed by Lewis, Jones, Gibbs, Ross,

Stewart, Crudup and finally JT Lewis. Watching it all happen was fascinating, because the horns — and Branch in particular — seemed to be conducting the whole thing. When she decided it was time, she'd murmur something to Jones, standing to her right, and they'd step up to the microphones and blare out that high-energy fanfare, as if to say, "All right, that's enough out of you — next!"

Everyone played in a relatively "free" mode. Branch and the saxophonists came off hard and fierce; Gibbs used an array of pedals to create a doomy sound reminiscent of his early 90s work with alternative metal group the Rollins Band; Stewart took an almost noise-rock approach to his attack on his upright bass; Ross shredded harder than he usually did with Tubman, going for out-rock fervor rather than arty clouds of sound; and Crudup's drum solo was positively apocalyptic. Consequently, JT Lewis's decision to follow the younger man with a series of delicate taps on cymbals and snare rim — he got louder eventually, of course — felt smart, and attention-getting.

James Brandon Lewis's career as a leader has taken him down a variety of paths. Born in Buffalo, New York in 1983, he studied at Howard University and later at Cal Arts in Los Angeles, ultimately moving to New York City in 2012. His first album, 2010's *Moments*, was self-released and featured a piano-guitar-bass-drums quintet, plus a harpist on one track. His playing felt freighted with a youthful desire to convey significance, most obviously on its opening track, "Reflection." He seemed to be aiming for John Coltrane circa 1963-64, but came closer to Joshua Redman circa 1994 (still not a bad place to be).

He signed with OKeh and made two albums. The first, *Divine Travels*, was released in 2014. On it, he was backed by bassist William Parker and drummer Gerald Cleaver, but he opened the record solo, worrying at and eventually wandering from a short foundational phrase as Parker's bass throbbed intermittently behind him, not so much setting up a groove as providing a counterweight to the saxophone's explorations. The second track, "Desensitized," took a similar approach, albeit at greater speed, with Cleaver playing a sort of shuffling free time. Throughout the album, the drums were assertive but soft, never truly erupting, and Parker served as both anchor and pivot point, balancing while driving the music forward. Lewis's long phrases were knotted and obsessive enough that without the bassist there, he might seem to be floating in space, legs pinwheeling madly like Wile E. Coyote after running off a cliff.

His next release, 2015's *Days of FreeMan*, found him backed by electric bassist Jamaaladeen Tacuma, a veteran of Prime Time, and drummer Rudy Royston. The music was inspired by late 80s/early 90s hip-hop, and by Lewis's upbringing in Buffalo (his grandmother narrated several interludes sprinkled throughout the 19-track disc), but avoided programmed beats and samples. Instead, he seemed to be channeling the head-nodding feel and thoughtful lyricism of A Tribe Called Quest or the Jungle Brothers, without consciously imitating their sound. As the bass and drums looped and loped, he ducked sideways, bobbing and weaving, finding places to wander and explore, floating atop the groove like an MC.

I spoke to Lewis by phone in late spring 2020; he was far from New York, hiding from the coronavirus with family. I had written down many questions about his discography and career, but our conversation went almost immediately off the traditional "interview" track and into a broader, deeper discussion of the disappearance of historical knowledge, the polemical value of instrumental music, the generational impact of large-scale social phenomena, and many other subjects. But he also seemed eager to dispel misapprehensions about his work.

"When I think about *Divine Travels*, or before that *Moments*, you hear many different styles, many different ranges," he said:

When I'm playing with Luke and Trae, that's a specific kind

> of thing...there's a specific hip-hop influence, and funk, so yeah, there's some riffs, but then if you listen to me playing with William and Gerald on *Divine Travels*, none of that's riffs, all of that is within the jazz tradition language. Then you fast-forward and I made *Days of FreeMan* with Jamaaladeen Tacuma and Rudy Royston, and all of those compositions were written out, thoroughly thought-out...so then after that, after the Sony situation, I wanted to come with something that was in your face.

He mentioned having read pianist Hampton Hawes' 1975 autobiography *Raise Up Off Me* around that time, and indeed there's a track on *No Filter* by that title. He also cited a slew of musicians from Buffalo, including fellow saxophonists Charles Gayle and Grover Washington Jr., who might seem to be polar opposites — hardcore, unfettered free jazz on the one hand, and R&B-laced smooth jazz on the other. But to Lewis, they're both part of the same picture.

> I know the lineage of players, I borrow things from different people. When I think about the low register, I think about Dexter Gordon; when I think about high-register screaming sounds, I think about Coltrane; when I think about a mellow, dark sound, I think about Wayne Shorter; when I think about going off the overtones and fundamentals, I think about Charles Gayle or Frank Lowe, Frank Wright...it just depends.

Some of his most explicit nods to predecessors have come on two duo albums with drummer Chad Taylor, 2018's *Radiant Imprints* and 2020's *Live in Willisau*. On the former, a studio album, the track "With Sorrow Lonnie" is a reimagining of "Lonnie's Lament," from John Coltrane's 1964 album *Crescent*. On it, Taylor plays a mbira (a small African thumb piano) while Lewis murmurs soft, mournful lines. At other times, the interplay between the two men is titanic, and the saxophonist is happy to stand back periodically and let the drummer rampage all over the kit.

Live in Willisau is even more keenly aware of history. The Willisau Jazz Festival in Switzerland has been the site of many amazing avant-garde jazz performances, including some notable sax-drums duos. Archie Shepp and Max Roach recorded *The Long March* there in 1979, and Dewey Redman and Ed Blackwell recorded *Black & Red* there a year later. Lewis and Taylor knew, when their tour in support of *Radiant Imprints* took them to Willisau, that they would have to reckon with that history. They did so in part by performing a version of "Willisee," the opening track from *Black & Red*. Their take was a rip-roaring, stomping free jazz eruption, with a lot of blues at its core. Taylor slammed the kit like he was trying to demolish it, while Lewis went out into zones typically occupied by Fred Anderson or David Murray. They also performed a version of the gospel song "Come Sunday" and closed with a version of "Over the Rainbow" that brought to mind free jazz drummer Sunny Murray's interpretation of that tune, which featured David Murray on tenor and Byard Lancaster on alto sax, plus vibraphonist Khan Jamal and bassist Fred Hopkins. (It's on *Wildflowers*, the five-volume set of live LPs released in 1977.)

Lewis collaborated with Taylor again in 2020, recording *Molecular*, a quartet studio session that featured Aruán Ortiz on piano and Brad Jones on bass. It was extremely muscular music, at times recalling 1990s albums by David Murray or even David S Ware. Lewis's playing throughout was rooted in strong, anthemic melodies, but worked its way over and over to an unrelenting pitch, striving for freedom like an eagle with one leg chained to a post. Taylor was in a hard-driving mode, slamming out the rhythm, and Ortiz's playing was full of flourishes and rippling waves of notes, while Jones served as the anchor, a throbbing pulse at the center of the music.

Once upon a time, David Murray was seen by some prominent critics as a man for all seasons. He could play in trios or quartets, lead a big band, experiment with Latin or West Indian music and juxtapose reverent treatment of standards with the wildest of free jazz blowouts. Lewis, a player with equally wide-open ears, a massive sound and a voracious appetite for collaboration, seems ready to assume that mantle in the twenty-first century.

Essential Listening

James Brandon Lewis, *Divine Travels* (OKeh, 2014)
James Brandon Lewis, *Days of FreeMan* (OKeh, 2015)
James Brandon Lewis, *No Filter* (Independent/Self-Released, 2017)
James Brandon Lewis/Chad Taylor, *Radiant Imprints* (Off, 2018)
James Brandon Lewis, *An UnRuly Manifesto* (Relative Pitch, 2019)
James Brandon Lewis/Chad Taylor, *Live in Willisau* (Intakt, 2020)
James Brandon Lewis Quartet, *Molecular* (Intakt, 2020)

Matana Roberts: Child of the Wind

The first time I saw Matana Roberts perform, I didn't know who she was. It was Thursday, May 27, 2004, and I was at a venue on Mulberry Street in downtown Manhattan simply known as the Center for the ninth annual Vision Festival. I was there to see Burnt Sugar the Arkestra Chamber, a large ensemble (membership and size varied from recording to recording, gig to gig) run by critic and musician Greg Tate and bassist Jared Nickerson. Burnt Sugar's methodology involves conducted improvisation led by Tate, inspired by and modeled after the work of the late Lawrence "Butch" Morris. Their work treats all of the music and methodologies of the African diaspora as a vast river into which they dip at will; there are elements of rock, jazz, funk, soul, hip-hop, modern composition and pure sound art, and at its best it's transportive, even transcendent.

That evening, they performed a single nearly 50-minute piece that featured at least two guitarists, two and possibly three bassists (some acoustic, some electric), three drummers, violin, cello, alto sax, flute, synth and several vocalists. It began with simmering strings over a patiently building rhythm, with a male singer uttering a kind of post-soul incantation up front. After about 10 minutes, it shifted into a strutting, Isaac Hayes-esque funk zone, with the alto saxophonist — Roberts — murmuring strong, free phrases as the guitars and keys vamped.

Seven years later, I interviewed her for *The Wire*. After several conventional "free jazz" albums, under her own name and as a member of the trio Sticks and Stones, she had just released the first in what was to become an ongoing series of albums (four volumes have been released, of a planned twelve).

The *Coin Coin* project is a chronicle of her family's history through slavery and Jim Crow, presumably up to the present day. The music on the first disc, subtitled *Gens de Couleur Libres*, was performed live in Montreal with a 16-member ensemble that included four horns, two violins, piano, two basses, drums, doudouk (an Armenian flute made of apricot wood), prepared electric guitar and musical saw. It wasn't a big band album, though; the ensemble was rarely heard all together at once. The music had a pulsing rhythm, surging and receding like the tide, and the horns had the sardonic quality of mid-60s Charles Mingus, seeming to comment bitterly, like a disillusioned Greek chorus, as Roberts and second vocalist Gitanjali Jain recited poetic lyrics about slavery, liberation, migration and more, a history written in blood and corpses.

"The text on [Chapter One] is a text that I created myself, imagining myself as a slave woman and telling this story," Roberts told me:

> And I've tweaked it over the last four or five years, I've changed some things. I used to do theater, I did theater in Chicago, God, mid-90s, early 90s, and one play I was involved with more on the musical side, not the poetry side, though, was Ntozake Shange's *for colored girls who have considered suicide when the rainbow is enuf*. And I got to sit and listen to that poetry — I think that show ran for 6 months at the Steppenwolf Theater...and the way it infused me was really, really powerful. And I wanted to figure out a way to do that with my own work. So the words that you hear, I'm speaking by memory and trying to infuse them and trying to become. The second chapter of *Coin Coin*, that text is actually an interview I did with my 80-year-old, paternal, Mississippi-born grandmother, where you hear her answers but not my questions, and I read it like prose.

Coin Coin Chapter Two: Mississippi Moonchile was released in 2013. It was recorded in a studio, with a small ensemble: trumpet, piano, bass, drums and a male operatic tenor vocalist.

Roberts recited her grandmother's words, while the male singer, Jeremiah Abiah, sang lyrics by the composer Joseph D. Howard. Her biting, earthy saxophone was shadowed and countered by Jason Palmer's virtuosic yet blues-drenched lines, as pianist Shoko Nagai, bassist Thomson Kneeland and drummer Tomas Fujiwara laid down a loose, bouncing backdrop.

The second time I saw Matana Roberts live was at the Whitney Museum in New York. An exhibition called *Blues for Smoke* had been running since February, exploring contemporary art through a filter of the blues. Some of the pieces had an extraordinary power, like Melvin Edwards' sculpture made from a steel cuff and chain welded together and given the multilayered, gut-punching title *Write When You Can*. Throughout the run, there were lectures and workshops, musical performances and poetry readings. Roberts was one of three performers on Saturday, April 20, 2013; the other two were Loren Mazzacane Connors and Keiji Haino.

Connors is a guitarist whose work is derived from blues and Celtic folk, but pushed through such a dense cloud of reverb and sustain that it becomes a kind of shimmering, dark atmosphere. Haino, too, works in darkness; he wears all black, never removes his sunglasses and often plays a kind of improvised psychedelic rock at extraordinary volume, sometimes on solo guitar and sometimes with bands, most notably his long-running trio Fushitsusha. He also makes more droning, meditative music on the hurdy-gurdy, a violin-like instrument played by turning a crank, which rubs a wheel against the strings. He deployed the latter at the Whitney, moaning and unspooling long rippling tones. Roberts performed on solo alto saxophone, with some visual elements (lights, projections); it wasn't an elaborate multimedia spectacle, but it was more than a mere avant-jazz recital. She struck an imposing figure, tall and tattooed with almost military clothing, and while she was friendly with the small audience, mingling before performing rather than lurking in a back room (as Haino did), there was a perceptible distance that one could almost, but not quite, reach across.

Coin Coin Chapter Three: River Run Thee was released in 2015. It reflected Roberts' increased interest in solo performance; although it was broken into 12 tracks for listener convenience, it was a single 45-minute work. And while she was the only person making the sounds, it was very far from a "solo album" in the way jazz listeners are accustomed to using that descriptor. The first track, "All is Written," laid out what was to come. She sang, recited texts, played saxophone and created background drones with loop pedals and field recordings, giving the piece the feeling of having been recorded outdoors. At times, there were as many as five Matana Robertses existing simultaneously in the immersive sonic world she had created: two were playing saxophones, but separately, as though passing each other in dark woods unaware and unable to connect, while two more recited texts that, again, did not match, and a third sang ominous lyrics in a soft voice that occasionally cracked at the end of a phrase.

Roberts had adopted the phrase "panoramic sound quilting" to describe her methodology and her art, and it was more accurate than ever on *River Run Thee*. The layers were impossible to separate; individual sounds (a baby crying, what could be footsteps on gravel, the thick hum of a harmonium, and always, always, the multiple voices, singing and talking and howling as the saxophone emitted fierce cries and sharp-edged runs). Heard on headphones, it was almost like going insane. It was sensory overload, too much to pick apart or summarize as a single thing with one central message. She seemed to simply want you to live in her head for a while, to experience what that was like.

The third time I saw Matana Roberts live was at Le Poisson Rouge in 2017. She was opening for the Norwegian improvising trio Supersilent, who were playing in the US for the first time since 2004 (and since losing their fourth member, drummer

Jarle Vespestad). It was a very stripped-down show, much different from the Whitney Museum appearance. There were no loop pedals or video projections; she simply stood near the lip of the stage, somewhat off center because of the amount of equipment Supersilent had laid out, with her saxophone and two microphones. In between passages on the horn, she delivered extended and surprisingly personal monologues. She talked about the deaths of her parents and how it had affected her and brought home even more strongly the importance of documenting her family's history through the *Coin Coin* project. She talked about how her father had gotten her into avant-garde jazz through his own enthusiasm for it, even though she hated it as a child. She also engaged even more directly with the audience, roping us into the performance. She asked us all to hum, demonstrating at first until we were all more or less together. When she had us "tuned up," she conducted us with one arm, asking us to hum higher or lower pitches as she played sax lines that harmonized with us.

Two years later, and five years after its predecessor, the fourth volume in the *Coin Coin* series, *Memphis*, arrived. The cover photo was a mugshot of her grandmother. For the recording, she was joined by an entirely new cohort of musicians: Hannah Marcus on guitar, fiddle and accordion; Sam Shalabi on electric guitar and oud; Nicolas Caloia on bass and Ryan Sawyer on drums, vibraphone, jaw harp and bells. Guests appeared on a few tracks: trombonist Steve Swell, vibraphonist Ryan White and singers Thierry Amar, Nadia Moss and Jessica Moss.

As with *River Run Thee*, the tracks on *Memphis* all blurred together, creating a single hour-long work. But given the collective personnel and their backgrounds — Shalabi came from the Montreal psychedelic rock scene, and Sawyer had played with former Sonic Youth guitarist Thurston Moore and free improv trumpeter Nate Wooley, among others — it was, unsurprisingly, the most aggressive album in the *Coin Coin* series. On the nearly 10-minute "Trail of the Smiling Sphinx," the combination of Marcus's fierce fiddle and Roberts' squalling saxophone, backed by Caloia's thunderous bass, had all the fire and fury of Albert Ayler's mid-60s band with violinist Michael Sampson. The energy level of the music seemed to infect Roberts when she read the texts she had written and/or assembled for the project too. One of the key passages, returned to again and again, was a diary or a transcribed memory, perhaps from Roberts' grandmother; she said, "I am a child of the wind; even Daddy said so. We used to race and I would always win. He'd say, 'Run, baby, run; run like the wind! That's it, the wind!'" She read the words in an excited voice, almost giddy, almost out of breath as though she'd been running through a field herself.

Roberts' mastery of editing and sound design was on display throughout, particularly on tracks like "Shoes of Gold," where plucked violin and bass shimmered through reverb like air coming off hot pavement as a vibraphone chimed and rang, or "Wild Fire Bare," where guitar and violin scraped as the horns flared up periodically from the background and the drums seemed to explode in a never-ending solo; it sounded like one of John Zorn's collage pieces, throwing free jazz, hillbilly music and blues into a blender and assembling the shards into something entirely new in the world.

There has never been anything in jazz with the scope of the *Coin Coin* series. Each volume fits with the others, but possesses its own unique identity; were they not titled as chapters in a series, one could easily understand each as a coherent and self-contained statement, both worthy of and requiring extended, careful listening. Her ability to play with language and rhetorical structure is on the level of a writer like Samuel Delany, and the recordings are masterfully constructed and arranged, the combinations of instruments as important as the themes; the playing and the production as detailed as a Joseph Cornell box. And onstage, she is a charming and compelling performer who draws the audience in with a combination of disarmingly personal storytelling and rough-hewn but fascinating music. Her narration of her family's journey through America mirrors her own journey out of jazz and into a multi-disciplinary dreamworld of her own creation. There's no one like her in jazz – there's no one like her in American art.

Essential Listening

Burnt Sugar the Arkestra Chamber, *If You Can't Dazzle Them With Your Brilliance, Then Baffle Them With Your Blisluth* (Trugroid, 2005)

Matana Roberts, *The Chicago Project* (Central Control International, 2007)

Matana Roberts, *Coin Coin Chapter One: Gens de Couleur Libres* (Constellation, 2011)

Matana Roberts, *Coin Coin Chapter Two: Mississippi Moonchile* (Constellation, 2013)

Matana Roberts, *Coin Coin Chapter Three: River Run Thee* (Constellation, 2015)

Matana Roberts, *Coin Coin Chapter Four: Memphis* (Constellation, 2019)

Kassa Overall: Finding Something in Everything

Musicians under 40 have grown up in an entirely different world than their elders. The most notable shift, as discussed earlier, is the omnipresence of hip-hop. Anyone who was aware of pop in the early 1980s can remember that one day there was this thing called rap music, but that was all it was at first: one thing among many. It wasn't until the late 1980s, or even the early 1990s, that it was truly everywhere. First it began to seem like an R&B song couldn't be a hit without a guest rapper. Then the rappers started having hit singles with R&B singers on the choruses. Then R&B and soul began to abandon the urbane, nightclub feeling that had marked the genre for decades, embracing the look — and the lyrical vocabulary — of the streets. Many decried this shift, but it was inexorable.

In the twenty-first century, hip-hop is pop music, and pop music is unimaginable without hip-hop. For anyone under 40, it's simply the air they breathe, the water in which they swim. Country artists rap. Pop and rock artists rap, in every country on the planet. The looping structures of hip-hop and its lack of interest in chord changes, bridges and harmonic complexity, coupled with its willingness to cannibalize any sound that might make a diverting hook, have permanently altered the practice of songwriting.

Other than Christian Scott, drummer and beat programmer Kassa Overall may be the most hip-hop-oriented musician in this book. Although he went to Oberlin College, where he befriended and worked with Theo Croker, he could just as easily have developed his style alone in his bedroom, as many of the greatest hip-hop producers have done.

"Because my brother was four years older than me," Overall told me by phone, "I heard some of the stuff I wasn't really supposed to be hearing so early." He recalled a time when his older brother asked their father for a copy of DJ Quik's *Born and Raised in Compton*.

> My dad got it for him for Kwanzaa, and the night before he gave him the tape, he listened to it...and he said, 'I listened to this tape last night, and there's a lot of stuff on here you shouldn't be listening to.' There was a lot of cussing, a lot of violence, a lot of hyper-sexual stuff, but he said, 'I'm gonna give you this tape, but remember that this is art, and this music on here is one person's experiences and it's a certain part of reality that artistically needs representation, but this guy is not a role model and this doesn't mean go out and do this stuff. But there is something to learn from people that live this life.' I remember my dad giving me that lesson early, and I think it stuck with me, because I listen to a lot of different kinds of music, with all kinds of messages, the whole positive, negative polarity, and I try to find something in everything, you know.

Both of Overall's parents were amateur musicians, and they passed their interests on to their sons:

> My brother got a drum set when he was four, and I was born, so I was trying to learn drums as soon as I could get up there on the set. I was just trying to emulate the drums from Charlie Parker to playing a one-drop rhythm from the Bob Marley records to even messing around with a few beat machines at a pretty young age. It was like I understood the idea of what was going on really early.

They were also wide-ranging listeners whose tastes ran beyond contemporary pop:

> more jazz and Indian classical music and reggae and folk and stuff. It was kind of a different bag of stuff in comparison to my friends, and because of that, the way I hear music, when something sounds too straight, rhythmically or harmonically, too down the middle, it doesn't sound right to me. For me, when I hear some of those chords that [Thelonious] Monk would play, the clusters and the parts where it sounds a little dissonant...that sounds normal [to me].

This has led Overall to blend sophisticated compositional structures with the psychedelic echo and reverb effects of dub, and leavening it all with precisely deployed crudity and what can even sound like mistakes. Like Thundercat, he often writes R&B songs that have a personal, quotidian lyrical perspective and are sung in a soft, conversational voice, but he warps them into unexpected shapes, frequently wrong-footing the listener. On "My Friend," from his 2019 album *Go Get Ice Cream and Listen to Jazz*, the beat starts out steady but begins to stutter and glitch, the sound drops out at various points, the piano is chopped up like a sample and his vocals dissolve into echo and reverb. The whole thing ends with a voice mail from a friend.

> There's certain things I do well and I try to do as good as I can and keep getting better at, and then there's certain things where I like to just throw the paint at the wall and just let it be raw and ugly, and then I spend hours putting a frame on it or coloring it in right or whatever. That's a nice balance for me.

Overall moved from Ohio to New York after graduating from Oberlin, at the invitation of trumpeter Wallace Roney. Through him, he met pianist Geri Allen, who brought him into her band and was his first strong advocate. "Wallace didn't hire me to be in his band right away — it was kind of like hang out, hang around — but Geri was like, 'You sound good; are you busy this summer?'" He spent the summer of 2007 on the road with her band in Europe, touring for the first time.

"I think she was a very understated artist, and an understated person, meaning she could play really aggressive and exciting [music], but some of the best stuff she played, if you weren't paying attention you could not notice," he told me.

> She had a real subtle quality to her playing, and even her harmonics. I'm not a really advanced harmonic person when it comes to the explanation, but I know that she could play some really outside chords or substitution chords, but it still didn't sound out. She could make out sound pretty, and had this really amorphous, cloudy quality to her playing. There was a lot of nature in her playing — things like clouds or the ocean, or rain.

It took Overall a while to learn what Allen actually needed from him:

> I feel like I didn't understand that you need different ingredients for a recipe, so when she would play she would be playing really floaty, around the time, and I kind of approached the time floaty as well, and so I would be out in floaty world with her and I realized [eventually] that she needed some of that Jimmy Cobb-like clarity in order for her to float around it. That was really hard for me to get together, because she'd be laying back behind the beat and different things and I would go with her, so the tempos would slow down a lot, and Kenny Davis, a very solid bassist, he would be like 'Kassa!' He'd be looking at me and nodding his head like, one, two, three, four, and I'm out in space with Geri. So I really had to learn how to go out in space but to keep an anchor...to get back, you know?

The final track on Overall's 2020 release *I Think I'm Good* is called "Was She Happy (for Geri Allen)," and features Vijay Iyer on synth or possibly Fender Rhodes. It's an atmospheric instrumental that sounds like the work of UNKLE or a post-rock group from the early 2000s. Electronically warped vocals moan over the simple rippling keyboard figure and slowly thumping beat, and in the piece's second half, Overall asks someone, "Was she happy?" The reply comes, "She was on a quest. She was on a journey."

I Think I'm Good is an album that deals explicitly with mental health struggles, something that became increasingly prevalent in hip-hop and R&B in the 2010s. Rappers have gone from talking about cocaine and partying to talking about antidepressants and isolation. Many of Overall's lyrics on the record center on images of confinement and even incarceration, and he told me that this came from concrete, real-life experience, but was also metaphorical:

> I went in twice to the mental hospital and spent ten days locked up, so to speak, and I guess after those experiences it feels like even though I've never been to jail, it feels like I have, and it's also kind of a metaphor because the idea of taking medication or taking anything to cool out your brain is kind of like a certain kind of confinement in itself.

He describes the periods when he was on medication — which he was not at the time we spoke, and had not been for several years — as artistically stifling. "One of the things that was frustrating was, I felt like I wasn't reaching my potential creatively. 'Man, I can't really get to it like I want to — I feel blocked.'"

He's a little suspicious of the overall trend toward expressions of psychological struggle in art, though, particularly pop music.

> I think that it kind of became a trend recently in the last

couple of years, especially in rap, and...I didn't like the fact that it felt like a put-on thing. Because if you're really dealing with that stuff, it's not something you're really proud of, you know what I mean? I don't know why it changed, but the fact that so many artists are dealing with some version or some level of mental sensitivity — it's so common. I hope we're getting to a place where you don't have to go down in flames to be a sensitive artist anymore. Hopefully society can change enough so where putting everything into your work doesn't mean you have to fall apart.

Essential Listening

Geri Allen & Timeline, *Live* (Motéma, 2010)

Vijay Iyer & Mike Ladd, *Holding It Down: The Veterans' Dreams Project* (Pi Recordings, 2013)

Kassa Overall, *Go Get Ice Cream and Listen to Jazz* (Independent/Self-Released, 2019)

Terri Lyne Carrington + Social Science, *Waiting Game* (Motéma, 2019)

Kassa Overall, *I Think I'm Good* (Brownswood, 2020)

Moor Mother & Luke Stewart: We All Come Together

The link between jazz and poetry is long established, but that's not always a good thing. Too many poets read in "poetry reading voice," that singsong cadence that turns every text into fortune cookie pseudo-wisdom at best, or meaningless phonemes at worst, and the music descends to meet them.

Fortunately, that's not always the case. The late Steve Dalachinsky, a fixture at avant-garde shows in New York for decades, conveyed a palpable joy and love for the music in his writing, and his delivery onstage was both pugnacious and welcoming. He wasn't performing for an audience, he was talking about his friends to his other friends, and if you were there, you were in that group.

Camae Ayewa, who makes music as Moor Mother, is a fierce, clear-eyed observer of America's slow-rolling demise. Based in Philadelphia, she has released two albums, *Fetish Bones* and *Analog Fluids of Sonic Black Holes*, that combine samples and field recordings with pulsing electronic noise, over which she declaims verses that contain an icy rage. The music is both dense and challenging, drawing the listener into a fever dream of darkness and terror that offers no solutions, only the challenge to resist with all one's might or be swallowed by Moloch.

Originally from Maryland, Ayewa moved to Philadelphia to study photography and began making music, first in more conventional rock bands like the indie/punk The Mighty Paradocs, then as Moor Mother. But she was also presenting her poetry in various contexts, many of which nudged up against jazz, though she says "it was never fully tucked into a genre — that's just not how it works in Philly, you know?"

"I've been playing with and read with many of the jazz legends here," she continued by phone one afternoon in

September 2020, shortly after recording a webcast that would appear on a Nebraska art institution's site. "I've played with [Sun Ra Arkestra saxophonist/bandleader] Marshall Allen, I've played with [poet/saxophonist/flutist] Elliott Levin, a lot of the Cuban-African drummers that are here in Philadelphia. Live music all comes together in this kind of way, whether it's African rhythms mixed with jazz and horn players, we all kind of come together."

Ayewa also curated and ran a weekly performance series that brought musicians together with no thought for genre. So from her point of view, forming Irreversible Entanglements was a natural progression, particularly since it involved working with longtime friends and collaborators. It was only from the outside, where the work leading up to the group's formation was invisible and she was only known for the industrial Black noise of *Fetish Bones*, that it came as a surprise.

Ayewa, saxophonist Keir Neuringer and bassist Luke Stewart (also a member of James Brandon Lewis's group and Jaimie Branch's trio, among many other projects) got together for a 2016 performance at Silent Bar, a now-defunct venue in Brooklyn, at a Musicians Against Police Brutality event put together by vocalist Amirtha Kidambi and trumpeter Peter Evans. After their performance, trumpeter Aquiles Navarro and drummer Tcheser Holmes played a duo set, and Stewart told me, "it sounded like it could be one set, so we linked up real heavy and basically determined that we would play together. So we booked the recording session a couple months later and essentially what you hear on our first album is the first time that we played together, at that recording session."

Irreversible Entanglements was improvised free jazz in the 1960s tradition; listening to Moor Mother's furious verses on its four tracks, particularly the opening one-two of "Chicago to Texas" (which began with a martial drum roll from Holmes) and "Fireworks," it was easy to think of Archie Shepp albums like *Blasé* or *Poem for Malcolm*, or the New York Art Quartet's "Black Dada Nihilismus," on which they were joined by Amiri Baraka. Indeed, Stewart acknowledged the NYAQ as an explicit model, and Ayewa called Baraka "a great inspiration to me...I can't even think about him and not think about jazz."

Her words were furious, but delivered with exquisite control, never letting the listener off the hook with showy displays of emotion. She seethed. And behind her, the music surged and flared, the horns coming in and out like she was conducting them, the bass and drums driving it all forward with a kind of marching swing. It was Albert Ayler-style free jazz, parade melodies warped into uncanny howls, and it sounded like the kind of thing one might hear at the front of a protest march.

The group created a sensation almost immediately, touring North America and Europe, playing clubs and prestige festivals. Live recordings from fall 2018 tour stops in Berlin, Germany and Mantova, Italy have been released, and it's possible to hear the music shifting and changing, their all-acoustic free jazz sound augmented by splashes of electronics and manipulations of Moor Mother's voice.

Ayewa's increased profile brought new opportunities. In addition to her solo work, she collaborated with producer Kevin Martin and Godflesh founder Justin Broadrick in the dubby, industrial noise project Zonal, and was invited to do residencies and curate events. For the 2018 Le Guess Who? Festival in Utrecht, in the Netherlands, she collaborated with flautist Nicole Mitchell on an entirely improvised performance.

Mitchell had originally been slated to perform solo, but she invited Moor Mother to join her. "So then the time comes, her showtime, and it's like, all right, do the soundcheck, OK, well, I guess I'm gonna be up here for the whole time; let's just play. So that's how it happened. We just played. I had no idea what words I would even say."

The 45-minute collaboration possessed a frankly terrifying

energy. Mitchell pushed her flute through echo and reverb, turning it into a massive whooshing roar like an elephant's exhalations, as Moor Mother created electronic hisses and rumbles like a spaceship disintegrating around its occupants. Over that bed of nightmare sound, she asked over and over, with increasing urgency, "Did you see the vultures laughing? Did you see the hawk circling, looking for flesh? Have you been walking around with open eyes?"

"It was kinda nerve-racking, because I admire Nicole Mitchell so much, so this was a huge deal for me," she told me.

> I didn't want to mess up, and I ended up in my mind — 'cause I'm hard on myself — replaying these moments of the set where I felt like I messed up. There's one part where my synthesizer just comes in really strong, you know?...I didn't think that it went so well until I heard the recording, and I heard the part where I thought I messed up and I loved it, and I sent it to Nicole and said, I thought I messed up on that part, and she was like, "I loved when you did that."

She's also worked extensively with saxophonist Roscoe Mitchell as a duo, and as a member of the Art Ensemble of Chicago, appearing on their album *We Are On the Edge* and touring with them.

> We went to Australia and it was only six of us including me, and...it was so great. It's great all the time, but...my thought was, OK, there's no other person to hide behind, you know? It's six of us, this is the Art Ensemble of Chicago, we need to push it, that was my thought. So when I got onstage, I just went off. I didn't hold back or just "play my part," and the communication really reminded me of playing with Irreversible, because it was just so driving, and we were constantly talking to each other through sound...You never

want to be taking up too much space within a group, at least I don't want to be taking up too much space unless it's my group, but I really like to have the conversation with sound.

The second Irreversible Entanglements studio album, 2019's *Who Sent You?*, displayed some of the changes heard in the live recordings, though they were subtle; a ripple of echo here, a sudden squiggling zap there. The music was slightly more danceable than it had been, while still both free and swinging. There was even some lyrical optimism; on "No Más," Ayewa said, "Infinite possibilities/Coming back around/I know we are more than circles/Coming back around to love ourselves fully," as the band created a bouncing, swirling leaf storm of sound.

Stewart is more than one of Ayewa's backing musicians. He's one of the busiest people on the current jazz scene. He works with James Brandon Lewis – primarily in a trio with drummer Warren Trae Crudup III, but occasionally a quartet and sometimes a quintet – and he and Crudup also perform and record as Blacks' Myths. He's in another out-jazz trio, Heart of the Ghost, that's made four albums; he's in trumpeter Jaimie Branch's trio with drummer Mike Pride, a group that has yet to record; he released a solo album, *Works for Solo Bass and Amplifier*, in 2018; and offstage, he's been a DJ on Washington, DC station WPFW and presented shows all over that city, from tiny DIY spaces to the Kennedy Center (where he presented Roscoe Mitchell and Moor Mother's duo piece, *The Black Drop*).

Watching him play the upright bass is hypnotic. He balances the instrument's long neck on his shoulder gently, like a dance partner who's fallen asleep, and leans an ear in as if it has something to tell him. When the music is fast, he bounces his upper body up and down, whipping his head toward the neck, then yanking it away as if trying to apprehend the notes he's just played. When he's playing electric, by contrast, he wears the instrument right at his waist, eschewing low-slung punk-rock cool in favor of a harmolodic intensity, again cocking one ear down toward the strings as he yanks and plucks them with his fingers.

Stewart has the friendly, open demeanor of someone who's spent years attempting to bring seemingly "difficult" music to as many people as possible. His own path to jazz came through punk and indie rock; he started on electric bass, in high school, as a way to make music with friends. "I didn't have access to the Grammy bands or even a jazz band in high school, I didn't go to [New England Conservatory] or Berklee — I didn't major in music at the university of whatever," he told me by phone, driving from Washington, DC to New York. "It's all been experiential for me, and part of a deep, engaged practice of passion, almost."

He grew up in Mississippi, and attended the state university there, known as Ole Miss, before transferring to American University in Washington, DC. That move transformed his life, setting him on his current path. He earned a degree in international relations, with a minor in audio production, and got a job at WPFW, a legendary station with the motto "Jazz and Justice."

"I was working there as the production coordinator and then assistant production manager, I had a show, it was a big part of my life for a good eight years," he said:

> Music-wise at least, it's a collection of people who are passionate about the music and are playing from their own personal collections. There's not a library, or a program director telling you what to play during a time slot. That's one aspect of that being my graduate school, was interacting with that community, as well as the very deep social justice activist community that also found a home at the station.

Since the mid-2000s, Stewart has booked shows all over DC,

in venues like DC Space, Gold Leaf and Union Arts. Some still exist, others are gone. He and writer Giovanni Russonello started the website CapitalBop and the DC Jazz Loft Series of concerts, to better promote and document the jazz being made under the radar in the nation's capital.

> My underground scene, which is the indie scene, all they could talk about was the latest indie band representing the DC underground, and I was like, "Wait a minute, there's the Young Lions playing at Café Nema every Tuesday and y'all never even heard of these people, and this is the best band in DC in my estimation." I saw that, so when I had the opportunity I wanted to put that music back in that conversation. And the result was, people of my generation who were coming to the DIY spot to see the indie show [started] coming to the DIY spot to see the jazz show.

It was via his indie rock band Laughing Man that Stewart first connected with Ayewa. "I actually knew Luke way before I met Keir," she recalled. "We were both in punk bands...so we developed a kinship.

"I feel like that's the beauty of the spirit of Irreversible," she continued.

> It wasn't something we had meeting after meeting about, it was like, OK, we're all doing the work outside of academia...I mean, some of the guys in the band went to school for music, but that wasn't the face they presented. I didn't know until we were in the band and started having different discussions about things, but yeah, we all have the energy of self-motivated versus self-taught.

Stewart's other projects are just as interesting as Irreversible. Heart of the Ghost is a more old-school free jazz trio, with him as the fulcrum, balancing between saxophonist Jarrett Gilgore and drummer Ian McColm. Their squawk-and-squeal, clatter-and-throb music recalls the work of players like Jemeel Moondoc, Charles Gayle, TEST and Other Dimensions in Music from the 1990s and early 2000s. He describes them as "the young, scrappy band that would get in the van and drive to Chicago and play all the crazy places along the way." Their home base was the DC space Rhizome, which closed in 2020; their fourth release, on which they were joined by trumpeter Dave Ballou, was recorded there.

In 2018, saxophonist Dave Rempis invited Stewart to participate in the Exposure Series of concerts in Chicago. In addition to playing with his own groups, he was asked to anchor an ensemble featuring Ken Vandermark and Ed Wilkerson Jr. on reeds, Jim Baker on piano and Avreeayl Ra on drums. They performed a fully improvised, one-off set of music, which he recorded and took home with him. Later that year, he returned to Chicago, having listened back to the music and transcribed peak moments, adding new ideas to the mix. He reassembled the quintet and recorded this new music, partly in the studio and partly live. Both sessions are represented on the album *Luke Stewart Exposure Quintet*.

Some tracks, like the opening "Awakening the Masters," were fierce and blaring, with a bluesy edge, like the work of Frank Wright or Giuseppi Logan. By contrast, "Harp and Concrete Silhouette Pt. II" was a trance-like, droning marathon, with Stewart's bass at the center; it sounded more like experimental Krautrock than jazz.

To Stewart, the point is to break away from the hierarchy — still prevalent even in supposedly free music — of the composer and the musicians who execute his vision. "When you listen to a field recording of a pygmy ensemble in the Congo, the question's never 'Whose song is that?' or 'Who is that?'," he explained:

> It's more "What is that?", which I think is a better question to ask when it comes to music and doing this work of breaking down hierarchies. Because when you're asking who, you're placing it in an individual [zone], where even if there's an ensemble of five, nine, eighteen, up to a full orchestra of music, the question is always, who wrote this music? And even if they did write it, is that music still theirs if someone else is playing that music and putting themselves into that music? How much of it can you say is yours? The band is improvised, and it's a group. It's not just me, it's this band, and it's me versus the collective legacies of these four titans of music, so it's like the concept of instilling your will upon a musician, upon a person's imagination, upon a person's creativity and then calling it yours. That's sort of the concept that I'm thinking about and trying to fight against...to highlight the non-hierarchical nature of free improvisational music ensembles and also in essence [challenge] the concept of the capital-C composer and how it affects our perceptions of music, for better or for worse.

Camae Ayewa takes a similarly anti-hierarchical approach to her non-musical work. She's a community and political activist in Philadelphia, founding the organization Black Quantum Futurism with her partner, Rasheedah Phillips. "It's not just 'this is my band' or 'this is my music' in one box, 'this is where I live' in another box," she told me. Her art is inextricably bonded with her politics, which are radical but intensely local.

> In Philly we've done a lot in BQF around housing. In 2016 we opened a community space called Community Futures Lab, which was about activating communities. We collected...oral histories of what's been happening in the neighborhood. We created an online map of different historical sites and did research to find artists that were in the community, to make

sure that they were not erased, while documenting ongoing redevelopment that's happening in our communities. Your neighbors are most times the most informed people about the community that they're living in. There's a trend of having outside people come in and delegate what a community needs, without asking the people that live there. You can hear a lot from my poetry — I speak about how people are becoming more paranoid, more antisocial, people are staying inside more...this kind of thing where you don't have to care about what's going on around you until it comes to your front door.

Essential Listening

Moor Mother, *Fetish Bones* (Don Giovanni, 2016)

Irreversible Entanglements, *Irreversible Entanglements* (International Anthem, 2017)

Moor Mother, *Analog Fluids of Sonic Black Holes* (Don Giovanni, 2019)

Irreversible Entanglements, *Who Sent You?* (International Anthem, 2019)

Irreversible Entanglements, *Irreversible Live in Italy* (Independent/Self-Released, 2020)

Irreversible Entanglements, *Irreversible Live in Berlin* (Independent/Self-Released, 2020)

Nicole Mitchell and Moor Mother, *Offering — Live at Le Guess Who* (Don Giovanni, 2020)

Moor Mother, *Circuit City* (Don Giovanni, 2020)

CULTURE, SOCIETY & POLITICS

The modern world is at an impasse. Disasters scroll across our smartphone screens and we're invited to like, follow or upvote, but critical thinking is harder and harder to find. Rather than connecting us in common struggle and debate, the internet has sped up and deepened a long-standing process of alienation and atomization. Zer0 Books wants to work against this trend.
With critical theory as our jumping off point, we aim to publish books that make our readers uncomfortable. We want to move beyond received opinions.
Zer0 Books is on the left and wants to reinvent the left. We are sick of the injustice, the suffering and the stupidity that defines both our political and cultural world, and we aim to find a new foundation for a new struggle.

If this book has helped you to clarify an idea, solve a problem or extend your knowledge, you may want to check out our online content as well. Look for Zer0 Books: Advancing Conversations in the iTunes directory and for our Zer0 Books YouTube channel.

Popular videos include:

Žižek and the Double Blackmain

The Intellectual Dark Web is a Bad Sign

Can there be an Anti-SJW Left?

Answering Jordan Peterson on Marxism

Follow us on Facebook at https://www.facebook.com/ZeroBooks and Twitter at https://twitter.com/Zer0Books

Bestsellers from Zer0 Books include:

Give Them An Argument
Logic for the Left
Ben Burgis
Many serious leftists have learned to distrust talk of logic. This is a serious mistake.
Paperback: 978-1-78904-210-8 ebook: 978-1-78904-211-5

Poor but Sexy
Culture Clashes in Europe East and West
Agata Pyzik
How the East stayed East and the West stayed West.
Paperback: 978-1-78099-394-2 ebook: 978-1-78099-395-9

An Anthropology of Nothing in Particular
Martin Demant Frederiksen
A journey into the social lives of meaninglessness.
Paperback: 978-1-78535-699-5 ebook: 978-1-78535-700-8

In the Dust of This Planet

Horror of Philosophy vol. 1

Eugene Thacker

In the first of a series of three books on the Horror of Philosophy, *In the Dust of This Planet* offers the genre of horror as a way of thinking about the unthinkable.

Paperback: 978-1-84694-676-9 ebook: 978-1-78099-010-1

The End of Oulipo?

An Attempt to Exhaust a Movement

Lauren Elkin, Veronica Esposito

Paperback: 978-1-78099-655-4 ebook: 978-1-78099-656-1

Capitalist Realism

Is There No Alternative?

Mark Fisher

An analysis of the ways in which capitalism has presented itself as the only realistic political-economic system.

Paperback: 978-1-84694-317-1 ebook: 978-1-78099-734-6

Rebel Rebel

Chris O'Leary

David Bowie: every single song. Everything you want to know, everything you didn't know.

Paperback: 978-1-78099-244-0 ebook: 978-1-78099-713-1

Kill All Normies

Angela Nagle

Online culture wars from 4chan and Tumblr to Trump.

Paperback: 978-1- 78535-543-1 ebook: 978-1-78535-544-8

Cartographies of the Absolute
Alberto Toscano, Jeff Kinkle
An aesthetics of the economy for the twenty-first century.
Paperback: 978-1-78099-275-4 ebook: 978-1-78279-973-3

Malign Velocities
Accelerationism and Capitalism
Benjamin Noys
Long listed for the Bread and Roses Prize 2015, *Malign Velocities* argues against the need for speed, tracking acceleration as the symptom of the ongoing crises of capitalism.
Paperback: 978-1-78279-300-7 ebook: 978-1-78279-299-4

Meat Market
Female Flesh under Capitalism
Laurie Penny
A feminist dissection of women's bodies as the fleshy fulcrum of capitalist cannibalism, whereby women are both consumers and consumed.
Paperback: 978-1-84694-521-2 ebook: 978-1-84694-782-7

Babbling Corpse
Vaporwave and the Commodification of Ghosts
Grafton Tanner
Paperback: 978-1-78279-759-3 ebook: 978-1-78279-760-9

New Work New Culture
Work we want and a culture that strengthens us
Frithjoff Bergmann
A serious alternative for mankind and the planet.
Paperback: 978-1-78904-064-7 ebook: 978-1-78904-065-4

Romeo and Juliet in Palestine
Teaching Under Occupation
Tom Sperlinger
Life in the West Bank, the nature of pedagogy and the role of a university under occupation.
Paperback: 978-1-78279-637-4 ebook: 978-1-78279-636-7

Ghosts of My Life
Writings on Depression, Hauntology and Lost Futures
Mark Fisher
Paperback: 978-1-78099-226-6 ebook: 978-1-78279-624-4

Sweetening the Pill
or How We Got Hooked on Hormonal Birth Control
Holly Grigg-Spall
Has contraception liberated or oppressed women? *Sweetening the Pill* breaks the silence on the dark side of hormonal contraception.
Paperback: 978-1-78099-607-3 ebook: 978-1-78099-608-0

Why Are We The Good Guys?
Reclaiming Your Mind from the Delusions of Propaganda
David Cromwell
A provocative challenge to the standard ideology that Western power is a benevolent force in the world.
Paperback: 978-1-78099-365-2 ebook: 978-1-78099-366-9

The Writing on the Wall
On the Decomposition of Capitalism and its Critics
Anselm Jappe, Alastair Hemmens
A new approach to the meaning of social emancipation.
Paperback: 978-1-78535-581-3 ebook: 978-1-78535-582-0

Enjoying It

Candy Crush and Capitalism

Alfie Bown

A study of enjoyment and of the enjoyment of studying. Bown asks what enjoyment says about us and what we say about enjoyment, and why.

Paperback: 978-1-78535-155-6 ebook: 978-1-78535-156-3

Color, Facture, Art and Design

Iona Singh

This materialist definition of fine-art develops guidelines for architecture, design, cultural-studies and ultimately social change.

Paperback: 978-1-78099-629-5 ebook: 978-1-78099-630-1

Neglected or Misunderstood

The Radical Feminism of Shulamith Firestone

Victoria Margree

An interrogation of issues surrounding gender, biology, sexuality, work and technology, and the ways in which our imaginations continue to be in thrall to ideologies of maternity and the nuclear family.

Paperback: 978-1-78535-539-4 ebook: 978-1-78535-540-0

How to Dismantle the NHS in 10 Easy Steps (Second Edition)

Youssef El-Gingihy

The story of how your NHS was sold off and why you will have to buy private health insurance soon. A new expanded second edition with chapters on junior doctors' strikes and government blueprints for US-style healthcare.

Paperback: 978-1-78904-178-1 ebook: 978-1-78904-179-8

Digesting Recipes

The Art of Culinary Notation

Susannah Worth

A recipe is an instruction, the imperative tone of the expert, but this constraint can offer its own kind of potential. A recipe need not be a domestic trap but might instead offer escape – something to fantasise about or aspire to.

Paperback: 978-1-78279-860-6 ebook: 978-1-78279-859-0